The Inland Waterways Manual

Third edition

The complete guide to boating on rivers, lakes and canals

Emrhys Barrell

Adlard Coles Nautical
London

I would like to dedicate this book to the crews of the *Crudgington Comet, Catspaw*, and all the other boats that have carried us round the waterways of Britain and Europe. To my wife Linda, and all our family and friends who have put up with the endless stops for just one more photograph, or the marathon trips to reach just one more river or canal.

This edition published by Adlard Coles Nautical
an imprint of A & C Black Publishers Ltd
38 Soho Square, London W1D 3HB
www.adlardcoles.com

Copyright © Emrhys Barrell 1993, 2001, 2006

First edition 1993
Second edition 2001
Second edition revised 2003
Third edition 2006

ISBN-10: 0-7136-7636-1
ISBN-13: 978-0-7136-7636-5

A CIP Catalogue record for this book is available from the British Library.

A & C Black uses paper produced with elemental chlorine-free pulp, harvested from managed sustainable forests

Typeset in 10.5/12.5pt Finnegan
Printed and bound in Spain by GraphyCems

Note: While all reasonable care has been taken in the preparation of this book, the publisher takes no responsibility for the use of the methods or products described in the book.

CFN

The Inland Waterways Manual

Cove

Contents

Acknowledgements

Photographs: Emrhys or Linda Barrell unless individually credited.

Artwork: Pages 110, 115 from *Ups and Downs of a Lockkeeper* by Jake Kavanagh published by Adlard Coles Nautical; page 113 reproduced from *Nicholson Waterways Guide North*, 1981 edition by kind permission of Bartholomew, Edinburgh; page 146, illustrations reproduced from *The Adlard Coles Book of EuroRegs for Inland Waterways* by kind permission of Marion Martin; page 180, map courtesy of Richard Fairhurst.

We would like to thank Paul Hanson of *Motorboats Monthly* for the detailed handling drawings, pages 49–67, 76, 83–106, 118, 130.

The author swaps tales of the journey outside a popular waterside watering hole.
Photo: William Payne.

Introduction

The inland waterways of the British Isles offer some of the most diverse and beautiful boating areas imaginable. They range from majestic rivers, such as the Thames, Severn and Shannon, to the secret winding canals of our man-made system. In between are lakes and Broads, with the whole network giving thousands of miles of ever-changing scenery and surroundings. Many people cruise them all their lives, without ever tiring of them. This book is to enable you to join them in their pleasure.

For most people, the whole purpose of going boating is for relaxation. Even competitive sailors, rowers or canoeists are doing it to get away from the stresses of modern life, and the rest of us are looking for pure pleasure. So it would seem that the idea of planning and preparation is at variance with the theory of a laid-back life afloat. But in practice, if you are to get the most benefit from your time on the water, you should spend enough time on the groundwork to ensure the minimum of problems afloat. This book helps you to make the right decisions on which boat to buy, which waterways to use it on and how to make the most of both of them.

A busy Thames lock on a sunny summer's day.

The Lapworth Flight, a system of narrow locks on the North Stratford Canal.

1 | *First Decisions*

I f you have bought this book, it is to be assumed that you have already made the decision that you want to go boating on inland waterways, rather than the sea, but if you are just browsing, here is a brief recap of the pros and cons. Possible boating areas can be broadly divided into tidal and non-tidal waters. Tidal waters include estuaries and the sea. Conditions here are likely to be more unpredictable, and potentially more severe. Wind, waves and tides, and the distance from safety mean that both your boat and crew need to be stronger and better prepared and equipped.

Inland waterways, on the other hand, are generally more placid and peaceful. Currents, if any, are likely to be slow; waves will be small, and tides only encountered at the seaward end of our large rivers. The bank will rarely be more than a dozen yards away, and depths of water often little more than that of the boat. As a result of this, stresses on vessel and crew will be much less severe, and the level of equipment required will be reduced. This is not to say that you should not be properly prepared and equipped – it is as easy to drown in three feet of water as in a hundred – just that the degree of preparedness needs to be less.

Three key points in favour of inland waterways

◆ The first benefit is cost. A boat used solely on rivers or canals will be much cheaper to buy and run than its sea-going counterpart. It can be smaller, have a lower-powered engine, and require much less sophisticated equipment, both for safety and navigation. Running costs – fuel, moorings, maintenance and insurance – will also be less.

◆ The second benefit is that the fitness and age of the crew is less important. One or two people can happily handle a modest-sized inland waterways boat and many owners graduate to rivers and canals from the sea as they advance in years.

◆ The third, and less obvious, advantage is that you will generally get much more use out of your boat on inland waters than if you have a sea-going craft. The weather is unlikely to stop you getting afloat, whereas it can severely curtail the operations of a boat on the sea – a Force 8 will keep coastal boats pinned in their marinas, but on the river or canal it just requires a bit more caution when handling your craft. Similarly, cold weather is less of a problem, and many owners use their boats right up to and sometimes through the winter. Modern heaters ensure you will be snug and warm on the coldest of days, and even the rain is bearable with an enclosed cockpit.

An increasing number of people are selling up their houses and taking to the waterways permanently, or for one or two years, and they are happily living afloat throughout the year.

Which waterway?

The possible boating areas can be broken down into a small number of general categories. We will be looking at specific waterways in more detail in Chapter 9, but at this stage we can define them broadly as rivers, canals and lakes.

Rivers

Rivers are generally wide – from 30–100ft (30m), and have a flow of current (usually small). They will either have no locks, or the locks will be at wide intervals. The individual locks will normally be of wide beam, that is to say usually 10–12ft (3–3.6m) or more, allowing correspondingly wider boats. The locks may well be manned, as on the Thames, and will usually take more than one boat at a time; thus operating them will be less onerous. Individual rivers may be isolated from the rest of the system, limiting your cruising range, though they will be connected to the sea, allowing you to travel out along the coast, or across the Channel if you have a suitable craft. Depth of water will normally be at least 3ft (1m), headroom 7–10ft (2.1–3m) and maximum speed 5–8mph, allowing a wide variety of boat types and sizes to use them.

Canals

Canals divide into two categories – narrow and broad. The narrow canals are so described because their locks are only approximately 7ft (2.1m) wide, and generally a maximum of 72ft (21.9m) long. They were built around the end of the 18th century and the beginning of the 19th century, to carry the cargoes of the industrial revolution, and the standard size determined the dimensions of the barge that could use them. In later years, some parts of the system were widened, with the locks being increased to 14ft (4.2m), and some canals were built from the outset with broad locks, but the pattern was not continuous, so in order to be able to travel the whole of the system, you will need a narrow-beam boat.

The whole network of canals at one time stretched for more than 5000 miles (8000km), and linked nearly all parts of England and Wales. Even so, it is still extensive – over 4000 miles, as the map on page 180 shows. Locks on canals will be unmanned, and can occur in considerable numbers. Up to 29 in one flight is possible, and because they will usually only take one or possibly two boats at a time you will have to expect to work them yourselves. They are also manually operated, so be prepared for some effort. Depth of water will be around 2ft 6in–3ft (0.75–0.9m), and the top speed allowed is 4mph. Because of the size restrictions, only purpose-built craft can use the whole of the canal system. This restricts many, but not all, river boats from travelling on the canals, though the reverse does not apply, and most canal craft are quite suitable for the rivers.

When locking down, the helmsman can take care of the stern line.

Lakes

Finally, we have lakes. Those found in the North West of England are popular boating areas. Some craft are left there permanently, on moorings and in marinas, but many are trailed for the day or weekend. The full range of types and sizes of craft can use lakes, as there are no problems of beam or draught. There are no tides or currents to worry about or locks to negotiate. However, they can get rough in very windy weather.

Which type of boat?

So, now you are convinced that you are doing the right thing, what should be your next step? Well, before you rush out and start looking at boats, it is important to decide just what you want from your boating. Where do you want to go? How much time do you want to spend? How much can you ~~?~~ And – often forgotten – who will be going with you?

Boating naturally divides into four broad categories: day-boating, week-ending, longer cruises and living aboard. Some people only want to do one of these things, while others will want to do two, three or all four. Similarly, some boats will be suitable for one category, whereas others will manage all four, though with varying degrees of suitability. It is important to decide on your requirements if you want to avoid buying the wrong boat – a boat with a lot of accommodation may often have only limited outside space, making it poorly suited for day trips, while its size may make short journeys and secluded moorings a chore. Similarly, a weekender, with no separate toilet compartment or shower, will quickly try the patience on longer holidays.

In general, while most people dream of long-distance cruising, reality suggests that the average boat will only spend two or three weeks a year on long trips. To this can be added three or four overnight weekends, with the rest of the outings being day trips.

However, as we have said, living aboard permanently is quite feasible, and a growing number of people these days are choosing a boat as their home. This can either be on a fixed mooring, or you can travel round the system. Some people sell their house and move on to the boat permanently. Some keep their house as a base, or downsize to a more manageable property, and use the capital released to buy the boat. This allows you somewhere to go back to if the weather gets really bad, and also keeps a foothold on the property ladder.

Choosing a boat for long-term living requires more thought and planning, and even deciding whether you can cope with the restricted space needs consideration. It has been suggested that the best test is to spend a week with your partner living in the kitchen of your house. If you can survive this then you can probably put up with each other on a boat.

We have mentioned the possibility of river boats going to sea; this is perfectly feasible, but we must stress that the vessel must have been built for this purpose. It is not safe to take just any river boat out into tidal or coastal waters, and you should bear this in mind when choosing your craft. In practice, some boats can comfortably be used in either waters, but most are best at home on one or the other. Also, considerably more safety equipment, navigation and boat-handling skills are required on tidal waters, and you should not venture on to these without the appropriate tuition.

Before we go any further on the selection process, you should bear in mind that, whatever boat you finally decide on for your first craft, you are likely to change it within one or two years. Very few people get the choice completely right first time and your ambitions expand as you get progressively caught by the bug. Many owners go through up to a dozen or more vessels during their boating lives, as family and financial circumstances continuously change, and you gradually learn what is best for you through experience. The purpose of these early chapters is to shorten the learning process, and to prevent you making any time-consuming or costly mistakes.

Because you are likely to move on quickly from your first boat, the first lesson to learn is that unless you are very sure of yourself, do not buy a craft that will be difficult to sell later. Choose well-known models and makes, and buy a boat in good condition. This might mean a slightly smaller craft than you might have preferred, but the benefit will pay off when you come to sell it. The bargain boat in need of repair will become a millstone around your neck. It will also spoil your first boating experiences. There are enough things to cope with in this new sport, without having to deal with a recalcitrant engine, or leaking hull.

The logic of buying a smaller craft has another benefit if you are new to the water. It will be easier to handle and operate, and allow you to find your feet and learn with fewer problems. After all, you would not learn to drive on roads in a lorry or bus, so apply the same thinking on the water.

We have already mentioned your age, and again this has to be borne in mind. If you are young and active, you can balance easily on the smallest of boats, or run up and down and jump off large ones. As you advance in years, you will look for something more stable which is safe to walk around. But, just as important, it still has to be small enough to handle and tie up – it can be a long drop down to the lockside from a large boat, and there may be no one to catch the ropes. You may have young families to help you on most occasions, but be careful you do not tie yourself to a vessel that needs a crew to handle, or you will have lost your independence – the whole reason for getting afloat.

In this respect, choosing the right specification and equipment can make the boat much easier to operate and handle. Bow-thrusters are a boon when coming alongside; diesel inboards are more reliable and safer than petrol outboards; self-stowing anchors are a considerable safety factor, and so on.

This 19ft Shetland Four Plus Two is a popular trailable family cruiser.

Similar comments about fitness and age apply to the waterways you choose. Canals require more physical strength and agility, which is why older people find rivers more appealing, but this does not mean that they cannot travel the canals – they just have to be prepared to move more slowly, and be more careful in their actions.

At the other end of the age spectrum, you may have to give consideration to babies, children and growing families. Again, the layout and design of the boat has considerable bearing on this. Deep cockpits keep crawlers from becoming swimmers, while separate cabins allow parents and children privacy and quiet. You should bear in mind that few boats are designed specifically for young families and most will need some modifications to guardrails and perhaps the addition of netting. Similarly, be aware that your young and enthusiastic crew will become bored by a waterborne life when they become teenagers, so do not rely on their support indefinitely.

Many people share their boating with other couples or friends, and again this can mean a compromise in the vessel that you choose. If you are only having parties aboard for day-trips, then a single sleeping/living area will suffice. If, however, you are intending longer cruises with other people, two cabins, preferably separated, are a necessity. Bulkheads in boats are notoriously thin and, unless you are very broad-minded, cabins at either end of the boat are a must. Similarly, even for a dayboat, some sort of toilet or changing facility is needed with a reasonable degree of privacy.

Where you live has an important bearing on where you do your boating. We may not all be fortunate enough to have ideal cruising waters on our doorsteps but even so, do not choose a base for your boat that is too far from home. An hour's drive is the most you should consider if possible. Any more than this, and much of the spontaneity and pleasure goes out of it. And remember, everyone else will be getting away from it all on the same weekends that you are, so do not turn your boating into a few hours' 'relaxation' sandwiched between two motorway jams. There is nothing worse than drifting down the stream listening to the reported chaos on the radio and knowing that you will have to face it on the way home!

If you want to cruise waters farther afield, it is quite possible to move your boat round the system during the season. You can leave it at safe marinas or moorings which will enable you to cover a new area every year, without a marathon trek on the annual holiday. In this respect we find that there is never any shortage of volunteers from family and friends to bring the boat back home if we should run out of time, or take it on the first legs of the trip.

Hiring or buying?

We now come to the key decisions in the buying process. The first, surprisingly, is should you buy at all? Boats are available for hire to suit all budgets and size of parties all over the system, and many people never buy a

This 35ft Dutch-built steel cruiser offers spacious accommodation in a sturdy hull that can make occasional coastal passages in good conditions.

boat at all. Look at the costs of owning and running a boat – if you are not able to use it for more than two or three weeks of the year, it is rarely cost effective to own your own. At the same time, by hiring you avoid all the worries and problems that can crop up with your own boat, all through the year. Certainly, hiring a boat for your first few trips is an excellent idea, and it is probably true that many owners have their first introduction to the waterways as a result of a hire-boat holiday.

Hiring will enable you to get an idea of the type of boating you would prefer without the commitment to a purchase. It will allow you to sample the diverse range of waterways: rivers, canals and lakes, before you make your final decision to buy. It also has another benefit: you will be learning to drive on someone else's boat, not your own. The first few trips can be damaging to confidence and boat alike, so it is a good idea to learn boat-handling on a boat designed and built for novices.

Sharing

The next option is sharing. This can either be done via the formal approach of a time-share or shared ownership, or on a more casual basis. The advantages are that it spreads the cost of buying and running the boat over a greater number of people, yet because most boats are under-utilised, everyone still gets as much time afloat as they want. The disadvantages are that you have to pre-plan your time on the boat, and may not be able to take it away for the weekend on the spur of the moment.

With time-share you buy one or more weeks on the boat over a period of up to 30 years, for a fixed initial sum. In addition to this you pay an annual management charge. You do not own the boat, or any part of it, and, at the end of the period, the scheme managers sell the boat.

Shared ownership divides the ownership of the boat between a set number of people, usually twelve, but sometimes less. In return they get four weeks' use of the boat every year, usually divided into two weeks in the summer, and two more individual weeks. Depending on the scheme, these weeks vary every year, according to a pre-agreed rotation. You pay an annual maintenance fee for the upkeep and running of the boat, and a management fee to the organisers of the scheme. However, the boat belongs to the group of owners, and they make decisions on a majority basis, on where to keep it, and whether to sell it.

Sharing can also be done on an informal basis between two or more individuals or families. Here the parties get together to buy and run a boat between them, sharing the costs as they arise. The advantages over time-share or shared ownership are more flexibility in choosing the periods of use of the boat, and often the parties will use it at the same time together. You also gain the benefit of use of the boat at weekends or short notice. The disadvantage is that the overall cost will be higher, because you will be sharing between a smaller number of people. Sharing can have considerable benefits. At a stroke, it cuts the cost of ownership by half or more, allowing you to invest in a more expensive boat than would otherwise be possible. It reduces the impact of unforeseen bills, and spreads the load of maintenance and repair. Clearly you have to choose your partners carefully, and complications can arise if one party wishes to pull out, but in the main these are not insurmountable. Surprisingly, few people seem to consider sharing, but I can assure you that it definitely can work.

Joining a club

Another intermediate step to full ownership is to join a club. Many types of boat clubs flourish on our waterways today. At their simplest they are just communal mooring associations, aimed at existing owners only. However, more sophisticated organisations have clubhouses, training schemes, competitions, and organise cruises. If you are undecided as to your first steps, you can go along to these in a non-owning capacity, to get the feel of different boat-types and cruising conditions. You should also occasionally be able to crew for other owners which will help you to learn the ropes. Obviously you will be expected to buy your own boat at some stage, but again the club can help, as secondhand craft are often advertised on the notice-board first, or change hands through word of mouth. Once you have bought your boat, the club will again help you, providing training and information. Communal club cruises are invaluable in helping you to

*The Freeman 27, now out of production, is still very popular for river use.
It has an inboard engine and four berths in the cabin, plus a galley and enclosed
toilet compartment.*

start, whether it is just up the river, or further afield. Eventually the wheel will turn full circle; there will be new members available as crew if you find yourself shorthanded.

The bottom line – costs of boat ownership

We will now look at the basic costs that are involved in owning a boat. This will help you to decide which size and type of craft is for you, and on which waterways you will operate it. Obviously the purchase price is a vital factor in your choice, but you should also carefully consider the running costs involved. Maintenance and fixed annual costs can mount up and can have a significant effect on your ability to use and enjoy your boat. A boat must be maintained to a certain standard, otherwise it will deteriorate rapidly, and cause endless problems during its use. These problems may just be a nuisance, but they may affect the safety of your craft and crew, and others around you.

Clearly, the first cost to consider is the purchase price. What proportion of this you put up as cash and how much you borrow depends on your personal circumstances; we will be looking at finance in Chapter 2. However, you should also take into account depreciation, and selling costs. A new boat may depreciate between 10–30% in its first one or two years (depending on the make) which is why it is a good policy to choose a well-known make, with a better re-sale value. Used boats depreciate less, and by a certain age, usually between 5–10 years old, the value of a popular model will level out. Of course, it has to be remembered that the price of its replacement will be increasing with inflation. Also, if you sell through a broker or dealer, you will pay 5–10% commission on the selling price.

Mooring fees

The next highest cost is usually mooring. Unless you are lucky enough to have a riverside garden, you will have to pay to moor your boat. Moorings vary considerably, the simplest being along a river or canal bank, the most sophisticated a marina berth, with costs increasing accordingly. Most moorings are charged on the basis of the overall length of the boat with, in some cases, a minimum overall length; they are usually quoted on the basis of a cost per foot (or metre) per year. For the humblest canalside mooring you could be paying (at the time of writing) as little as £12 per foot per year, or £600 for a 50ft boat, while the grandest of the marinas will be up to £80 per foot, or £4000 for a 50-footer, per year. Obviously, the facilities offered and convenience vary considerably between the two, and this can be an important factor in your boating.

A bankside mooring may mean a long walk down a muddy towpath to the boat, which can be a chore when you are carrying equipment, provisions and gear. It can also have attendant problems of vandalism or theft. You are unlikely to have electricity or water alongside, which, initially, might not appear to be a problem, but can become important. A marina, on the other hand, should have good access from pontoons and nearby car parking. Electricity and water should be at least nearby if not alongside and there will probably be other facilities such as showers, a shop, a chandlery and even a club. In theory, security should also be better though this cannot be guaranteed. Obviously you are paying extra for the convenience and facilities provided by marinas, but for many owners, particularly older people, or those with children, the benefits outweigh the costs. Bear in mind also that it might be worth opting for a slightly smaller or cheaper boat, and spending the difference on a better berth. Or conversely, putting up with a cheap mooring might allow you to justify a bigger boat.

Precise costs will also vary from area to area, with the south-east, particularly the Thames, commanding the highest rates. There also tends to be a general shortage of moorings throughout the country and most of the popular moorings still have a waiting list. The classified pages of the national boating magazines carry adverts from a representative spread of moorings, with current costs, while the British Marine Federation (BMF) can supply you with a comprehensive list of what is available. The navigation authority for a particular waterway will also have moorings.

Of course, if you buy a trailable boat, you can store it at home, and save mooring costs altogether. You will have to add the cost of the trailer, but this can be looked on as an investment rather than a running cost. Some people compromise, by storing the boat at home for the winter, and paying for a short-term berth in the summer. You will also have to check that nothing in your local byelaws prevents you from parking a boat outside your house.

Insurance

A minimum of Third Party insurance is now compulsory for virtually every craft that uses the waters under the control of British Waterways, and most of the other authorities have similar requirements. Also, most marinas require your boat to be insured. However, on all but the cheapest of boats, we would strongly recommend you take out a comprehensive policy, because the extra premium to cover fire, theft and damage is not large, and could save you money later; you never know when your boat might be stolen or damaged. Rates vary depending on the value and type of boat, and whether you intend using it on the sea but, as a rough guide, you can expect to pay an annual premium of between 0.75–1.25% of the value of the boat. Specialist companies handle most boats, and advertise in the boating magazines, but for small dinghies you may be able to extend your house contents policy.

Licences

Licences come next. On virtually every inland waterway you will need some sort of licence for your boat, however small it is. These are usually levied by the authority that administers the navigation and, in theory, are meant to cover the costs of dredging, bank maintenance and repairs. With the privatisation of the water companies, control of several waterways changed hands, and this prompted the government to look at the whole question of navigation authorities. At the time of publishing this book, most of the canals, and some of the rivers, are run by British Waterways, with 2000 miles under their control. After them comes the Environment Agency, with about 500 miles of rivers, including the Thames, the Medway, the Great Ouse and the River Nene. The Norfolk Broads are controlled by the Broads Authority. There are then a further 23 smaller authorities, usually controlling individual rivers or canals, with a total of 300 miles or so under their jurisdiction.

Costs vary considerably between different waters, and are dependent on the length, and sometimes beam, of your boat. A 50ft (15m) craft will be paying between £300–500, with smaller craft accordingly less. In some cases, you will need more than one licence to travel between one system and another, though short-term visitors' licences are sometimes available. In theory, the rationalisation of the system was meant to encourage single licensing, or at least concessions for craft licensed elsewhere, but progress towards this goal has been slow, with individual authorities wanting to protect their own revenues. At the time of writing, the different authorities are still issuing their own licences, which most owners will buy, but there is now the option of a so-called Gold Licence, issued by British Waterways and the Environment Agency, which allows you to travel the combined waters of both authorities. Short-term visitor licences are also available for every water-way, for periods of one day up to one month. At the time of writing, British

Waterways were considering charging shared ownership boats an increased licence fee, of between 1½ and 2½ times the standard rate, but this has not been finalised.

Driving licences do not exist at present for UK use, and are unlikely to do so in the foreseeable future. However, we do strongly recommend that complete newcomers undergo some form of training. The Royal Yachting Association (RYA) administers a training scheme, with approved schools, and it issues an Inland Waterways Helmsman's Certificate. Courses are one or two days, and the cost is money well spent, for you and for all your crew members. (See page 47.) If you wish to take your boat abroad you will almost certainly require a licence, but you can do the training and take the tests for this in the UK. Adlard Coles Nautical publishes the *RYA Book of the International Certificate of Competence* by Bill Anderson which will take you through the course.

Running costs and maintenance

To the fixed annual costs you will have to add running costs. The largest of these might appear to be fuel, but in practice this will not be considerable for an inland craft. Our own 45ft (13.7m) narrowboat consumes around 50–100 gallons of diesel per year, at a cost of between £1.75–2.50 per gallon (at 2005 prices). At present, due to an anomaly of the system, diesel for use in boats is not taxed to the same level as road-going fuel, though some boat-yards take advantage of the difference to increase the profit margins. The net price to them is probably around £1.35–1.50 per gallon, from which you can estimate the mark up. However, in their defence it has to be said that the fire regulations applying to waterside fuelling facilities make them expensive to maintain and staff, for a comparatively low turnover. Also, the tax concession on diesel fuel for boats is under constant review by the European Commission, as it does not apply to most countries, and it may disappear at any time.

Petrol is taxed at road rates, and is even more costly to store and insure, resulting in it being increasingly hard to find on the riverside. A petrol outboard will use around ½–1½ gallons per hour, which over a 50–100 hour cruising season will add up to £100–400.

Maintenance and repairs must not be forgotten. A boat operates in a hostile, damp environment, and spends long periods inactive, contributing to neglect and decay. The precise amount you spend on maintenance will depend on the size of the boat, and how much work you do yourself. You must assume, however, that it will have to be lifted from the water, at least every two years, for the bottom to be inspected and painted at a cost of £200–500 for a 30–40ft (9–12m) boat. To this must be added engine servic-ing, of £50–200 per year, depending on size and sophistication. Every second year you can anticipate repairing or replacing one major item of equipment such as fridge or water heater at around £300–500 each, plus smaller items such as batteries, pumps etc, every 2–3 years at a cost of another £250–350.

Fibreglass boats will not need painting, except perhaps after 10–15 years, but they do need cleaning and polishing to maintain their looks, while any woodwork will need varnishing. Steel boats will need painting, usually every 4–6 years, depending on the area where they are used. Pollution in the air around industrial towns reduces the efficiency and appearance of paint more quickly. To these will have to be added general running costs, such as gas for heating and cooking, pump-outs for the toilet, and other items which will depend on how much you use the boat.

Boat types

We will be looking at detailed boat models and types in Chapter 2, but a brief run-down here of what we are talking about will help you in coming to your major decision of what type of boating is best for you.

Dinghies and inflatables

The simplest way of getting afloat is with an inflatable dinghy. Store it at home, carry it in the boot of the car, and have a lot of fun on a sunny day. Inflatables can be rowed or paddled but it is a good idea to try and buy one with a transom so that a small outboard can be fitted to extend your range. You can choose a different waterway every trip, and explore small ones that other boats cannot reach, but make sure that you are allowed on them, and obtain the necessary licence.

You can hire or buy this traditional Thames camping skiff and follow in the footsteps of Jerome K. Jerome's heroes. Note the Edwardian wine cooler!

A 12ft (3.5m) dinghy will carry 3–4 adults, or two adults and two children. For safety's sake, make sure you buy a reputable make, and insure it under your household policy. And remember that non-swimmers and children need lifejackets or buoyancy aids. Inflatable dinghies cost between £200–1000, depending on whether new or secondhand, plus £150–400 for the engine. Modern inflatables are robust and, if well looked after, will give five or even ten years of use; they are suitable for rivers, lakes or canals.

You may prefer the solidity of a rigid dinghy, but it will have to be carried on the roof of the car, or on a trailer. Again, you can either row it for short trips, or fit the smallest petrol outboard, or you may prefer to glide silently along powered by an electric engine. A 10–14ft (3–4m) GRP (glass reinforced plastic) dinghy will cost £250–1500, plus £200–500 for the engine. It will be suitable for rivers, lakes and canals.

Or you can go the whole hog and buy or hire a classic Thames camping skiff and re-enact *Three Men in a Boat*.

Dayboats

The next step up is a dayboat. This can be a 13–16ft (3–4.8m) outboard-powered runabout or dory, or an inboard-powered craft, again petrol, diesel or electric; it will require either a trailer, or a summer mooring. You may have the benefit of a fold-down canopy to keep off the rain, or excess sun! It will carry 4–6 adults plus gear – you will be moving into the area of cool-boxes or fridges to keep the picnic fresh.

This 13ft dory is an ideal dayboat, being stable, with plenty of room for two- and four-legged passengers.

The outboard will need to be 6–10hp for rivers, lakes or canals, but with a bigger engine, the boat may also be suitable for use on estuaries or the sea. The cost of a dayboat varies from £1000–15,000 depending on age and engine. The construction material is usually GRP, sometimes wood.

Trailable cruisers

If the idea of mooring up overnight appeals to you, then you will be looking at 16–20ft (4.8–6m) cruisers. Depending on size, you will normally have two berths in the cabin, plus an optional two for children in the cockpit, under a fold-away canopy. A chemical toilet will normally be sited in the cabin, but not always in its own separate compartment. A two-burner bottled-gas cooker, with either a portable or fixed sink, will enable you to do simple cooking.

A portable fridge or ice-box, cooled at home or in the car, will keep food and drinks fresh for one or two days. A trailable cruiser is ideal for day trips or weekends and makes a good introduction to family cruising. Suitable for rivers, lakes and canals, with 10-20hp, many models with a large enough engine (40–60hp) can also be used on the sea in sheltered waters. Costs range from £1000–18,000 depending on age and engine. The construction material is normally GRP.

Small cruisers

You are now moving up in size to 20–22ft (6–6.7m), with 2–4 berths in the cabin, and usually a separate toilet compartment, and fixed galley. The headroom will be getting close to 6ft (1.8m) now. It will be powered by either an inboard or outboard engine. If the beam is under 6ft 10in (2.08m) it will be suitable for use on rivers and broad or narrow canals. You will need a permanent mooring unless you own a powerful tow vehicle. The prices will range from £3000–20,000. Construction material is usually GRP, sometimes wood.

Medium cruisers

A cruiser of 24–30ft (7.3–9m) will give you 4–6 berths, two or more cabins, full standing headroom and separate toilet and shower. The engine will be either inboard or outboard. Again, this craft is suitable for rivers and broad canals, or the narrow canals if under 6ft 10in (2.08m) beam. Prices are now in the £6000–30,000 bracket. Construction material is usually GRP, some-times steel or wood.

Larger cruisers

Cruisers of 30ft (9m) upwards will provide 4–8 berths, two or more cabins, full headroom. Power will be from an inboard diesel engine, either single or twin. Some are purpose-designed for river use only, but many can also be used for coastal or offshore cruising. Prices range from £10,000–150,000. Construction material is usually GRP, sometimes steel or aluminium.

Canal narrowboats

Purpose-designed for our narrow canals, these craft have a 6ft 10in (2.08m) beam and length ranging from 25–70ft (7.6–21m). They can also travel on rivers and broad canals, plus the tidal lower sections of some rivers for short connecting hops, provided they have enough power. They are not, however, designed for use at sea, though some have ventured across the Channel at Dover, but only with a fully experienced crew, a support boat, permission from the Coastguard, and fine weather conditions. Usually made from steel, but sometimes aluminium, these boats are built to take the knocks of frequent locking on our narrow canals, and occasional collisions with bridges and other boats. Despite its narrow beam, the interior is remarkably spacious, with full standing headroom throughout, and most boats are fitted out to a high standard, with many of the creature comforts we expect in our homes. These include full-size gas cookers, fridges, central heating, continuous hot water, with showers and even baths, flush toilets, TV and stereo. Some will have generators or inverters, to give mains electricity. A 30ft (9m) craft is usually comfortable for two berths, 40ft (12m) will give 4–6 berths, while the bigger boats can go up to 8 or even 10. A 35ft (10.6m) narrowboat is easily manageable by two people, 45ft (13.7m) needs a crew of two, or preferably three, while 50ft (15.2m) upwards needs an active two, preferably more.

The narrowboat was designed originally for our narrow canals, but it can also happily cruise on rivers. Made from steel for strength and resistance to damage in locks, or sometimes aluminium, it comes in all lengths up to a maximum of 70ft (21m). An inboard diesel gives reliable economical power, and interior comforts can be as good as in your home. Some people live on narrowboats all year round.

Single-handed boating

Single-handed boating on the inland waterways is possible, but you must be experienced and completely confident in your abilities. A narrowboat up to 40ft (12m) can be handled by one active person, but your progress through locks will be slow, and you should not venture out after dark, or in adverse weather conditions.

Construction materials

We have mentioned some of the materials used for boat construction and we shall briefly explain the benefits and differences of each.

At one time nearly all boats on inland waterways were wooden. Today some of these still remain, but few new craft are made of wood. This is because it is expensive for construction, and needs continuous maintenance and care if it is to retain its appearance and soundness. Wood is still used in classic boats but these are a subject in their own right, which are not covered in this book.

GRP

One of the preferred materials used for boats today is glassfibre or GRP. This consists of layers of glassfibre mat or cloth laid up inside a mould with a liquid polyester resin. The resin sets to form a hard composite material. The thickness and strength depend on the number of layers of mat or cloth. A 20ft (6m) boat will probably have 4–6 layers, and a thickness of ³/₈in (10mm). A 35ft (10.6m) boat may have 8–12 layers, and a thickness of ¹/₂–³/₄in (13–19mm). The thickness used in the hull will be greater than that used for the cabin or decks.

The outside has a hard, shiny layer, known as the gelcoat. This is designed to improve the appearance of the rough glassfibre that you see inside the hull. It also protects the GRP against water ingress, and the effects of ultraviolet light.

Cheap to manufacture, requiring minimal maintenance, and relatively easy to repair, GRP is the favoured material of today for sea-going boats and river cruisers. Once the mould has been made, complex curved shapes are as easy to produce as flat panels, allowing considerable scope to the designer.

The only drawback is osmosis, a form of underwater blistering, due to water absorption through the gelcoat. In most cases it is a surface defect that can be successfully treated, restoring the hull to its original condition or better; it is rare for it to affect the structural integrity of the boat.

Steel

Steel is used for some sea-going river cruisers (particularly those built in Holland) and for most canal narrowboats and broad-beam boats built in the

UK. It is extremely tough, withstanding more collision damage than GRP. This makes it particularly suitable for boats that are regularly going to be passing through narrow locks and bridges. Because it is supplied in flat panels, it is more difficult to form into complex curved final shapes, though this is not a problem with the flat-bottomed, square-sided narrowboats. Steel also has a tendency to rust, requiring more care in its maintenance and protection than GRP. However, provided that initially it is correctly prepared and painted using the best-quality modern paints for priming and undercoating, it will give excellent service. You also need to fit sacrificial anodes to a steel hull to prevent electrolytic corrosion, as we will discuss later in the book. As an example of its durability, the hull of our narrowboat is now over 20 years old, and has only suffered a 5–10% corrosion.

The designation of narrowboat plate thicknesses needs some explanation. A typical specification today will be described as 10:6:4. This indicates that the bottom of the hull is made from plate 10mm (3/8in) thick, the sides of the hull are 6mm (1/4in) thick, and the cabin sides and top are 4mm (3/16in) thick. The different thicknesses are used because the hull bottom takes the brunt of the wear and corrosion, and gives the boat most of its strength. The sides take less wear and corrosion, while the cabin has no wear, and little corrosion. These thicknesses can vary, depending on the overall length of the vessel, with 12:8:4 being the maximum for a 70ft (21m) boat, though there can be some mystique attached to massive dimensions such as these. As an example, our own 45ft (13.7m) boat was only built to 6:5:3 specification, with consequent savings in cost and weight, but as described above it is lasting the course well, due to good construction and maintenance.

Other materials

Aluminium and ferro-cement were two materials occasionally used for boat construction, but the former has recently undergone a resurgence, with one company, Sea Otter, specialising in the material. They initially used aluminium for a range of trailable narrowboats, with its light weight being the main benefit, but now build larger narrowboats and Dutch barges, with low corrosion being the main advantage, offsetting its higher initial cost.

2 | *Buying Your Boat*

New or secondhand?

Assuming you have now decided to buy your boat, do you go for new or secondhand? The first point you should understand is that buying a boat is not like buying a car. In the case of the latter, it gradually deteriorates and depreciates, from the moment it is sold. As a result of this, secondhand cars have acquired an unfortunate reputation of unreliability. Secondhand boats, however, should be viewed in a similar way to houses; after all, most of us live in a secondhand house. Whilst a boat is not quite as long-lasting as a house, it is closer to it than a car. A boat may even improve with age, as more equipment is added to it, engines upgraded, and many of the initial 'bugs' are ironed out.

Clearly there are some benefits in buying new, and many people choose to go this route. You will be able to specify the exact options and equipment you want. You will have the benefits of any warranties on engines and equipment, and you will get back-up from the manufacturer or dealer. You will also have the satisfaction of owning the latest model, with the most up-to-date equipment. On most GRP production boats you will not have much say in the design or layout, which is fixed for all examples of the same model. On a one-off steel vessel, however, such as a canal narrowboat, you can design your ultimate dreamboat, tailor-made to your own requirements, and this is the goal which many owners eventually aspire to.

Engines

We touched briefly on the subject of the different engines that are available for inland waterways boats, and a further explanation of the benefits of the various types would be of assistance in helping you to make up your mind on which boat to buy. The options are petrol or diesel, inboard, outboard or outdrive, and steam or electric.

Outboard motors

Most smaller craft, up to 20ft (6m), will have an outboard motor. This can be either two-stroke, four-stroke, diesel or electric. The advantage of the outboard is its simplicity of installation, and ease of removal for storage or repairs. It is also easy to get at the propeller if it should become clogged with weed.

Until recently, the commonest units were petrol-driven two-strokes. These are relatively cheap to buy, and simple to maintain. The oil for lubrication is mixed with the petrol which can give rise to a smoky exhaust, especially on older models where the mixture has a ratio of 25:1 or 33:1. This may also lead to problems with plugs oiling up at slow speeds, together with poor tickover and starting. Modern two-strokes use 50:1 or even 100:1 mixtures and these, together with electronic ignition, have largely solved both problems. Two-strokes have a comparatively high fuel consumption, almost double that of four-strokes or diesels, but the low-powered engines used on the rivers make this less of a problem.

Until 15 years ago, there were few makes of four-stroke petrol outboards and they were only available up to 15hp. Now, spurred on by impending legislation requiring lower emission engines throughout Europe, all the major manufacturers have full ranges of four-strokes, up to 250hp and more. The advantages of the four-stroke are smooth running, low noise and vibration, low fuel consumption, lower exhaust emissions and no need to mix oil with the fuel. They will idle along at tickover with no oiling of the plugs, and are easy to start. They carry their lubricating oil in their sump, the level of which has to be regularly checked. Their disadvantages are: a slightly higher initial price, higher weight, and more expensive service and repair costs.

Diesel outboards are available, but their development has been sporadic. They are expensive, heavy and noisy, with the only advantage being reduced fuel cost. As such they have not yet made an impact on inland waterways.

Electric outboards provide the ideal solution for dinghies and small day-boats. They are completely silent in operation, do not vibrate, and of course do not smoke or pollute the water. They also start immediately every time. The disadvantage is the cost and weight of the batteries, which limit their range to 4–8 hours on average. They are also low-powered, in the range of $1/2$–1hp, though new models being developed now offer greater powers, up to 3–4hp, and longer range, provided you fit enough batteries.

Inboard motors

The inboard motor drives through a shaft and propeller either directly, or indirectly through a hydraulic drive – an arrangement that enables the engine to be mounted anywhere in the boat. It is more expensive to install than an outboard, and requires a weedhatch over the propeller to allow you to get down to remove weed, plastic bags or rope from around the prop. However, it is usually fairly reliable, cheap to run, and its drive system is relatively cheap to maintain and repair. An inboard can be either petrol or diesel, with steam or electric as an option.

Petrol engines are cheaper to buy, quieter and lighter than diesels. They used to be common in boats up to 25ft (7.6m), but few are fitted as new today. The problems are the flammability and explosive nature of petrol plus

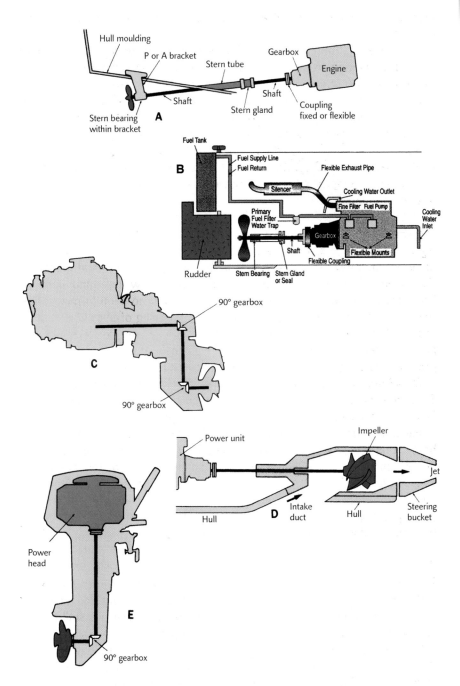

Fig 1 The different methods of propelling a motorboat. (A) Conventional inboard installation.
(B) Keel-cooled narrowboat inboard diesel.
(C) Sterndrive or outdrive. (D) Jet-drive (the intake usually has a
protective grill. (E) Outboard motor.

Pike is a classic Thames launch. Built in 1899, it was completely restored in 1996. It was originally an electric launch, and with the latest motor and batteries set a world endurance record of 135 miles in 30 hours on one charge.

its higher cost than diesel. Although a petrol engine is cheaper to buy than a diesel, when you take engine installation into account in the overall cost of the boat this is a relatively small saving and their use is gradually being phased out.

Diesels are reliable and long-lasting. Provided they are flexibly mounted, and well soundproofed, the noise and vibration are not a major problem. Larger models, over 40hp, are usually based on automotive or lorry engines. Below this they can be either specialised marine engines, or marinisations of general purpose units.

Electric motors are now making an impact on inland waterways. Their benefits are silent running, no smoke or vibration, and no pollution of the waterways. At the same time they are also cheap to run, and qualify for reduced-rate licences. They need virtually no maintenance, and start every time. Until recently their use has been restricted to dayboats, with running times of 6–12 hours, as they have to return to their charging points to recharge the batteries; but improved technology and a greater number of charging points along the waterways has allowed them to be fitted to cruising boats. The present endurance record held by a 30ft (9m) electric boat is 135 miles on a single charge in 30 hours, enough to get most of the way up the Thames, for instance, without recharging. Hybrid systems are also now available, with combinations of diesel main engines or generators, and electric motors, which give silent cruising at normal speeds, but with power available for strong flow conditions or for reaching a distant charging point; these are now being fitted to canal narrowboats. British Waterways have recently taken delivery of a 57ft (17m) narrowboat with a hybrid diesel/electric system, developed by the Thames Electric Launch Company, while the Environment Agency and Broads Authority have similarly powered diesel/electric patrol boats.

Steam engines are the province of the enthusiast only and are not practical for anything but dayboats and traditional classic craft.

Outdrives

The outdrive is basically a combination of an inboard and outboard, hence its other names of inboard/outboard, sterndrive, or Z-drive. It consists of an inboard engine, either petrol or diesel, mounted just in front of the transom, and driving through an outdrive leg. Benefits are easier installation, plus keeping the engine out of the saloon. You get the extra steering control of an outboard, plus the ease of reaching the propeller. On the downside, the unit is vulnerable to damage, and expensive to repair compared to a conventional shaft and prop.

Buying a new boat

New boats are usually either sold through dealers or direct from the manufacturer. If a boat is sold through a dealer, it will have a profit margin built into the quoted retail price to allow for his costs and overheads. This margin can be anywhere between 5–30%, depending on the make and type of boat, and the size of the operation involved. More usually it will be 10–20%. In return for his profit, the dealer will be expected to buy and stock one or more models from the manufacturer's range. He may produce his own advertising in magazines, and may fund some or all of the cost of exhibiting at boat shows. The dealer will give you your demonstrations, and will be expected to provide after-sales service, and handle any warranty claims, passing the cost of these on to the manufacturer.

Warranties

Warranty claims for specific items of equipment on board are usually dealt with by the maker of that equipment. In particular, this applies to the engine, though in many cases a good dealer will act as the liaison in these situations. It should be noted that this is a fundamental difference from buying a car, or almost any other consumer item, where component parts are usually the responsibility of the overall manufacturer.

If the dealer fails to satisfy a customer on a warranty claim on the boat or equipment, the ultimate liability rests with the manufacturer. This is an important point as, in most cases, it will be the dealer you buy the boat from, and pay the money to.

In an ideal world, problems of warranty should not arise, but in practice they will, and it is important to ascertain who is responsible for the various items. This becomes particularly important with boats manufactured overseas, where it may be time-consuming and difficult to get a response from the builder. In this instance, it should be remembered that many of the major items of equipment, the engine in particular, will have a UK distributor, who can be approached if you are having problems with either the dealer or the manufacturer, though it should be borne in mind that they will not have supplied the equipment if it was installed in the country of manufacture.

Dealer service

At the end of all this, there are several benefits from buying through a dealer. He will be geared up to selling boats, and looking after the customer, whereas the builder will be more concerned with the mechanics of production. Thus the dealer will be open at weekends and bank holidays, whereas most builders like to take some time off. The dealer will have models afloat and ready for trials at their premises, whereas the builder will frequently be on an industrial estate miles from the water, and only have boats under construction. This is an important consideration, as it is always best to look at a boat in its natural environment if possible, and to try it out under the conditions in which you will use it.

A dealer should have more than one model from the range available for inspection. He may also have secondhand versions of the same boats for sale at his premises. This is important, because often people will not be able to afford a new boat at first, but will buy a used model to start with, and trade up as the funds allow it, or as they get a better idea of exactly what they want. In this case, the dealer will usually handle the selling of the old boat, or take it in part exchange, considerably simplifying the process of moving up the range.

The dealer should also be able to arrange finance and insurance, and will be able to supply and fit any extra items of equipment you require. Good ones will also arrange any training or tuition you might feel you need if you are completely new to the sport.

Buying from a boatbuilder

So what are the benefits of buying direct from the builder? Well, of course, you do cut out the profit that would otherwise be paid to the dealer, thus reducing the cost of the boat, though the builder might add on a percentage to take account of this. You will also be better able to specify exactly what you want in the boat, in terms of layout, equipment, materials and colour. You will probably be able to watch your craft through its various stages of construction, though do not overdo the number of visits you make to the yard, as the builder will not want the customer looking over his shoulder all the time. In any case, you will probably be horrified at what your dream boat looks like in its early life.

Narrowboat builders, who will rarely produce more than 5–10 boats a year, will mostly deal directly with their customers, whereas the makers of production GRP craft will usually tend to work through dealers.

Boat shows

So if you are buying new, how should you go about it, and what are the points you should look at? For many people, the starting point is a boat show. Here you can see a number of makes and models on display, and can browse between them, comparing features as you go. Be aware, though, that because boat show stands are expensive, the smaller companies with low turnover may not find it cost effective to exhibit. This does not necessarily imply that there is anything wrong with the company or its product. Large national shows tend to be very expensive, and prohibitive to smaller craft builders, who you should find at regional shows.

If you are going to a show, try to find a preview in one of the magazines, as it will help you to draw up a list of makes and models before you get there; this saves you time wasted tramping around, or missing possibly suitable boats. Once at the show, make it clear to the demonstrator that you are a serious buyer. Tell them what sort of boat you are looking for, and how much you have got to spend. They will then be better able to advise you, and more likely to give you their time than if they think you are just a spectator.

Obviously you should be collecting brochures and price lists, but as you do this, check what levels of standard equipment are supplied with each boat, and what the actual price will be with equivalent levels of gear on board. This applies to major items, such as the cooker, fridge and engine, but it also applies to basic running gear. Before you can go afloat, you will need such items as mooring lines, fenders, anchor, boathook, fire extinguishers, horn, gas bottle, lifejackets and so on, and the cost of these can mount up. Some companies include them, others do not.

Check on the options of layout, finish and materials that are available, and whether they will involve extra cost. Some makes will be restricted in this area, others will be generous.

Ask whether the boats have been tested by any of the boating magazines and, if possible, get hold of a copy carrying the results. Alternatively, when you get back home, ask the magazines to send you photocopies of reports they may have on boats you are interested in. Most will do this for a small charge, and it is well worth it. Be aware that the depth and objectivity of such reports will vary. Some will be little more than rewrites of the brochure, but most will give you fair comment, and some background on the company. At the same time, while you are at the show, ask how old the company is, and how many boats it builds each year. Clearly, there is nothing inherently wrong with new or small companies, but it is still good to get a general feel of the operation.

While you are at the show, try to get an overall impression of the quality built into the different models. Look past the first impressions, with the wall-to-wall carpet and four-speaker stereo, and check behind the scenes. Open the cupboards, and lift some locker lids; check whether the standard of finish inside is anywhere near as good as outside. You do not need perfection in a locker, but you do need a coat of varnish or paint, and no rough edges to snag clothes or bedding. Look at the engineering – are the nuts bodged where they were tightened with the wrong spanner? Are the welds smooth or rough? Is the wiring neat and clipped out of the way in looms, or straggling round the inside of the hull like multi-coloured spaghetti? Double hose-clips on important piping such as through-hull fittings, bilge-pumps and engine cooling are a good sign. Batteries should be secured in boxes with lids. Is a bilge-pump fitted as standard, and is it a sensible size? Also, can you get to it in an emergency? It is surprising how many builders do not consider a pump to be an essential item, or fit one that is totally inadequate and nowhere near large enough for the job.

Is the inside of the hull painted out, or is it just rough steel or GRP? This is not just cosmetic – it will affect the future life of the boat and is a good indication of the level of care of the builder. Step back outside, and look along the length of the hull. It should be smooth and fair, with no ripples in a GRP hull, and no welds showing in steel plate. Having said that, some builders do not believe in grinding off their welds. This will save them time, and hence make the boat cheaper. It is not structurally unsound, but again it gives a general indication of their approach to the job, and where they see their boat in the market.

Similar comments apply to the interior finish of the boat. Seven coats of varnish cost more to apply than two, and do not significantly add to the longevity of a vessel, just its overall appearance. At the same time, one coat or none at all will affect both the durability and attractiveness of the boat in later life, which will have a bearing on its resale value.

Finally, take your camera with you to the show, and snap off a couple of shots of each boat you are interested in, or any particular features you noticed on board which are not illustrated in the brochure. They will remind you of some of the good points of each craft, though do make a note of which boat you have photographed – include a copy of the brochure in the shot as a reference.

If you do not have a convenient show at the time you are making your first decisions, advertisements in magazines will give you the names of companies producing the type of boat you want; many run lists of makes and models available, on a regular basis. Alternatively, the BMF Boatline Information Service will provide you with a similar list.

Drawing up a shortlist

Once you are back home, the next stage of the selection process takes place. Go through the brochures, and draw up a shortlist of models. Again, be careful to compare like with like in terms of the standard equipment, or the cost of including this. Be careful that the prices you are using are the normal retail price, as many boats will be marked at a lower price for a quick sale at the show. Also, be careful that all prices include VAT. Boats are still one of the surprising areas that have many of their prices displayed excluding VAT. This practice is gradually being phased out, and is technically at variance with the

Price Markings Act, but just scrapes through on the basis that many new boats are sold to overseas customers, who will not necessarily pay UK VAT. Also, some dealers argue that many UK buyers are VAT-registered commercial users.

Be cautious about comparing boats on the basis of length. It is tempting to use the quoted length as a yardstick, but this can be confusing. The Searunner 24 may, in fact, only be as long as the Wavecruiser 22 – it is just that Searunner include bathing platform and pulpit in their designation, whereas Wavecruiser do not. In fact there is no law stating that the 24 has to relate to any particular dimension, though in practice, length is the one they will take. Even the specifications have to be read carefully. Overall length would appear to be obvious, but again it can include bathing platform, fenders, pulpit and so on. American boats can be even more confusing, sometimes measuring overall length as the length round the gunwale, and sometimes as the centreline length.

In practice, the specification should state whether overall length includes the bathing platform. However, today's design trend towards integral platforms, particularly found on fast, sea-going boats, where they are part of the overall structure of the boat, is adding its own complication. Similarly, canal boats, and some river cruisers, will have permanent bow and stern fenders. These should not generally be included in the measurement of over-all length, though you should be warned that some marina operators may think otherwise when they come to charge you for your berth. (Similar comments may apply to davits and dinghies on the transom.) So, apply your own formula, and mark all brochures with what you consider to be the realistic length of the model described.

Similarly, you should make a note of the beam of the boat. As we have already said, certain craft are designed to fit into the standard locks of our narrow canal system, and their beam will be a maximum 7ft (2.1m). (In fact 6ft 10in (2.08m) is normally used for the maximum beam, to give the necessary clearance.) Boats used on wider waterways do not have this restriction, and will accordingly have greater beam. Typically, a 24ft (7.3m) boat will be around 8–9ft (2.4–2.7m) wide, while a 30ft (9m) vessel can be 9–11ft (2.7–3.3m) or more. Clearly, the greater beam will give greater internal volume, and hence increase the apparent value of this boat over its narrow-beam counterpart. Some of the extra beam may be used to give wider side decks, not just extra accommodation.

Finally, when making your first comparative assessment, you should also consider the possibility of discounts. A price reduction will depend partly on the time of year, partly on the state of the economy, and partly on the popularity of the model and make. Clearly there are times of the year when a dealer wants to move his stock. At the end of the season, or when a model is about to change, he will be more receptive to an offer of a lower price. Be aware, however, that squeezing the last penny out of the seller is likely to make him less concerned with after-sales and the invisible back-up that can be so essential to enjoyable boating. This is particularly important if you are new to the sport, and want as much help as possible in your first year. Similarly, a lavish discount could indicate a dealer whose financial structure is not so sound, or one who is just wanting to clear out his stock, then leave the business. Also, remember that the discount is probably being offered to every other customer, so the resale value of that model or make is going to suffer accordingly.

Cancelled orders can be another fruitful area. Providing you are prepared to take a boat built to a completed specification with no alterations, the builder may be interested in negotiating a special price.

Demonstrations

Once you have drawn up your shortlist of boats, you should book yourself some trial runs. It is obviously impossible to predict the weather for these, but try to take this into account when later assessing how a boat measured up. No boat looks its best in the rain, though having said that, the weather-proofness and ease of erection of the canopy is an important factor in our climate. Similarly, windy days can tax the handling of any craft, and you should take this into account when assessing a real-life situation.

Make mental notes on the whole approach of the dealer to the trial. Is the boat ready for you to take out? Has it been cleaned and prepared? Is there fuel in the tank, and does the engine start and run readily? All these might appear obvious points, but it is surprising how casual some sellers can be, which may reflect on their overall approach. It is usually sensible to let the demonstrator take the boat out of its berth – even if you think you know what you are doing, every craft and mooring has its quirks. And in any case, this will allow you to handle the lines, and get a feel of how safe the decks are to move around on. Incidentally, go to the trial in your boating gear, not your Sunday best, so you feel comfortable when stepping aboard and moving about.

If possible, take along a knowledgeable friend who can give you some impressions of the boat, though this is not essential. Whether or not to take children is a difficult question. They may well be part of your boating plans, but while you are trying to control them, you will be missing important points about the boat. Remember at best you will only have half an hour or so to assess the suitability of the craft.

Once out on the river, check how easily the boat handles. Does it steer in a straight line, or does it require continuous attention to the helm? Does it stop quickly, and how tightly does it turn? What is the view like from the helm, and from other seats in the cockpit? What are the noise levels like at maximum and cruising speeds? This can be particularly important on a narrowboat, where the helm position is usually above the engine; high levels of noise and vibration can become wearing after a long period at the tiller. Once you have assessed these points, do not hog the helm. Let someone else drive, and then move around the boat yourself, checking noise levels and general comfort underway.

Entering the basin at Stratford-upon-Avon, you can expect an audience of interested spectators.

Back in the marina, you can check how easily the boat handles if you wish, but it may be wise to let the salesman drive it back into its berth, as again, this manoeuvre can be tricky and your handling of the helm might not give a fair indication of the boat's capabilities if you are trying it for the first time. Alternatively, if the berth is a tight one and you still want to get a feel for mooring the boat, ask if you can take it alongside an easier stretch of pontoon.

Once you are safely tied up, ask to see how easy it is to put the canopy up, and how effective it is. Can you see out with it up, especially astern? Is there enough headroom, and how well does it stow away? Can you get in and out of the cockpit easily with it up and is it safe to move forward on the sidedecks? Often the canopy will cover any grab rails on the cockpit side, leaving you short of handholds just when the conditions most require them. Of course, on a narrowboat you will have no problems with the canopy over the steering position – there isn't one. All you can do is check the condition of your waterproofs, and invest in an umbrella.

You are now free to make a general inspection of the boat. We cannot go into every detail that you should be checking, but a few basic principles apply. You will spend a lot of time tying up, and manoeuvring in locks on both rivers and canals, so check the mooring equipment. Cleats should be large and well fastened. They should be easy to reach for fastening your lines. Sidedecks should be as wide as possible, preferably with some sort of non-slip finish. Hand rails should be provided at as many places as possible. On small boats, these will normally be inboard, for you to hang on to, but larger craft will have guard rails around the gunwales. Guard rails should be well secured – lean on them to see if they move – and have a lower rail or wire to stop you sliding underneath. Narrowboats will have rails or raised handholds along the length of the cabin top. Make sure that these are easy to hold on to, with no obstructions as you slide your hand forward – it is not unknown for ventilators or gas heater vents to be sited under the rails, just where your hands go. For river use, an anchor should be stowed readily to hand, either in the cockpit or on the foredeck, in case you have to use it in an emergency.

Gas bottles and portable fuel tanks should be stowed in purpose-made lockers, with drains in the bottom to let out any leaks of gas or fumes. These lockers should not be shared with anything else, to avoid risk of damaging the tanks or piping.

On the subject of safety, the Environment Agency and British Waterways have drawn up the Boat Safety Scheme that all boats over four years old must comply with (see page 42). New boats will also have to comply with the EU Recreational Craft Directive, of which more later. The rules are, in the main, sensible and well thought out, resulting from many years of experience, so it is in your interest that the boat complies, quite apart from the legal side.

Down below you should look for features relevant to how you intend using the boat. If you are expecting to do some serious cruising, storage space is a must. Try to envisage how much you will need for provisions, crockery and

The interior of this narrowboat shows the comfort and luxury that these modern craft can provide.

pots, and for stowing clothes. Work out how many people will normally be on board, and make sure there is enough room for all their gear. Bedding may have to be stowed during the daytime so look for large lockers with easy access. The galley is always an important area. Check the size of the cooker and the fridge. How much worktop area is there? Many sinks have hinged lids over them. This gives a tidy look to the galley area particularly if it is in the saloon and gives an impression of worktop space; bear in mind, however, that the lid will usually be raised when you are using the galley. The size of the sink is important, as is the supply of hot and cold water. Check how large the water tank is – often you will find it is only 5 or 10 gallons (23–45 litres) capacity, which may be all right for day-trips or overnight stops, but will quickly run out on longer cruises.

Satisfactory toilet arrangements are also a key to happy cruising. The smallest craft will have a portable chemical WC which you empty at disposal points strategically located along the waterway. The modern units are a far cry from the old bucket-type Elsan, having flushing water reservoirs built in, and sealed lower chambers. Even so, the process of emptying them is not

Bathroom arrangements on boats range from the simplest portable chemical toilet to all the facilities of home including flushing toilets, domestic basins and heated towel rails, plus showers and even baths.

very salubrious; also they will usually fill up every second day if there are four people on board. The more sophisticated option is a holding tank system. This is built into the boat and has a capacity of up to a week or more, depending on how many people are aboard. Disposal is by pump-out at designated points along the waterway, usually at marinas. Each pump-out will normally cost you £5–10, but you may consider this more desirable than tottering across the tow-path with your containerful of effluent.

Paradoxically, some of the most expensive narrowboats being built today for long-term liveaboards are being fitted with cassette versions of the Thetford Porta Potti. The reasoning being that if you should be forced by winter maintenance lock closures to spend several months on a stretch of waterway without a pump-out, you can at least carry or wheel your cassette to a disposal point.

Showers are also standard on most boats which have a separate toilet compartment. The method of heating the water will either be a gas or diesel heater, or a calorifier tank heated by the cooling water of an inboard engine. In either case, check the headroom in the toilet compartment, plus the elbow room. Also check to see that there are enough lockers for everyone's washing gear, plus the necessary bathroom cleaning products – many boatbuilders seem to fall down in this important area, with inadequate space allowed.

Check how wide the berths are, and also how long. On a small boat you will not expect to find beds as large as you have at home but, even so, some manufacturers' idea of a double berth would be more appropriate for children than adults. The double bed on a narrowboat should be 4ft wide, or even 4ft 6in. Check how easy it is to keep the boat clean. Stuck-down carpets are the very devil if they get wet. Also it is important that you can get access to the inside of the hull under the floor in case of damage. A good boat will have removable hatches to allow you to do this.

Linings and overhead ceilings should be on removable panels, to allow you to get at the underside of deck fittings. Steel boats should be lined on the inside with insulating foam, to keep them warm in winter and cool in summer, and to prevent condensation. Insulation is also useful for GRP boats but less critical and less common.

Some of the windows should open, or preferably slide, to give ventilation in hot weather. There should also be an opening escape hatch forward (and aft in an aft cabin boat) for emergency exit in case of fire. Channels should be present under the windows to collect condensation which will always occur, especially when people are sleeping in a cabin. Adequate permanent ventilation should be provided in the form of overhead vents to help prevent condensation and also the build-up of suffocating gases if gas-powered appliances are used on board.

The Recreational Craft Directive

This is European Commission legislation that applies to all new boats built after June 1998. Its provisions are detailed and complex, and are beyond the scope of this book to describe. However, briefly it covers virtually all vessels between 2.5–24m (8–79ft) in length, with certain limited exemptions for historic replica craft, canoes, and personal watercraft. It also does not apply to a boat you build yourself, providing you do not sell it within five years.

As the purchaser, you should receive certain documents. These include a Certificate of Conformity, signed by the builder or the person putting the boat on the market. You should also get a detailed Owner's Manual, with operating instructions, and full information on all the equipment installed, including wiring diagrams and drawings of the positions of all major items. You should be given details of all the warranties that apply to the boat and its equipment.

The boat should have a plate permanently displayed, stating who built it, the number of people it is designed to carry, and the category of waters it is to be used on. There are four categories, but most inland craft come under D: sheltered inland waters, including small lakes, rivers and canals. Alternatively, they may be classed Category C: coastal waters. However, you should note that these categories of waters are only advisory, and the decision as to whether you set sail at any time is still up to you.

The boat should also have a CIN (formerly HIN) number (Craft/Hull Identification Number). This will be welded into the plating of a steel hull, and moulded into a GRP hull. It consists of a series of letters and numbers which uniquely identify the craft, and when and where it was built.

It will consist of 6 letters and 8 numbers, as follows:

ABCDE12345F678

AB	Country Code (GB for Great Britain, NL for Netherlands etc)
CDE	Builder's Code
12345	Builder's Serial Number
F	Month of Construction (Jan to Dec = A to L)
6	Year of Construction (Final Digit)
78	Model Year (Final 2 Digits)

Even a part-finished hull for home completion should have a CIN number.

The purpose of the RCD was originally to ensure that all boats sold throughout the European Community were built to the same standards, to give level trading conditions for all manufacturers. But the safety and construction requirements it has brought in work to the benefit of all owners, and now the initial teething problems have been ironed out, it is seen as a generally beneficial piece of legislation.

Incidentally, it may appear to be connected to the Boat Safety Scheme that we will be describing later, but this is not the case. The RCD applies only to new craft. The BSS applies to all craft, new or old, and once a new boat becomes four years old, it will have to be inspected and awarded a Boat Safety Certificate, even if it was built to conform to the RCD. For more

information on the RCD you should contact the British Marine Federation: 35
01784 473377.

Buying Your Boat

Finance

Whilst some people may be able to buy their boat outright using capital, most of us will have to borrow at least some of the purchase price. There are various methods available, depending on how much you need, and how quickly you are able to repay it. The interest rate payable will be dependent on the size of the loan, the repayment period, and whether it is secured or not.

If the amount required is relatively small compared to your income (eg say £1000–2000 payable within a year) a bank overdraft is often the quickest and simplest to arrange. Above this figure, the bank will usually try to sell you a personal loan, with a fixed interest rate up to £5000 and a variable interest rate, tied to the bank's base rate, for amounts above that. These loans will normally be unsecured. Above these figures, a bank is likely to want a charge over a major asset which is normally your house. Building societies are becoming more interested in the personal loan market, in addition to their traditional mortgage business, and are worth approaching.

However, the commonest route for most people, especially when the amounts are over £10,000 or so, is to go to one of the specialist marine finance houses who advertise in the boating magazines. The advantage of going to these companies is that you will be dealing with experienced staff who understand the problems involved. The finance houses will require the loan to be secured by a charge on the boat itself. This is often termed a marine mortgage, but the expression needs explaining.

At one time, a marine mortgage required that the vessel be officially registered, as a British Registered Ship. The mortgage was then entered on the register as a charge against the vessel. If the craft was sold, the charge could be seen by the prospective buyer. Most finance houses still require a vessel to be registered in this way if it is of high value. However, the high cost of registration – around £400 or more – has led to a simpler and cheaper form of registration, the Small Ships Register (SSR): 02920 448800. For £12, this provides a form of documentation sufficient to satisfy officials in foreign countries of the identity of the boat. The SSR can also form the basis of a secured loan, though not one recorded in the statutory fashion of a full Registered Vessel. Some companies are prepared to accept this system, in return for the simplicity and cheapness of the SSR. The security for the lender is deemed to be sufficient this way, though there is no protection for a prospective buyer.

Marine mortgages will normally have a repayment period of between 5 and 10 years. Their interest rate will be comparable to the best secured personal loan from a bank.

Obviously, interest rates vary all the time but in general an overdraft will have the highest interest rate. This is followed by an unsecured personal loan, then a secured personal loan, and finally a marine mortgage.

Depreciation

Provided that the boat has been regularly maintained, it will keep its value well. Of course, its price will gradually fall, with the most pronounced drop being in the first year or two, but then the value will gradually stabilise as the price of new boats increases.

Buying a secondhand boat

As we have already said, many people opt to buy a secondhand boat. In fact statistics show that of all the boat sales every year, 75% are used craft, and many people never own a new boat in their lives.

First you have to decide where to find your boat. The main sources of used craft are: brokers, dealers, private classified advertisements in magazines and newspapers, websites, club noticeboards, and auctions. We will deal with these in turn.

Brokers

The distinction between a broker and a dealer is an important one, and has to be understood. Again, the analogies with selling cars and houses are useful ones. A broker acts in much the same capacity as an estate agent. He takes on the duty of selling boats for existing owners, for which he charges a commission, usually between 5 and 10%. He will sometimes, but not always, berth the boat at his premises and will in theory keep it in a clean, saleable condition. He (or she) will show prospective owners over the boat, arrange trials if required and can organise surveys and finance. However, the final transaction is between owner and customer. This is a significant point, because it means that the broker cannot subsequently be held liable for any faults which may occur after the sale. He also will include an exclusion clause on any details or specification he draws up for the boat, to the effect that any information contained therein is included in good faith, but based on information provided by the owner.

Again, this is an important point. Accurate information about secondhand boats is notoriously hard to come by. Speeds quoted will usually be based on estimates, or the vessel's speedometer, neither of which will be accurate; also speeds cannot be easily checked on a river. Engine hours, even the age of the boat, can be difficult to pin down, especially if the maker has gone out of business, or the craft has had several owners. Unless it is a Registered Vessel – unlikely with most inland craft – a boat has no equivalent to a car log-book, and historical information will be very hard to obtain or verify. This is not to say that the seller is intentionally going to deceive you, he may be just as ignorant of these details as the person he bought the boat from, but the principle of *caveat emptor* (buyer beware) is never more pertinent.

Having said this, a good broker should do his best to ensure that information he is passing on is as accurate as possible as he has a moral obligation to his customer if not a legal one. He should also have a general interest in preserving his reputation with both seller and buyer alike, as both are likely to be back in the market at some time in the future. Many brokers belong to the YDSA (Yacht Designers and Surveyors Association), as do surveyors, of whom more later.

Dealers

A dealer will own the boat outright and here the transaction is much closer to that of a secondhand car sale. Some dealers specialise in one make, and look for good used models to buy for their stock. Some will have simply taken the boat in part exchange for a new vessel. In either case, the transaction falls under the Sale of Goods Act, with the seller being responsible for verifying information given about the vessel if possible, and for ensuring that it is of basic merchantable quality. They may even offer a limited guarantee on some items of equipment, though this is unusual. In general, most secondhand boats will be sold on the brokerage basis, with the dealer system most commonly found for new craft, though this situation is altering slowly.

Private sales

Private sales are most often found advertised in the classified pages of the main boating magazines, or in other magazines such as *Exchange & Mart* or on the Internet. You may also find them advertised in your local paper, particularly those with circulations in the main boating areas. Another good source of possible sales are the notice-boards of boat clubs.

There is nothing wrong with a private sale, providing seller and buyer observe some simple rules to ensure that the transaction goes smoothly. The main benefit is that you save the 5 to 10% broker's commission. The drawback is that you cannot look at more than one boat at a time, and it is less easy to pin down both parties to a convenient time to view the boat. You will also have less comeback if any problems should subsequently occur although the seller must not make deliberately inaccurate or misleading statements.

Auctions

Boat auctions are uncommon, but the number is gradually increasing, mainly for smaller craft. It is impossible to give precise information about auctions as they have different practices of their own. In general, the same warnings apply as to any auction. Take along someone who knows something about boats. Look carefully at any craft you may be interested in. Check the price that it would normally sell for and set a maximum amount that you are prepared to bid. Some auctions will allow you to try the boat out before buying, and some will cover you against a serious defect that might occur immediately after purchase, but you need to find this out in advance. All auctions will charge some sort of commission, and some may charge VAT on this. Again, check before setting your price for a boat, and add this amount to get the final figure. Be particularly careful about verifying the ownership of a boat before you bid for it, in case it is subject to a finance agreement, or has been stolen.

What to look for

When assessing a secondhand boat, whether it is a private sale or brokerage, the most important factor is how well it has been looked after. A boat will suffer more from neglect than from over-use; this is what affects its value and saleability. As an example, a marine engine will rarely get a fraction of the use that its road-going counterpart does and will hardly ever wear out. If, however, it isn't serviced at regular intervals by the owner, it will quickly become unreliable.

The signs of care or lack of it are easy to spot, even for the amateur or newcomer to the sport. If you are at all unsure what to look for, take along a knowledgeable friend and once you have decided on the right boat, get it surveyed before the final sale. Remember, be tough enough to turn down a boat that does not look right – there will be plenty more to look at. Unless you are enthusiastic about repairs, avoid buying a bad example, even at a low price – boating is meant to be fun.

First impressions count for much in assessing the condition of a boat. Is it

Bold as brass – the highly polished horn and tunnel light on a traditional narrowboat.

clean on the outside, and does it seem well looked after? Obviously, if the owner has been away for some time, or it is the end of the winter, expect some superficial dirt, but not too much. Look at the mooring lines – are they frayed, green with mould, hard with exposure to the sunlight, spliced, or full of knots – anyone who scrimps on this basic item will probably do the same elsewhere. Fenders should be clean and undamaged. Cleats, guard rails, fairleads, stem-head fitting and anchor should all be secure.

Look for damage to the hull. No river or canal boat can avoid the occasional scrape or bump but these should be minimal, and should have been repaired or touched in. Areas to look for damage are around the gunwale, especially at the forward shoulder of the boat and the aft quarter. The stem is also a vulnerable point, as are the topsides amidships, and the corner of the transom. Again, some scratches and chips must be expected, especially on an older boat, but if it is GRP, these should have been filled in neatly with a good match to the original gelcoat. Similarly, if viewing a steel narrowboat at the beginning of the season, it should have its scratches and dents filled and painted.

The underwater sections of narrowboats will usually be painted in bitumastic which is a dull black tarry protective finish. Above the waterline, when new they will usually have been painted with enamel paint – the shiny gloss that you use on the outside of your house. As they grow older, and the topsides become damaged with collisions with locks, the temptation is to carry the bitumastic up the side of the boat to the gunwale, as its matt finish disguises the dents and marks. Unfortunately this is the lazy way out; the bitumastic leaves tarry black marks on anything it comes in contact with, including neighbouring boats and their fenders. The practice does much to generate antagonism between owners of fibreglass river boats, with their clean white hulls, and canal boaters, when they meet in the locks. More importantly, it often indicates a general lack of care in the maintenance of these craft.

Continuing our inspection of the outside of the boat, the canopy is the next important item. These are expensive to replace and do not last for ever. Five years or so will be their maximum lifespan, after that they generally become stiff to handle, cracked and leaky. Check on its condition, particularly the zips, fastenings and clear panels. Cabin windows should also be checked for damage, scratches or cracks. The best windows are made of toughened glass. Perspex is cheaper but discolours, crazes and cracks as it ages.

If the boat is out of the water, check the condition of the stern gear, and the underwater hull. Look for damage to the hull, particularly along the keel and the chines (the corners between topsides and bottom). You can check for osmosis in a GRP hull, which in its most obvious form appears as blisters in the gelcoat but unless you are sure of yourself this should be reported on by a surveyor. Similarly, with a steel boat you can check for obvious corrosion, pitting and rust, but only a surveyor will be able to give you the whole story.

Check the propeller for damage – bent blades and nicks out of the leading edges being danger signs. Try to lift the shaft, to see if it moves in its bearing – very slight movement is permitted, but nothing more. Similarly, check the rudder for looseness in its bearings or slack play either way. Check that the P-bracket that carries the shaft on some boats is securely fastened to the hull.

Check the anodes. These are lumps of silver-coloured magnesium or zinc, usually pear-shaped or rectangular, bolted to the hull. They are normally between 8–15in (20–38cm) long, and will be located underwater near the stern gear on a GRP boat, and at both stern and bow on a steel boat. Their purpose is to prevent electrolytic corrosion of the underwater metal due to its immersion in the water. They work by corroding away themselves, in preference to the bronze of the propeller or the steel of the hull, hence their description as 'sacrificial'. Anodes are more critical in salt water, but they are also advisable in fresh water, where they should be made of magnesium rather than zinc. They corrode away over a period of 2–4 years, and their condition is important to note. If they are smooth and uncorroded, they are probably not doing their job. If they are more than 75% wasted away, they should be replaced. Without them, a steel hull will pit and corrode, while the propeller will gradually lose the zinc content of its bronze. To check the latter, tap the prop with a coin. If it is in good condition it will ring like a bell. If it has lost zinc it will sound dull.

As we have already mentioned, some inland waterways boats will be fitted with outdrives rather than a conventional shaft and prop. You should ask to see the boat out of the water so that you can check the outdrive for corrosion or wear. They will be made of aluminium, which will eventually deteriorate and pit. This advice also applies to outboard motors.

Back on board, check the cockpit for signs of leaks from the cover. Check the gas locker and fuel tank locker. Lift up the floorboards and check for leaks in the bilge. A certain amount of water is inevitable, but a lot of it, or a layer of oil on top, should be a warning sign. Of course, the clever owner will have pumped the bilge before you arrive, but the giveaway is a black tidemark that the oil film will have left around the side of the boat. The higher this is, the more you should beware. The usual source of leaks will be the stern-gland. It is in order for this to drip slightly when the shaft is turning, but not at rest. Check the steering and engine controls. These should be free-moving, but with no slack or backlash.

The engine itself should be accessible through either the cockpit or the cabin. At this stage, it is not feasible to give the motor a thorough test, but a visual inspection will tell you much. The engine should be clean, with no oil leaks or rust. The bilge underneath should be similarly free from oil. Piping and wiring should be undamaged, and clipped out of the way. The battery should be clean, with no corrosion round the terminals. Tools and spare oil cans should be neatly stowed.

Inside the boat, dampness is a bad sign. This will be indicated by a musty smell, and can be the result of either condensation or leaks. Condensation is

Outdrives are made of aluminium which can suffer corrosion, particularly if they have been painted with a copper-based anti-fouling. Always use the right paint for this job.

With the boat out of the water, check the propeller for damage and corrosion, and the propeller shaft bearing and rudder bearing for wear.

caused by poor ventilation while the boat is closed up. Leaks occur most often round the window frames so check around these, and also underneath. The giveaway will be stains down the sidelining, or damp patches in the upholstery or carpet beneath. Leaks will also occur through fittings and hatches in the cabin top, or round the deck, where the join is to the cabin or the gunwale. One or two leaks are not necessarily a serious problem, as they can be cured, but if they have been occurring for some time, there may be water damage and rot.

A general check of all the domestic equipment will give you a good indication of how the boat has been treated. Cooker, fridge, toilet – all should be clean and working. Marks on cushions and damage to joinery are warning signs. You should ask how much of the interior fittings and equipment will be part of the sale price. Make a note of these, and take a photograph or two, partly as a reminder of what the boat looked like, and partly to fix what is there. It is remarkable how many items can vanish between inspection and handover. Under this heading come crockery, pots and pans, curtains, cushions, loose chairs, decorations on the walls, plaques, as well as running gear such as boat-hook, fenders, spare lines and so on. Many owners will remove these items innocently, not realising that you thought they were remaining, but the cost of replacing them can quickly mount up.

At this stage, if the owner or his representative is with you, ask to see any documentation that goes with the boat, including invoices for recent work done. A good boat will have been regularly serviced and repaired, and should have the bills to back this up. Be suspicious if these cannot be produced. Even if the owner does the work himself, there will be bills for filters and oil for the engine, paint for the hull, and the cost of lifting the boat from the water. As a guide, the engine should be serviced every year, and the boat lifted from the water every one or two years.

If you are shown a full cruising and maintenance log, you will know you are on a boat that has been cared for and loved all its life. The overall age of the vessel and its number of owners is not critical, providing each has kept up the standard.

The Boat Safety Scheme

This has been drawn up by British Waterways and the Environment Agency, to improve the safety standards of boats using their waters; the scheme is being adopted by most of the other navigation authorities. The full details are beyond the scope of this book, but more information and booklets can be obtained from British Waterways on 01923 226422.

Briefly, the scheme covers all powered craft that have cooking, heating or lighting facilities on board. Boats have to be inspected every four years, and a valid certificate is required before they can be licensed. The main areas covered are engine installations, electrical systems, gas systems, fire prevention and extinguishers, and pollution.

The importance to you as the potential buyer is to ensure that the boat you are looking at has a valid certificate. If this only has a short time left to run, it is worth considering having a new inspection carried out to ensure the boat has not fallen below the standards over a period of time. Alternatively you should make passing the scheme a condition of your buying the boat if you are putting down any deposit.

Trials

If you are fairly sure that you have found a boat that could be right for you, it is time to arrange a trial. Again, this can be with either the owner, or the broker acting as the owner's representative. All the comments under new boat trials apply, but in addition you should pay particular attention to the mechanics and the engine. Does it start easily, with a minimum of smoke at tickover and underway? Do the gears shift easily, with no stalling? Does the engine run smoothly, with no misfires or vibration? Your speed will be limited by the river restrictions, but a quick burst on an open stretch will tell you what the engine will run up to. Obviously you will not be able to do this on a boat with sea-going potential, and a planing top speed. Check the cooling water coming out of the exhaust, if appropriate, though some boats will have closed-circuit cooling, or will be air-cooled. Check the temperature and oil gauges if fitted, plus ammeter and voltmeter. Check the steering for slackness underway. Lift the hatches and check for stern-gland leaks, or leaks from the engine cooling piping.

Surveys

If all the above has proved positive, then now is the time to consider a survey. Marine surveyors are specialised professionals, dealing all the time with boats. You will find them advertised in the magazine classified sections, or can obtain a list from the YDSA. Their fees are based on the size of the boat,

Before you buy any boat bigger than a dinghy, always take it for a trial run.

Glassfibre boats can suffer from blistering or osmosis of the underwater hull.
Here a surveyor checks the moisture content of the laminate.

plus travelling expenses, so choose one who does not live too far away. Also, check that they specialise in the sort of boat you are looking at.

The purpose of the surveyor is to double-check the points you have looked at, then to look even deeper at the parts of the boat you will not be qualified to inspect. These will include gas systems, electrics, the structure of the hull and so on. The survey will cost you anything from £100–300 or possibly more, so should only be commissioned when you think you have found the right boat.

The survey report will indicate all the faults or wear that exist on the boat and will give you a valuation. With this information you should then be able to decide if the vessel is a good buy. In theory, if the survey uncovers faults, you can use this information to reduce the price you offer for the boat, but it has to be borne in mind that it is a secondhand craft and a certain number of problems will be expected. Similarly, the surveyor is bound to point out anything he finds, but you have to use your own judgement to decide how serious these are. A good example of this is osmosis. If the surveyor finds blisters in the gelcoat, he will state that this indicates the presence of osmosis. However, if the number of blisters is limited, and the boat is 5–10 years old, this is acceptable. If the boat is only 1–2 years old, though, it could indicate a serious problem. He should be able to carry out a moisture content test on the hull, to see how serious the problem is.

Similarly, on a steel boat, the surveyor will carry out an ultrasonic test on

Training is essential if you have never handled a boat before. You will be taught the basics of boat-handling, ropes and mooring. Photo: Roy Devereux.

the hull. This will tell you how thick the plating is, both under and above the water. It should be apparent what the original thickness of the plating was, since most steel is supplied in standard grades, so the amount of rusting or wastage can be surmised. Again, all hulls will gradually corrode away, but this is relative to the age. 10% in a 15-year-old boat is not a problem; 25% in a two-year-old vessel is. Occasionally the steel will pit, usually due to electrolytic corrosion. If the pits are deeper than 30% of the thickness of the plate, they should be welded up, and the cause investigated.

The survey can either be done with the vessel in the water or, more thoroughly, with it out of the water but you will have to pay for the lift. Most surveys will not describe the internal condition of the engine. If you are in doubt about this, it is a good idea to find the local authorised agent for that make, and ask them to come and give you a report on it.

The purchase

Assuming your boat still has a clean bill of health, you should be moving towards the formalities. The first priority is to ascertain the true owner. You may think this is obvious, but we have already explained that most vessels have no documentation to identify them. The exception is a British Registered Vessel, which has its identifying number carved on a bulkhead or permanently inscribed on a plate. With this you can be reasonably sure what you are dealing with, though even then you should be cautious. On transfer of ownership, you can ask to check with the Registrar of Shipping, who should be able to tell you whether there is a debt, such as a mortgage or loan, on the boat.

An alternative to full registration is the Small Ships Register, but be warned that this does not necessarily prove title to the boat.

It is important to establish ownership because the boat may be stolen, or have a hire-purchase loan on it. It is not possible to completely check out either of these, but a few simple precautions will cover most situations. First, ask to see the Bill of Sale or receipt from the previous sale. If this is not forthcoming, be suspicious. Then check names and addresses on any recent bills or the insurance policy if possible – a thief is unlikely to have these and in any case his address will not match. Incidentally, it is worth checking that his name, address and telephone number match with Directory Enquiries. If all this seems over-dramatic, be assured that every year a certain number of people get caught with shady deals, so make sure that you are not one of them!

The question of loans on the boat is less easy to resolve, though you can ask for a written statement from the seller that there are none. Again, if all the addresses and other information check out, you should be reasonably protected.

To secure the boat, you should pay a deposit, usually 10%, and receive a receipt. If the survey has not been carried out it is wise to annotate this as 'paid subject to suitable survey' or similar, to allow you to pull out of the deal if the boat should turn out to have a serious fault. When it comes to actually handing over the money, the usual arrangement is with a banker's draft, or building society cheque, which avoids delays while a normal cheque is cleared.

The handover can be accompanied by a simple receipt, with the names and addresses of the seller and buyer on it or, if you wish, you can use something grander. The BMF can supply you with their 'Form for the disposal of a secondhand boat'. This is a detailed document covering all foreseeable eventualities and probably only worth using if the craft is worth more than £5000.

It is important to remember that you should apply all these precautions even if you are buying through a broker because, as we have said, he is only acting on behalf of the vendor and cannot vouch for that person's honesty.

Insurance, licences and brokerage fees

Remember to insure the boat from the date you are taking over ownership. Be warned that most insurance companies nowadays will require a condition survey on a boat more than 10 years old, with periodic updates.

Also remember to license the boat, or notify the authority of the change of ownership. Remember also to check with the marina or mooring authority whether you can retain the berth on change of ownership – preferably before you complete the transaction.

You should also be aware that some marinas charge a commission of 1–2% on any sale of a boat from their premises. This is because they would prefer that you sold the boat through their brokerage. Whatever your views on this practice, it should be borne in mind, even if it is the seller who has to pay the commission, as any dispute here could affect their willingness to let you stay.

Training

We have already recommended that if you are new to the water, you should take some form of training course. You will enjoy your boating so much more for a small amount of time spent learning the basics.

To achieve this, the RYA has drawn up the Inland Waterways Helmsman's Certificate. This is a scheme that teaches you all you need to know to get started. It is run by a series of approved centres, and courses can be either one or two days. You can learn on the school's boat, or they will instruct you on your own. Typically they take only two or three pupils at a time, and we recommend both you and your partner or crew learn together.

The courses include simple theory in the classroom, but quickly move out onto the water. They will teach you the basics of boat handling, plus ropes, and the Rules of the Road. At the end of the course, if you have passed, you will receive a certificate that covers the UK inland waterways. If you take an extra simple written section, covering the European Regulations, the Certificate will be extended to International waters, important if you intend cruising abroad.

Costs are around £120–150 per person per day, which is money well spent to get the right start on the water. You will feel more confident and enjoy your boating so much more.

3 | *Getting Underway*

Driving a boat on our inland waterways is not difficult and almost anyone should be able to do it. Speeds are slow, there is no complicated navigation to understand, and the banks are never far away if things should go wrong. However, there are certain principles to be understood which, if properly applied, will make your outings enjoyable, safe and rewarding. If you neglect them, you will make progress up the river or canal but your trips will be a non-stop succession of disasters and dramas and may even lead to accidents.

At first glance, the controls of many boats are similar to those of a car and it is this that gives most people the confidence to set off. There is a wheel for steering (or a tiller) and gear-lever for forward and reverse. However, there are fundamental differences in how a boat moves, stops and turns and these should be understood by anyone who wants to approach the sport in a professional and competent manner. This chapter lays out the principles of handling a boat, whether large or small, on river, canal or lake and we shall start with the basic parts of the boat.

Nautical terms

Like most sports, boating has its own language and special terms. Some of these might seem archaic and unnecessary but they often describe things for which there are no equivalent terms ashore. In any case, learning them is part of the fun and gets the whole crew into the spirit of the operation.

Port and starboard Port is the left side and starboard is the right side when you are looking towards the bow. These terms also describe direction – 'I am turning to port' meaning 'I am turning the boat to the left'.

Forward and aft The front and rear halves of the boat, and also items found there – 'the forward cabin', 'the aft cabin' etc.

Bow and stern The bow is the forward part of a vessel while the stern is the afterpart (see also **stem**).

Transom The flat surface across the stern.

Midships or amidships The centre of the boat, either in the fore-and-aft sense, or side-to-side. Also relative position of the helm – 'the helm is amidships' meaning it is in its central position.

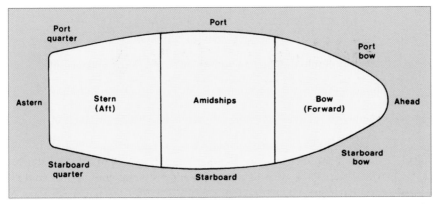

Fig 2 Principal positions and areas on the boat.

Ahead and astern These describe directions of movement – 'the boat was moving ahead', 'the boat was moving astern'. They also describe positions of objects or other boats relative to your craft – 'we could see the lock ahead', 'the other boat was astern'.

Abeam The position of objects or other craft on either side of your boat.

Length overall (LOA) The total length of the boat including bathing platform and anchor platform if any.

Hull The main body of a boat excluding superstructure and masts.

Hull length The length of the hull only, excluding platforms or projections.

Waterline length The length of the hull at the waterline.

Beam Overall width at the widest part.

Draught (sometimes spelt draft) The maximum underwater depth of the boat.

Air draught The vertical distance from the waterline to the highest point of the boat. Used to estimate if it can pass under a bridge.

Keel The lowest part of the bottom of the boat. Either the V-shape where the bottom sections meet or an extension below this.

Stem Forward member attached to the keel coming up to the front of the bow.

Topsides The sides of the hull above the waterline.

Bottom The immersed part of the hull.

Chine The corner between bottom and sides.

Gunwale The corner between the deck and the topsides.

Swim On a narrowboat, the shaped underwater section of the hull aft.

Cockpit An open-air part of the boat, protected by a raised coaming. It can be located forward, midships or aft. In the last two cases it may also include a helm position.

Displacement The weight of the boat.

Rudder Underwater plate that steers the boat.

Tiller Steering arm attached directly to the top of the rudder post.

Wheel Steering wheel attached remotely to the rudder stock.

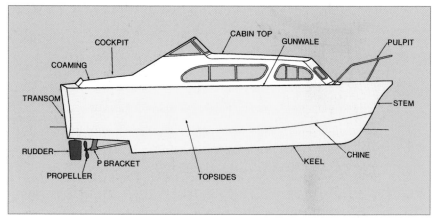

COCKPIT
CABIN TOP
GUNWALE
PULPIT
COAMING
TRANSOM
STEM
RUDDER
P BRACKET
PROPELLER
KEEL
CHINE
TOPSIDES

Fig 3 Parts of a typical cruiser.

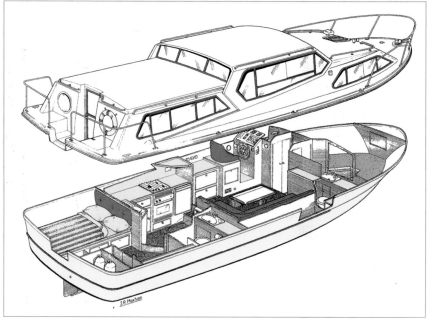

The Sheerline 31, a six-berth cruiser with two cabins and a sliding roof over the saloon, designed by John Moxham.

Helm Another word for the wheel, though it can also generally describe the steering system, either wheel or tiller.

Knots The speed of the boat, usually when describing sea-going craft. The speed of inland vessels is normally described in miles per hour; 1 knot equals 1.15mph.

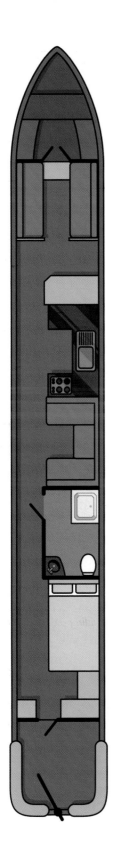

Layouts of two typical narrowboats. The top one has a cruiser stern, the bottom one a trad-stern, with enclosed engine room. Illustrations: Matthew Dartford.

Controls

The basic engine controls on a boat consist of gear-shift and throttle. Sometimes they are combined in one, in which case they are known as a single-lever control. Sometimes they are separated but contained in the same box, then they are known as twin-lever controls, or completely separated, as throttle and gear-lever.

The gearbox of a boat is different to that on a car. It has just three positions – forward, neutral and reverse. Forward has just one gear, and this is the same ratio as reverse. There is no clutch as such – you simply move the lever forward and it engages the gear. In fact there are what are termed 'clutches' in the gearbox, but these simply engage the gear, with no slip. The reason you do not need a slipping clutch is that, unlike a car, whose tyres are continuously gripping the road, your boat has a propeller which can slip relative to the water, reducing the shock as the gears engage. Even so, you should always engage gear with the throttle fully closed, to reduce the stress and damage to the gearbox and shaft. As you engage either forward or reverse, the engine revs will drop slightly as the load comes on. If the tickover is correctly set, the engine will not stall. However, this can sometimes happen if the engine is not correctly set up, and you should be on your guard against this. If it should happen, always return the gear-lever to neutral before restarting the engine, as the boat could suddenly shoot forward if you do not.

Single-lever controls

With a single-lever control, one lever controls both functions. With the lever in neutral, normally in the vertical position, the gearbox is in neutral, and the engine is at tickover.

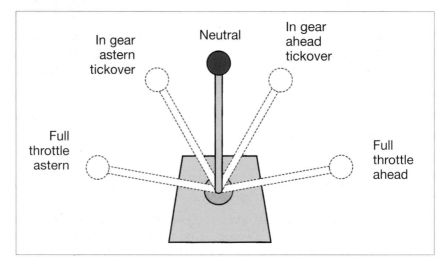

Fig 4 Throttle positions on a single-lever control.

- To engage the gears, move the lever slowly forwards. You can usually feel this at the lever in the form of a click. You will also feel the clunk as the gearbox engages, and a slight surge forward as the propeller begins to turn. As you move the lever further forward, the engine rpm will increase. It is important that you do not suddenly push the lever forward from the neutral position, as the engine can start to rev before the gears engage, with consequent damage to the transmission and a sudden leap forward of the boat which could dislodge your crew!

- Bringing the lever backwards to the first click position reduces engine speed to tickover, but leaves the gearbox in ahead.

- Back again to the vertical position, and the gearbox goes into neutral.

- Keep moving the lever aft and again you will feel the click position, and the gearbox will shift into reverse. Move the lever further aft, and the revs will increase.

Some older narrowboats have a slightly different single-lever system, where the lever moves in a control head with slots in the form of an E. The operation is similar, with forward and astern being up the vertical leg of the E, but increased throttle being to the right along the cross arms.

If you wish to open the throttle of your engine, without engaging gear, such as when you are starting the engine for the first time, it is possible to disengage the gear-change mechanism, usually with a button at the control head, or by pulling the lever sideways. When you return the lever back to the vertical position, this disengagement automatically drops out. Some modern levers have a latch mechanism in their head which you have to operate as you push the lever from neutral. This is to prevent accidental engagement of the gears.

Twin-lever controls

With a twin-lever control, the throttle and gear-lever are separate. The gear-lever has the same movements of forwards and backwards for forward, neutral and reverse but the throttle only moves forwards for increasing revs. With this system it is possible to leave the engine running at a high speed when changing gears which is a practice you have to beware of, for the reasons discussed above.

In some older boats, the gear-lever will go directly through the floor into the top of the box, with the throttle being mounted on the dash. Most modern craft, however, have the gear-lever remotely mounted, operating the box through a cable.

Outboard engine controls

Outboard motors can have two different systems. The simplest will have the throttle on a twist-grip on the tiller handle. The gear-lever will be mounted on the side of the engine. This is satisfactory for small dinghies and dayboats, but it means you have to sit at the back of the boat to steer and operate the engine. On most larger craft, remote controls will be fitted, either single or twin-lever, with their operation as described above.

Steering systems

Steering can be either by tiller or wheel. Most narrowboats use a tiller. This is directly fixed to the top of the rudder. It gives rapid and immediate control and allows you to know where the rudder is pointing at any time, both of which are important when manoeuvring. You are also standing at the back of the boat, and can clearly observe where bow and stern are swinging, enabling you to put your vessel precisely into locks that are only inches wider than your boat. The system is also very simple and reliable, with nothing to wear or break. The drawback is that you have to stand out at the back of the boat, in sun, wind or rain. It also means you cannot let go of the helm at any time, as it may swing to one side or the other. Some narrowboats are now being built with inside steering, but this is frequently frowned upon by the purists.

The other method of controlling the rudder is by a wheel. This will be remotely connected, either by cables or wires or, more recently, hydraulics. The wheel can then be mounted wherever is most convenient, preferably out of the rain. Some boats have them in an aft cockpit, with a hinged canopy to keep off the weather. Some have them inside the cabin, either amidships or forward. Some boats have two steering positions, with wheel and engine controls at each, allowing you to drive in the open air or under cover. Seagoing boats and some river craft will have a raised steering position on top of the cabin, known as a flying-bridge; this is less practical as it prevents you from passing under low bridges on rivers and canals.

If the helm is at the forward end of the boat, you have to be careful when manoeuvring, as the stern behind you can be swinging one way or the other without you realising it, making entering and leaving locks tricky. It is essential to keep a good lookout astern.

Preparation

The secret to all successful and troublefree boating lies in preparation. Having your boat ready and properly equipped with your crew knowing what to do is the key to competent manoeuvring. If difficult situations do arise, you can tackle them confidently.

The basic preparation starts with ensuring that your boat is properly maintained and equipped, which we will cover in later chapters. Here we look at the preparations you should make before setting off on every trip.

Basic checks

Before you cast off you should adopt the same approach as a pilot does before take-off: flight plan, cockpit check and crew instructions. Get into the habit of doing this and it will become second nature.

The 'flight plan' is simple. Decide where you are going, and ensure that the boat has everything needed for the trip. If it is a long journey, check that the gas bottles, water tank and fuel tanks are all full. If you are changing waterways, have you got the right lock handles (windlasses), maps and keys? Make sure that you have got an emergency tool kit and spares – buying these en route will be expensive and time-consuming. It is worth making a list of all items you think you will need such as dinghy, outboard, and waterproof clothing. Add to this list every time you forget something so that, eventually, everything is covered.

The cockpit check should be done before you cast off; this involves all the running aspects of the boat. If you are in the habit of turning off the cooling water inlet valve, make sure it is open. Start the engine and let it run for a few minutes to warm up – do not just start up and cast off. Never cast off before making sure the engine will start! Check the oil pressure, temperature gauge, ammeter and voltmeter if fitted. Check that cooling water is coming out of the exhaust on boats with wet exhaust; then keep an eye on all of these for the first few minutes of the trip, as this is when most problems occur.

Check the fuel gauge on a fixed tank installation. Check the portable tank on an outboard motor and check that the air-vent is open – we all forget to do this at some stage, resulting in the engine dying just as you get out into the middle of the stream.

Check steering and gears – with the boat still tied up, slip the engine in and out of forward and reverse and note that you have thrust from the prop. Turn the wheel fully either way, and if possible check that the rudder follows it. On a narrowboat, check that the tiller pin is in place – in fact remember to check that the tiller is fitted! It is not unknown for the tiller to be forgotten in the haste of a rapid departure to catch an open lock. If you have been tied up for some time on a river bank, a collection of weed and debris may have floated up against your stern. Clear it before it gets sucked into the prop. Check the depth of water under the boat. Water levels may drop overnight on rivers or canals, and leave you stuck on the bottom, or with your rudder and prop in the mud. Rock the boat to see that it moves. If in doubt, ease the stern out from the bank with boathook or pole before engaging gear.

Look around your craft to see that everything is in its right place. Boathook should be to hand next to the helm or on deck – on long vessels and narrowboats you should have one at each end. Have your guide book or map open at the right page next to the helm – it is amazing how your first bridge, lock or obstruction always seems to arrive just after you have cast off and the rest of the crew are engaged in tidying up the boat!

Check that the fenders are attached all round – they can work themselves loose with the rocking up and down overnight, finally slipping gracefully into the water just as you make the perfect departure. Some people prefer to lift the fenders while underway, but this is optional. It looks neater, but unless you are going to untie them every time, the fenders will usually have to lie on the sidedecks, where they could be an obstruction to anyone moving round the boat. Also, when going to sea, it is usual to remove the fenders, to stop them bouncing around, and eventually falling off, but on a river or canal it is perfectly acceptable to leave them down.

The anchor should be free and ready for use; pole and gang-plank securely in place; mops and buckets tidily stowed away; cushions, pillows and sun-bathing gear cleared off the cabin top. Ensure that the lifebuoy is in its holder, the canopy is properly stowed or secured, and see that crockery is stowed away or stacked in the sink.

In addition, all ropes should be neatly coiled and stowed; the mooring pins should be loosened ready to be pulled out. Finally, check that all the crew are on board (including pets); it is remarkable how often someone pops ashore for a last photo or bit of shopping, without telling the helmsman!

Briefing the crew

Now you are nearly ready to cast off. Before you do this, though, you should carefully work out the best way of leaving your berth, taking into account wind and current and then, most importantly, you should talk this plan through with the crew. Don't rely on telepathy or what seems obvious to you. If you are with your regular crew, they will be familiar with the way you operate but, even so, a short discussion on the bankside or in the cockpit will save arm-waving, shouting and confusion later. If you have new crew members on board, explain what is expected of them, and work out a simple system of signals. Once the engine starts it is often difficult to make yourself heard, particularly between helm and foredeck on a long boat; raised voices immediately attract the attention of onlookers and raise the tension on board.

A simple system of signals can be:

* 'Ready to let go' – from the crew – usually a thumbs-up.
* 'Let go' – from the helmsman – also a thumbs-up.
* 'Hold it as you are' – from either party – a raised hand.
* 'Come ahead' – from the crew – beckoning hand.
* 'Go astern' – from the crew – points astern.
* 'Push out' – from the helmsman – points away from bank.
* 'Pull in' – from the helmsman – points towards the bank.

Incidentally, for simplicity of writing, we will be referring to helmsman in the male person. This does not suggest that only men can drive a boat, and, for both practical reasons and enjoyment of all aboard, it is important that everyone can handle all aspects of the boat. It will rapidly become boring if only one person steers, both for them and the rest of the crew.

Steering techniques

Casting off may appear to be the simplest of manoeuvres but a good knowledge of how your boat steers is essential for success, especially if there is a wind blowing, current flowing or other craft moored ahead and astern.

Two principles of boat movement need to be understood. First, unlike a car, a boat is not operating on a solid surface; it can move sideways or in any direction of its own accord under the influence of current and wind, even if you are applying no power. Thus you cannot stop and take stock of a situation once you have cast off. At the same time, the thrust from propeller and rudder is not a positive and fixed one. It tends to propel you in a general direction rather than taking you from point to point – rather like driving on ice.

Secondly, a boat steers in a different fashion to a car. Instead of the steering acting on the wheels at the front and pulling that end of the vehicle left or right, the rudder is located at the stern; it pushes the rear of the boat one way or the other. The effect is similar to reversing in your car, except that, to add to the confusion, the bow also moves but in the opposite direction.

These effects govern all your movements in a boat, not just casting off, so we will look at them in detail with the aid of drawings. It is also important to note that outboards and outdrives act slightly differently to a conventional propeller and rudder, especially in reverse, and twin-engined boats are different again, so we will examine each in turn.

Steering single-engined boats

The principal turning effect for a single-engined boat with shaft-driven propeller and rudder is due to the flow of water over the rudder. This is partly caused by the forward motion of the boat, but is magnified by the thrust of water from the propeller.

Fig 5 (overleaf) shows the boat moving ahead, and the engine in 'ahead'. The flow of water from both the forward motion and the propeller acts on the rudder, and with the helm to port, the rudder pushes the stern of the boat to starboard. In fact, when any boat turns, it rotates about a point halfway along its length, so as the stern moves to starboard, the bow moves to port. You must understand this effect, to avoid the stern or bow clipping boats along-side you in tight situations, but you can also use it to your advantage. With the helm to starboard, the boat moves in the opposite direction to that shown.

At this point, we should explain the terminology we use when describing steering. If we say 'the helm to port', we mean the rudder is to port. To achieve this with a wheel-steered boat you turn the wheel anti-clockwise. With a tiller-steered boat such as a narrowboat, you push the tiller to starboard.

With a single-engined craft, you should also be aware of another factor, known as the *paddlewheel effect*, that will affect your steering. When the boat is going ahead, the propeller rotates in one direction, which can be either clockwise or anti-clockwise, depending on the particular engine and

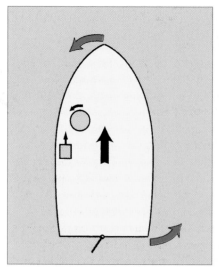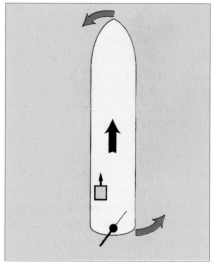

Fig 5 left: Boat moving ahead, wheel anti-clockwise, rudder to port; bow swings to port, stern swings to starboard. right: Narrowboat: tiller to starboard, rudder to port, bow swings to port, stern swings to starboard.

gearbox fitted. In reverse, the direction of rotation of the propeller itself reverses. The principle is the same as that of a screw going into wood. Turn it one way and it goes in, turn it the other and it comes out, hence propellers are sometimes known as screws. As the propeller rotates, it not only thrusts the boat forwards, but also to one side, depending on the direction of rotation. This sideways thrust is much less than the forward one, but it can have an effect on your steering at low speeds. It is also particularly significant in reverse. A right-handed propeller, ie one that rotates clockwise in ahead, will thrust the stern of your boat also to the right in ahead. In astern it will thrust the stern of the boat to the left. A left-handed propeller will have the opposite effects, ie pushing the stern to port in ahead, and to starboard in astern (see Fig 6).

In Fig 7, the helm is amidships, the boat stationary, and the engine put into ahead. In this case, a right-hand prop will give the stern a kick to starboard before the boat gathers way. A left-hand prop will kick it to port.

In Fig 8, the boat is stationary, and the engine is put into ahead, this time, with the helm to port. The thrust of water from the propeller over the rudder will push the stern of the boat to starboard, and the bow will follow to port. At the same time, there will be a contribution from the paddlewheel effect. This will either increase or reduce the turning effect, depending on the rotation of the propeller. A right-hand prop will increase the rate of turn to port. A left-hand prop will reduce it. If the helm is put over to starboard, the boat will turn that way, with the rate of turn being reduced with a right-hand prop, and increased with a left-hand prop.

You can check the handing of your prop by looking down at the propshaft with the engine in gear. This will enable you to work out the direction of the

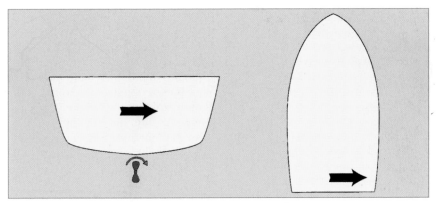

Fig 6 Paddlewheel effect. When the propeller turns clockwise, the stern of the boat moves to starboard. On a boat with a right-hand propeller, the prop turns clockwise in ahead, so the stern moves to the right when you engage ahead. When you engage astern, the prop turns anti-clockwise, and the stern moves to port. With a left-hand propeller, the motions are reversed.

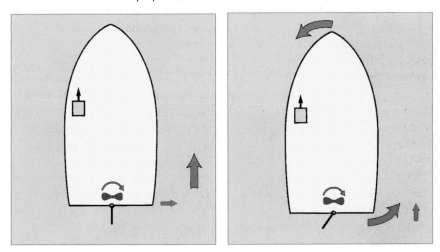

Fig 7 left: The boat is stationary with helm amidships. When the engine is put into ahead, the paddlewheel effect kicks the stern to the right (with a right-hand prop), then the boat gathers way ahead.
Fig 8 right: The boat is stationary with helm to port. When the engine is put into ahead, the bow goes to port, and the stern to starboard; the boat also moves slightly ahead. The paddlewheel effect increases the swing with a right-hand prop, decreases it with a left-hand prop.

paddlewheel effect, though you can also check this in practice. Since you will never remember this when you need it, it is not a bad idea to stick an arrow on the bulkhead next to the helm showing you which way the stern kicks when you go into gear. To avoid confusion, show the direction it moves when you go into reverse, as this is the most important situation, as we will explain later.

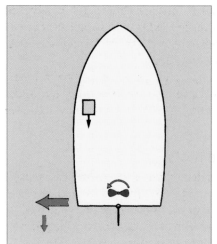 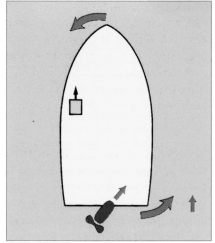

Fig 9 left: *With the engine astern, the paddlewheel effect pushes the stern to port (with a right-hand prop) and the boat moves aft. With a left-hand prop, the stern moves to starboard.*

Fig 10 right: *Outdrive or outboard boat with helm to port and engine ahead. The thrust pushes the stern to starboard and the bow to port; the boat moves ahead.*

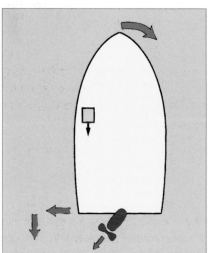 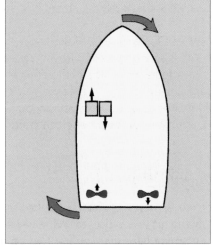

Fig 11 left: *Outdrive or outboard boat with helm to port and engine astern. The thrust pulls stern to port, and the boat moves aft.*

Fig 12 right: *Twin-engine boat with port engine ahead and starboard engine astern. The boat rotates on the spot with no movement forward or aft.*

Fig 9 shows what happens when you put the engine into 'astern'. If the boat is stationary, there will be no flow of water over the rudder from the motion, and no flow from the propeller, as it is pushing the water forward, past the keel. Thus the boat will initially kick to starboard or port, depending on the paddlewheel effect. As speed builds up astern, there will be a limited steering effect from the water passing over the rudder, but in practice this will not be sufficient to overcome the paddlewheel effect, explaining why most boats with shaft drives do not steer well in astern.

A similar situation occurs when you engage astern while the boat is travelling forward. Again, you will get a braking effect from the prop, but at the same time the stern will kick one way or the other. How you deal with this we will cover later.

Steering outboard and sterndrive boats

With an outboard or a sterndrive, a different set of circumstances applies. There is no separate rudder as such; instead the whole drive and propeller turns as you steer. This alters the angle of the thrust from the propeller, so turning the boat. This has two significant effects. Firstly, the turning effect of the thrust when the boat is in forward gear is much greater than with a shaftdrive and rudder (see Fig 10). However, when the engine is put in neutral, even though you have forward way on, there will be very little steering effect, something that you have to bear in mind when you come alongside. Secondly, in reverse, you also have a directional thrust from the propeller, which you can control with the tiller or wheel. This enables you to steer the boat in reverse, or pull it out of tight moorings with ease (see Fig 11). Also, any paddlewheel effect can be immediately countered by a small adjustment of the helm.

Steering twin-engined boats

With a twin-engined boat you can achieve another turning effect by putting one engine in ahead and the other in reverse. The boat will then rotate on the spot (see Fig 12). In practice you do not find many twin-engined boats on the river, and even fewer on canals, so we will concentrate most of our instructions on single-engined craft.

Casting off

Now we have explained the basics of how a boat steers, we can put our theory into practice to get away from our mooring. Incidentally, we are assuming here that you are tied up alongside a bank. If you are in a marina berth and can just drive out backwards, life is generally simpler, and we will not cover that situation here.

Letting go

At this point, a mention of techniques for letting go is needed. Prior to casting off you should let go all except the bow and stern lines. Each of these should then be shortened to either one length to the cleat or bollard on the bank with a couple of turns around it, or should be doubled down to the cleat (see Fig 13, overleaf) and back on board. Then the crew can either untie the

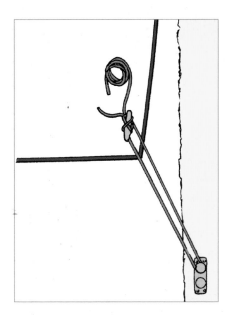

Fig 13 Slipped stern line. Take the line from the stern round the bollard and back on board when preparing to cast off.

line from the cleat or bollard and step on board, pushing off at the same time, or the crew can remain on board and pull the line from round the cleat.

If you choose the latter, it is essential that the line runs cleanly through. Before letting go, the crew should coil the loose rope, running it through their hands to ensure that there are no knots, loops or kinks that could catch on the cleat. They should keep the rope in their hands from then on, to ensure no tangles occur. The skipper should watch until the whole of the rope has run round the cleat before engaging gear. Too often the last inches of the line can snag or jam, and if the boat is moving forward by then, a dangerous situation can occur, with fingers being jammed, ropes breaking, or cleats being pulled out of the bank or off the boat. You should also see that the end of the rope is back on board to remove any risk of it dropping in the water and wrapping round the prop. All of this may sound dramatic, but experience shows that these things can happen, whereas if you adopt the right technique from the outset, you will avoid the risk of possible problems and injuries.

Leaving a river bank

The problem when leaving your mooring is that if you simply turn the wheel away from the bank, the stern will be pushed in towards it, and you will never pull away, simply scraping forwards along the bank. If you put the engine in astern, the same thing will happen, unless you have an outboard or outdrive, in which case the reverse thrust with the helm over will pull the stern out.

So we have to get the boat away from the bank. The simplest method, if there is no wind or current and plenty of depth of water under your stern, is for a crew member to stand forward to push the bow out gently, while you

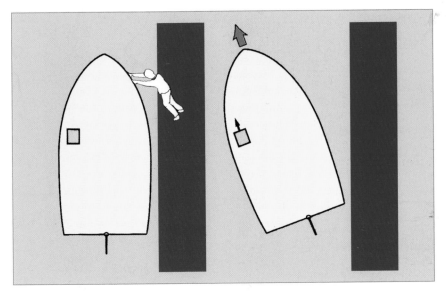

*Fig 13a Casting off. Put engine in neutral with wheel amidships. The crew
pushes off to 20–30°. With engine ahead the boat pulls away.*

keep the engine in neutral (see Fig 13a). When the bow is angled out by
20–30°, you go ahead, with the helm amidships, and the boat drives out in
a straight line. Beware of a slight kick from the paddlewheel effect but, in
practice, this should not cause a problem. If your crew is none too agile, they
can remain on the boat and push the bank. In this case they can either use
hands, keeping them well clear of being injured, or a boathook, but the latter
should be applied gently, against a secure point. If it slips, injuries can occur.
A greater push will be achieved by the crew member standing on the bank
and moving back amidships, where they will achieve a better angle, but they
need to be agile enough to jump aboard as you pull out. Again, do not
engage gear until they are aboard.

If the water is shallow where you have moored, you run the risk of hitting
the bottom with propeller or rudder. In this case it is preferable to go out
astern. Again, in calm conditions, with no current or wind, this can simply be
done by pushing out the stern, again until you are 20–30° from the bank,
then engaging reverse (see Fig 14, overleaf). In this case the paddlewheel
effect will have more relevance. In our diagram, if you have a right-hand
prop, the effect will be to increase your angle from the bank as you pull away,
which is good. If you have a left-hand prop, it will initially pull you back into
the bank, which is not so good. If you are moored the other way round, the
opposite will occur. In practice, once you are far enough out from the bank,
you can go ahead and straighten up. Make sure you are well out, though, as
the boat will tend to drive back into the bank until you have steerage
way, and the stern will swing in again, possibly hitting the bank, or other
moored boats.

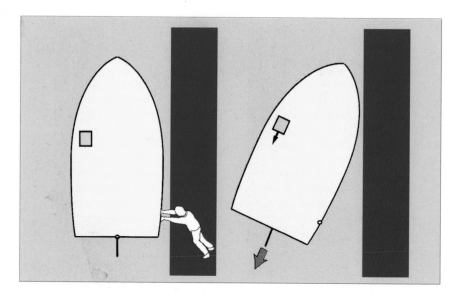

Fig 14 Casting off with shallow water under the stern. The engine is in neutral with the wheel amidships. Crew pushes off stern to 20–30°; engine is put astern and the boat pulls away.

So far we have dealt with the easy cases. In practice there will usually be complications to the situation. The first is that you will have other boats moored up ahead and astern. Again, if there is no wind and current, you can repeat either of the procedures above, but in this case ensure your angle from the bank is sufficient to clear the other boats before you engage gear. If necessary, hand yourself out past these craft to achieve the necessary angle. Do not stick boat-hooks into other people's boats, and keep hands and fingers well clear of being squashed. Do not engage gear until all hands are clear. As you drive out, take it gently, keep the wheel amidships and in the immortal words, 'Watch your stern'. It is invariably this that does the damage. Beware davits or dinghies on the transoms of the other boats, and allow room to clear them (see Fig 15).

The next complication will be caused by the wind. This will cause problems whether you are on river or canal. Check carefully in which direction it is blowing, by looking at ripples on the water, or pennants on boats. If the wind is blowing directly away from the bank, it will help you, but you must remember to get all the crew on board before you cast off, or they may be left behind. You must also be extra sure that no other boat is coming before you finally let go, as you will be committed by then.

Wind from ahead

If the wind is coming from ahead, then you can use it to your advantage. Leave by going ahead; as soon as your bow is clear of the boat in front of you, the wind will tend to take your bow round, increasing your angle and clearance. If the wind is strong, make sure it does not carry you back on to

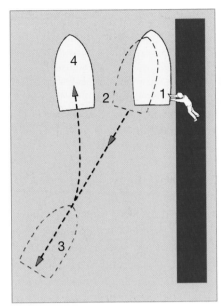

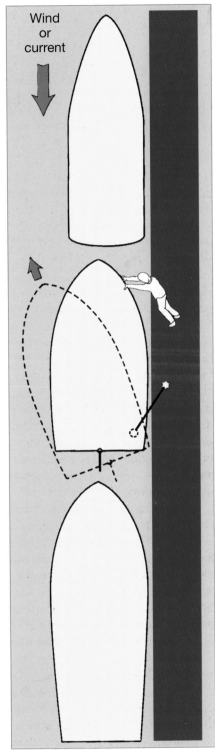

Fig 15 above: *Pulling out astern. Remember to go far enough out for your stern to clear any boats moored behind you when you go ahead.*

Fig 16 right: *Pulling out, with boats ahead and astern and the wind from ahead. Push the bow out, and keep a rope from the stern to the shore to stop the boat blowing backwards.*

the boat behind. If necessary, keep a rope from your stern going forward to a cleat, ready to be slipped (see Fig 16).

Wind from astern

If the wind is coming from directly astern (Fig 17), you can use the same technique in reverse, but make sure that it does not blow you right round as you pull out. A strong burst of astern throttle may be needed when the angle is right, with quick work on helm and throttle when you straighten out ahead.

Wind abeam

If the wind is abeam, blowing you on to the bank, it may be too strong for you to manoeuvre the bow out or it will push you on to the boat in front as you drive out in ahead. You will then have to use a special technique known as 'springing the boat out' (Fig 18). This entails taking a line from the bow back to a secure cleat or bollard on the bank amidships. This line, known as a spring, is doubled back to the cleat on the boat, with a couple of turns taken round it but not made fast. The crew member holds the end of the line, ready to let it go. All other lines are then released, and you engage forward gear, with the helm hard over towards the bank. The thrust from the propeller will then drive the stern of the boat out into the stream while the spring stops the boat from moving forward along the bank. If you are up against a hard piling, you may wish to lower a fender down to protect the boat where it touches but on soft banks this will not usually be necessary. The amount of throttle you have to use will depend on the strength of the wind, but you should be able to drive the boat out against it. When the angle between the boat and the bank is 45° or more, you put the gear lever into neutral. This relieves the load on the spring, which the crew member promptly releases and slips. You then apply rapid astern throttle to pull the boat out into the stream. The amount of throttle, and the angle before you let go, will depend on the strength of the wind.

The technique requires good timing between skipper and crew and smart work by both. Rather than waiting till the first time you need to do it, you should practise the manoeuvre on a quiet stretch of the bank, preferably with no boats nearby and no spectators. Then, when the situation really arises you may well surprise the experts watching, and amaze other amateurs alongside as they struggle to cast off.

River currents

Current has similar effects to the wind. It usually only comes from ahead and astern but some tricky moorings may have an eddy pressing you on to the bank. The techniques required are also similar, wherever possible using the current to help you out rather than hold you in. Again, you should be prepared to go out astern if the stream is from that direction, and you should be prepared to use enough throttle to hold you against the current if required.

There is no shame in using a lot of throttle if the situation demands it. The

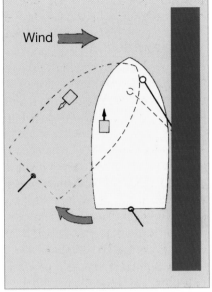

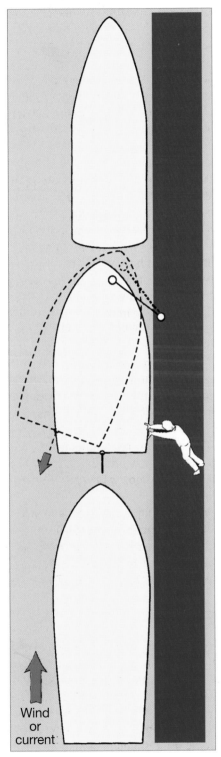

Fig 18 above: *Springing out the stern. Take a line from the bow back to the shore amidships. Put the helm hard over to starboard and engage ahead. The stern will drive out. When it is at 45°, put engine into neutral and release the spring; then put wheel amidships and engine in astern.*

Wind

Wind or current

Fig 17 left: *Pulling out, wind from astern.*

wrong tactic is to always use full power for the simplest manoeuvre. All this does is get you into tight situations quicker while the roaring exhaust merely alerts any spectators to a possibly entertaining situation.

Traffic safety

Make sure that before you cast off at any time, you check carefully for other boats moving on the water. If you are coming out astern, the correct signal is three short blasts on the horn but in practice it is best to wait till your way is clear. If you are in any doubt about getting out of a difficult spot, have a word with the skipper of the boats ahead or astern. This gives them the opportunity of putting a crew member with a fender at the likely contact point. It may also be possible to move their boat farther up the bank, or you may discover that they are also about to leave which removes the problem altogether.

If your boat is suitable, you may wish to take it into waterways frequented by large boats or even ships. If this is the case you will need to be familiar with the International Regulations for Preventing Collisions at Sea. You will find them listed in any good nautical almanac.

So far it has been assumed that when you cast off you are wanting to carry on in the same direction that you are pointing. If you want to go the other way, again you need to appraise the situation. If it is a calm day, and the river or canal is wide enough, without much traffic about, you can just pull out ahead, and turn round in the stream. If the waterway is congested with traffic, it may be best to follow the flow of boats until you find a convenient place to turn. If the waterway is narrow, it is often a good idea to turn the boat round where you are moored, before finally letting go. We will cover this situation in more detail in Chapter 4.

Bow-thrusters

The ease by which you carry out the operations we have previously described mainly depends on the size of your boat, and the experience and agility of your crew. On vessels up to 25–30ft (7.6–9m), the manoeuvres are easy: the boat is light to push; the deck is not high above the water which makes getting on and off simple. Above this size, especially on riverboats, the older or less active crews will start to find things difficult or even dangerous.

A development that solves all these problems is the bow-thruster. This consists of a small propeller, 5–6in (13–15cm) diameter, set underwater in a tube mounted across the boat at the bow. The propeller is powered by an electric or hydraulic motor, and can run in either direction. It is controlled by a lever next to the helm. When the thruster is operated, a jet of water drives the bow of the boat to either port or starboard.

It can be used when casting off or when coming alongside. When casting off, it removes the need for the crew to push the boat out. This means they can be safely on board, with the lines released, before the helmsman decides to thrust the bow. It also means he can carry on thrusting the bow out, past any obstructions ahead, before engaging gear. The unit chosen should be powerful enough to push the bow out against a cross wind.

When coming alongside, the thruster avoids the need for precision control of the engines and rudder to get the bow close enough for the crew to get off or put a rope ashore. All you have to do is bring the boat level with the chosen mooring, then use the thruster to bring the bow in just the right amount. Even if the wind is blowing you off, you can hold the bow in for long enough to get a line round a bollard.

The thruster also makes turning the boat round easy, which can be an important factor when manoeuvring in a congested marina, especially when the wind is blowing.

The Dutch are great fans of bow-thrusters; many of their river craft have them fitted as standard or options. They can be installed in either steel or GRP hulls and can be fitted in new or secondhand hulls, though obviously the boat will have to be lifted from the water. They make boat-handling so much easier that it is surprising that they are not more common on our rivers or even on canals for the longer craft.

Some of the prejudice comes from experienced helmsmen who somehow think that they are 'cheating'. Some resistance comes from boatyards who are not familiar with fitting them as they do need a large hole to be cut in the side of the boat, at just the right angle. Price is also a factor, as they can range from £1500–3000, depending on the model and the fitting costs. However, once you have tried one, you will never go back. They are ideal for older people or shorthanded crews, enabling you to tackle the most difficult part of river boating with complete confidence.

Lifejackets

There are no hard and fast rules as to whether or when you should wear a lifejacket, but sensible precautions should apply. All children, non-swimmers and the elderly should wear a lifejacket at all times when they are on deck, or walking around the boat, or around a lock. It is up to you whether you also make them wear them on the towpath, but out of sight they could easily slip into the water.

Everyone aboard should wear a lifejacket in strong stream conditions, or cold, wet wintry weather, or when the ground and decks are slippery with leaves, rain, snow or ice, or at night. You should also wear a lifejacket if you are handling your boat on your own, as you could fall in and bang your head on the way down. Even if you do not, the shock of hitting cold water unexpectedly will knock the breath out of you, and your first gulp could be your last.

There is some confusion over the terminology today. Strictly speaking, to be described as a lifejacket, an appliance must turn an unconscious person over onto their back, and hold their head above water. All other devices are termed buoyancy aids. Full lifejackets can be cumbersome, and unpopular with children, so a buoyancy aid can suffice, but only if the child is always in view or supervised.

The best solution for all the crew is to buy them the latest automatic-inflating

Mike Eagles, lock-keeper at Goring-on-Thames wearing an automatic lifejacket used by all river staff in strong stream conditions. The same lifejacket is ideal for general use by all boaters. Inset: Children and non-swimmers should always wear lifejackets particularly when working around locks.

lifejackets. These are completely unobtrusive when you are wearing them, quick to put on, and do not restrict your arm movements. If you fall in, they inflate within seconds, and will turn you over if unconscious. They are what all the professional boatmen wear, and are in many cases mandatory for lock-keepers and river-bank staff. They will be slightly more expensive than the foam-filled variety, but how much is the life of your family member worth?

4 | *Handling and Manoeuvring*

Once you have cast off, a different set of conditions and techniques for controlling your boat applies, depending on whether you are travelling on a river or canal.

Underway on rivers

Rivers are broader and deeper than canals. They have a greater variety of craft using them and they will normally allow you to travel at a greater speed. However, you should not travel too fast, even on a river. Maximum speed limits will normally be between 5–7mph, but it is not speed in itself that is the restricting factor. The problem is caused by the amount of wash your boat makes. Wash is the waves caused by your boat moving through the water. The faster you go, the bigger and more damaging the waves. These waves wash away the banks, injure wildlife and birds nesting there and cause damage to moored craft. Wash can even swamp other smaller river users such as rowing boats and canoes.

Effects of your wash

The amount of wash your boat makes increases out of all proportion to your speed. At 4mph, most boats will scarcely make a ripple. At 5mph the waves will be noticeable but not damaging, but by 6 or 7mph they will usually be too large. Thus you always have to check behind you to see that your wash is acceptable. If you see waves breaking or splashing against the banks, then they are too big and will be starting to wash the banks away. You should always slow down when passing moored craft, small dinghies and fishermen and where the river narrows or shallows. Remember also that an extra 1 or 2 mph will probably be doubling your fuel consumption, to little purpose. The average distance between locks on the Thames for instance is 3½ miles (5.6km). At a bank-breaking 6mph you will cover this distance only 7 minutes faster than at a leisurely 5mph, and will probably still be waiting to enter the lock when your peaceful neighbour comes round the bend.

The amount of wash your boat makes depends to a certain extent on its shape and size. Long thin vessels will make less wake than short fat ones, but in the main it is speed that causes waves, so slow down, relax and enjoy the countryside passing you by.

Rules of the road

The rule of the waterways says you travel on the right – the opposite to driving on roads in the UK. This applies to all waterways, in all countries of the world, and out at sea. In practice you do not have to drive right over by the bank – that will just annoy fishermen and owners of moored craft unnecessarily – but you should keep to the right of the centreline, particularly when meeting oncoming vessels. Be careful not to cut corners – it is easy to let your attention wander on a long bend and suddenly find yourself facing an oncoming boat!

The rule also says that overtaking boats must give way. If you have to over-take another craft, remember that its helmsman might not be aware of your presence. For preference, wait till you have a straight stretch ahead of you, then pass with as much clearance as possible, without unduly impeding oncoming craft. Try to wait until the boat ahead is aware of your presence and can move over to let you go through, though do not force him to pass too close to the bank. Similarly, in your turn, if you are aware that a faster craft is coming up behind you, move over and call him past at the appropriate moment.

On some rivers and larger canals you may encounter large commercial vessels. These can range from passenger trip boats to tugs, barges and ferries. The rules say that you should keep clear of these at all times. They will be less manoeuvrable than you in narrow waterways, and may be restricted by their draught. You should be aware that they may have to travel down the centre of the channel, or even on the outside of some bends, to have enough deep water. If you are in any doubt, pull over out of their way. When doing this, you should signal your intent, with one of the approved sound signals which we describe later on page 80.

Racing rowing boats should be given a wide berth. They are not so manoeuvrable as you are and need more room. However, they do travel in predictable straight lines, and by law should keep to the correct side of the river. As we have said, you should also slow down when passing them to reduce your wash, though in practice you will find that they are usually travel-ling faster than you!

Encountering sailing boats

Sailing boats are more of a problem. The smaller dinghies tend to congregate in stretches of water close to their clubs and sail round race courses marked by buoys. Some people, including many of their helmsmen, persist in think-ing that the rule of the road says that power gives way to sail, under all circumstances. In practice, this blanket rule went out with the Onedin Line. Today's interpretation says that in a narrow channel, any vessel restricted in its ability to manoeuvre has right of way. Thus, if a sailing boat is tacking properly to and fro across a river and making steady progress along it, then you should give way to it. To do this you should aim to go behind it, after it has gone about. Similarly, if it is running before the wind, it should keep to the correct side of the river, and you should treat it as another vessel, whether coming towards you, or travelling in the same direction. If, however, the sailing boat chooses to alter from its steady course simply to attempt to gain an advantage over a competitor, or to pass round a racing mark, then he cannot expect you to anticipate this, or take sudden evasive action. You then become the vessel restrained in your ability to manoeuvre – possibly restricted by the bank or the proximity of other craft; the sailing boat should then give way to you.

The problem is further complicated by the fact that many dinghies will be sailing together, all at different speeds, and on different courses. They will all be accelerating or slowing as the wind gusts and shifts. To a certain extent, they can control these changes in speed, by letting out or pulling in the sail, and should therefore attempt to maintain a steady speed as required in the rules; however, you must be alert for sudden changes. Also, they are actually more manoeuvrable than you are, and more aware of what they are going to do next.

The best solution when encountering sailing boats is to move over to the right-hand side of the river, thus giving them maximum room to manoeuvre. Slow down to a walking speed then keep a steady course, allowing them to predict your movements, but bear in mind the situations, given above, when you should give way. Obviously, if a collision should still seem about to occur then you should apply reverse but otherwise do not keep speeding up or slowing down. If there is more than one motorboat passing through a fleet of dinghies, be aware that the vessel in front of you may suddenly stop or slow down and keep a good distance. Do not try to overtake in these circumstances but keep in line astern.

Steering a straight course

Keeping a straight course is a matter of practice and experience. We have already explained that boats steer from the rear, and this can initially take some getting used to. It is also easy to oversteer – continuously correcting your direction and ending up zig-zagging down the river. The secret is to anticipate the swing, and to remember that a correction will take a few seconds to take effect. Try to apply the minimum helm every time and you will gradually get the hang of it. Some boats are harder than others to keep straight, with outdrives and outboards being the worst. Boats with a keel tend to travel straighter but, in the end, it is down to the helmsman to control the course.

Underway on canals

Travelling on canals requires different techniques and skills. The canal will normally be narrower and shallower than a river, frequently little deeper than the draught of the boat, and only four or five times as wide. It is important to understand the shape of the bed of the canal. To reduce the amount of material that had to be dug out, and to make it easier to seal the bottom and prevent leaks, canals were made with a saucer-shaped section. The deepest point is a channel down the centre, and they then shelve rapidly towards the edge. Because of this, it is best to travel down the middle of the canal wherever possible, unless you meet an oncoming boat. The only exception to this rule is when passing fishermen, when it is courteous to move towards the other bank. Having said that, today's anglers often use long poles that reach right across the cut, enabling them to fish close to the far bank; in which case, you cannot win!

Slow down when passing moored craft on canals and narrow rivers.

Speed limits

The reason for travelling down the middle is that you will be in the deepest water, thus causing the least damage to the canal bottom. When the canals were first made, the only means of propulsion for barges was the horse. Maximum speeds were 2–3mph, and there was no propeller to stir up the bed. Today's motorised craft are capable of greater speeds, and have the additional damaging effect of the prop. This causes two problems: there is the obvious one of stirring up the water, and scouring the bed. Also, as the propeller rotates, it sucks in water to create the thrust. This water comes from the side, and also from underneath. On a deep river this is barely noticeable, but in a shallow canal, the effect is to suck the boat down deeper in the water, by up to 3–6in (8–15cm), depending on the speed and the amount of water under the hull. Thus, you cause even more damage by dragging the prop deeper in the water and increasing its scouring effect, as well as dragging water from the canal edge. In the middle of the canal, where the water is deeper, this effect will be least.

This effect of the propeller drawing in the water can be observed by watching the canalside as you pass. At a point about amidships, you will see the water level at the bank going down, and weeds being sucked towards you. As you pass, they will go back to normal. This suction effect is, in fact, partly caused by the propeller and partly by the passage of the hull along a narrow, shallow channel but the end result is the same.

Of course you should not be travelling too fast in the first place. The maximum speed limit on all canals is 4mph, or a brisk walking pace. In practice, on many of them you should not travel more than 3mph, or less. The deciding factor is the wash you make. Look behind you frequently and keep the waves down to a minimum by adjusting your speed. The worst condition that can occur is when your stern wave actually starts to break behind you. At this point it is causing maximum damage to the bottom and bank and under no circumstances should you allow this to happen. The problem is a cumulative one; the washing away of the banks creates more mud which falls to the bottom of the canal, reducing its depth, and further increasing the size of the waves.

Losing steerage way

As you get closer to the critical breaking wave point, you will start to lose steerage effect from the rudder. The explanation of this is complicated; it relates to the fact that the stern wave starts to travel along with the boat which means that there is no flow of water over the rudder and hence no steerage effect but the practical considerations need to be understood. The first will occur if you stray towards the bank, while still maintaining the same speed. As you move into shallower water, you will start to lose your steering and get sucked in towards the bank. If this occurs, you should shut down your engine to tickover, though leave it in gear. Hopefully, the reduced suction from the prop will let the boat lift enough in the water; if you have caught it in time, you will regain steerage way and can straighten up.

If you have left it too late, you will run gracefully aground and will have to pole yourself off. If you try to use too much reverse to pull yourself off you will just drag the stern down deeper while if you try to do it in ahead, you will just drive yourself farther aground.

Oncoming craft

Another potential grounding can occur when you meet an oncoming boat. Remember that you are both travelling down the middle of the canal and, in theory, on a collision course. If you pull over to the side of the canal too early, you risk running aground from the causes we have just discussed. The technique, therefore, is to start to slow down well in advance as in Fig 19. Halve your speed to about 2mph. Then, just as the two boats approach, you should alter course slightly to starboard. Because you have reduced your speed, even

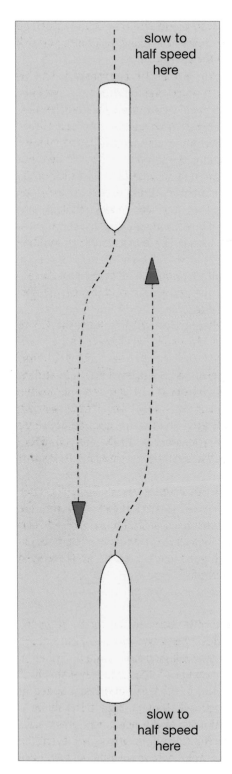

slow to
half speed
here

slow to
half speed
here

Fig 19 Passing on a narrow canal.
Because the deepest water will be in the
centre of the channel, you normally will
drive here, but on encountering another
boat, you both have to move to the side.
Always slow down sufficiently early to
maintain steerage-way and avoid
running aground.

though you are moving into shallower water, you should not lose steerage way and run aground. Do not leave the movement too late, or else you risk swerving into the bank or, worse, hitting the other boat.

The commonest fault in this manoeuvre is that the helmsman keeps his speed up for too long, then swerves to avoid the other boat. Fearing a collision, he then suddenly applies reverse. At this point the paddlewheel effect (remember that from earlier?) takes over and kicks the stern even farther to the side – invariably the wrong side – and magnifies the swerve. From this point, there are three possible outcomes. If the oncoming boat has judged it right and has already slowed down, it may be able to avoid you by maintaining steerage way. You, however, will run aground. Alternatively, the oncoming boat may not have enough room or may have to stop suddenly and you will both run aground. Thirdly, it will swing towards you and you will collide and run aground. So slow down well in advance when meeting oncoming boats.

Clearly, on the wider and deeper canals, the above effects will be reduced, but even so it pays to adopt the 'safety first' approach because even broad canals can be deceptively shallow at the edges.

If you encounter one of the goliaths of the system, the 70ft (21m) converted working barges, be aware that they will normally be of the maximum draught and will be very restricted in their ability to manoeuvre. In this case, on narrow stretches it is a good policy to pull over to one side and let them pass. Do not do this suddenly, as you could run aground and swerve into their path. Instead, let your way drop off gradually, without needing reverse, and ease gently into the edge. Even if you do run aground, it will be softly, and you will be able to pole yourself off easily and continue. Remember to signal your intentions to the oncoming helmsman to let him know that he can hold his course.

On bends, barges will need to keep in the deepest water. This will usually be on the towpath side, which will not always be the 'correct' side from the rule of the road point of view, so be prepared to pass on the 'wrong' side and look for a signal from their helmsman. Also these boats will often travel in pairs, with the motorboat towing the other, engineless 'butty', so leave even more room, and pull well over to let them pass.

Overtaking

You will occasionally have to overtake another boat on the canal. In theory, both of you should be travelling at the ideal speed and this should not occur. There will, however, still be times when you will gradually come up behind a low-powered craft or one whose size or draught forces it to travel slowly. If you have a shallow draught vessel that can travel safely at a faster speed, it may be appropriate to overtake. Be warned, though, that this can be a deceptively difficult task. You should only pass if the helmsman ahead calls you on. Do not just drive past and force him into the bank; in any event, he will normally have to slow down. If you simply try to accelerate past, you will find the combined suction effect of both craft will cause you both to lose steerage way and you will either be sucked together, or swerve into the bank. You should only carry out the manoeuvre on a long straight stretch, to avoid the risk of meeting an oncoming craft. Also, you should check your map to make sure that there is no lock coming up – if there is, the manoeuvre will be unnecessary and it is most discourteous to barge past someone just to steal a lock.

By the same token, if you are travelling more slowly than the conditions allow and another boat comes up behind you, do not obstruct them but wait for a straight stretch, slow down and call them past. If you are on a broad canal, with double width locks, you will, hopefully, find that the overtaking craft will have emptied and opened the next lock for you, and you can drive straight in.

Stopping

Stopping may sound simple, but you need to understand the principles. There are no brakes on a boat. Instead, you have to put the engine in reverse to slow yourself down. You need to bear several things in mind when you do this. First, except in an emergency, do not slam the engine from full ahead to full astern. Put the gear lever into neutral, then into reverse; when you feel the gears have engaged, gradually open the throttle. If you do not do this, the gearbox, engine and shaft may be damaged.

Also, unless your crew are prepared for your action, they could be thrown off their feet or even overboard. This is particularly relevant when you are coming alongside, when the crew may be poised on the deck edge with ropes in their hands ready to secure the boat and not expecting a sudden stop. Try to think ahead and keep your crew informed.

A second consideration is that even with the engine in reverse, the boat's momentum will keep it going forward. The distance it travels before stopping depends on the weight of the boat and how fast it was going. For these reasons, always moderate your speed when you approach places where you know you are going to stop. Bear in mind also that, if the wind or current are behind you, you will take longer to come to rest.

Finally, always remember the paddlewheel effect. This will kick the stern of your boat the same way every time you go into reverse. You will find out the direction through experience. The effect should be remembered and used to your advantage – if the kick is towards the bank that you are approaching, it can bring your stern neatly in but only if you have approached at an angle. If you come in parallel to the bank, it will swing you in with a crunch. Similarly, if it is taking you out, it can leave the aft crew member desperately stretching for the shore! To reduce the paddlewheel effect, apply reverse gradually – not suddenly – and turn the wheel against it while you still have forward motion, and just before you go into reverse. Turning the helm once you are in reverse will have virtually no effect at all.

Except in an emergency, always use the engine to stop your boat. Do not use a rope thrown over a bollard on the bank, as damage or injuries may occur. The rope may snap, the cleat on the boat may pull out or the boat will be dragged suddenly into the edge of the lock or pier. If you have to make an emergency stop if, for example, the engine has stalled when coming into a lock or the propeller has fouled, use a rope from the stern, not the bow. This will stop the craft parallel with the wall. If you use the bow line, it will drag the bow in with a crash, leaving the stern to swing out and hit other craft alongside.

The prudent skipper will always check reverse gear before approaching an obstruction, rather than when he is on top of it. You can drive for hours along an open stretch of river or canal without realising that the pin may have dropped out of the gear linkage. You will only find out when you try to engage reverse, by which time it may be too late. Incidentally, if this should happen, bear in mind that if the gearbox is stuck in ahead and you think it is in reverse, opening the throttle will simply make matters worse. In this case you should shut the engine down and shout a warning to the crew. Equally, engines can stall when going into reverse, particularly after a long run at one speed, so do check in advance.

Accident avoidance

It is vital that, before you set off on any trip, you clearly brief everyone on board that in the event of a potential serious collision, no one should try to stop it by fending off or pushing with a boathook. Boats and locks are tough and their damage can be repaired. Hands, arms and legs are tender and precious. It may seem wrong at the time to let the accident occur but if anyone is injured it makes the damage to the boat seem irrelevant. Even minor bumps can cause serious harm to fingers and if you see someone about to put themselves at risk, it is your duty to warn them to stand clear.

The experienced crew will always keep a fender ready to hand and if they see a crunch approaching, this can be dropped in the gap, but that is all. Obviously, if your boat is travelling slowly or moving about in a lock, keep it away from other craft, but again, well-shod feet or fenders are the best for this purpose.

Turning

Turning involves understanding and using all the functions of engine, gears and rudder. Let us remind ourselves of the three factors that cause a boat to turn:

1 Waterflow over the rudder caused by forward motion of the boat. With the helm to port, the vessel will turn that way. The speed of the turn depends on the speed of the boat through the water and the amount the helm is turned. This latter is an important point – up to about 30° of rudder angle, the rate of turn increases with angle of rudder. Turn the rudder further and it may stall, reducing the turning effect, while beyond

45–60° it may have little or no effect. Most wheel-steered craft have a stop to prevent the rudder going beyond 35° but on a narrowboat you can turn it through 90°, though with little effect at this point. The rudder effect will be greatest in ahead, least in reverse.

2 Waterflow over the rudder caused by the propeller. The rate of turn from this is dependent on the engine revs, not the boat speed. This is an important point, as we will discover later. Propeller effect only applies in ahead, not in reverse, as then the thrust is going forward, and not over the rudder.

3 The paddlewheel effect. This operates in one direction in ahead and in the opposite direction in reverse. The particular directions are dependent on the way the propeller rotates. The paddlewheel effect is proportional to engine speed. It is the same force in either ahead or astern, though it is usually greater in reverse, as the other two forces will then have little or virtually no effect.

The simplest turn is in a wide empty river. Here you just put the helm over, with the boat travelling forward, and round it goes. Your actual turning circle will depend on your boat and speed – practise a few times to find the circle of your own particular craft. To give yourself maximum room you should pull over to the right-hand side and preferably slow down to half speed to make the turn. Remember to look behind you and, if necessary, signal your intentions.

Official sound signals

The officially correct signals when manoeuvring are as follows:

◆ 1 short blast of the horn	– I am altering course to starboard
◆ 2 short blasts of the horn	– I am altering course to port
◆ 3 short blasts of the horn	– My engines are in astern
◆ 5 short rapid blasts	– I am uncertain of your actions
◆ 4 short blasts followed by 1 short blast	– I am turning right round to starboard
◆ 4 short blasts followed by 2 short blasts	– I am turning right round to port

Approved sound signals vary from waterway to waterway, but the first four are universal. The last two are used on the Thames, but understood elsewhere. Signals for European waterways are covered by international regulations.

In practice, when manoeuvring at slow speeds at close quarters, if you know the skipper of another boat is watching what you are doing, a simple hand signal will often suffice. If, however, you are in any doubt, use the official sound signals. Do not assume that because you have given a signal, you have the right to turn regardless. Equally, if your turn is not going to affect any other craft, do not disturb the peace by unnecessary use of the horn.

A simple one-point turn

Wide open river turns are easy. In practice, the situation will be complicated by a narrow channel, other boats and wind or current. These will require application of one or more of the turning principles we have discussed above.

A simple one-point turning circle will be improved by bringing your speed right down – to rest if necessary – then applying hard-over rudder, followed by a burst of power in ahead. This will give you maximum propeller turning effect but with minimum forward speed. The size and length of the power burst will depend on how tight and quickly you want to turn. On most vessels this should give you a turning circle of 2–3 times the length of the boat. Be also aware that the paddlewheel effect means that most boats will turn tighter one way than the other as paddlewheel and rudder effect work together. With a right-hand prop, you will turn tighter to port. Try this out some day just to see for yourself. Once you have found which way is your best one-point turn, try to go this way every time if other traffic allows. If this is still not tight enough, you will have to do a three-point turn or more. The procedure for this is as follows:

- ◆ Slow down and pull over to the right-hand side of the channel.

- ◆ Apply hard port helm and forward engine throttle. The boat will start to turn to port. (Watch your stern at this point as it may get too close to the bank or moored craft.)

- ◆ As you approach the left-hand bank, you apply full reverse. (The point at which you do this depends on how fast your boat stops.) Its momentum should keep the boat swinging to port, even though it is slowing down.

- ◆ Once it has stopped, usually at right-angles to the channel, and has then started to move backwards towards the bank, you re-apply forward throttle with the helm still hard over to port; the boat will continue to turn.

- ◆ The number of times you carry out this procedure depends on the width of the channel and how fast your boat reacts. (For channels only slightly wider than the length of your craft we will describe a different technique later.)

While making a turn, it is useful to have a crew member at the bow telling you how close you are getting to the bank but they should hold on tight to prevent the reverse thrusts from dislodging them. You should also be careful not to let your stern swing in too close to the bank, as you may damage rudder or prop on the bottom. In practice, most craft have much less draught at the bow than the stern, allowing you to take them closer at that end.

Turning with a right-hand prop

As we saw, every boat will have a direction in which it turns best, due once again to the paddlewheel effect. Let us look at a boat with a right-hand propeller and start with a turn to port as in Fig 20. As you apply the first burst of ahead power, the paddlewheel effect will be assisting the turn to port slightly, by kicking the stern to starboard. This will only be a small benefit compared to the prop thrust over the rudder. However, as you apply reverse to stop the boat, the paddle wheel effect will counteract the turn as it is then kicking the stern to port. On some vessels, with small rudders, this can lead to a situation where the boat never gets round in a narrow channel.

Turning with a left-hand prop

If we look at a left-hand prop boat (see Fig 21) turning the same way – to port – the first burst of power swings the stern to starboard which easily overcomes the paddlewheel effect the other way. When we come to apply reverse though, the paddlewheel effect kicks the stern to starboard, assisting the swing, and giving an overall tighter turn.

So you will find, annoyingly, that for every boat, the best direction to turn when you need to make more than one movement is the opposite one to the best direction for a single-point turn. You therefore need to know in advance whether you will make it in one go or not. Preferably do some practices on a quiet stretch of water to enable you to gauge your boat's turning circle.

Turning with an outdrive

So far we have assumed you are in a single-engined shaftdrive boat. Outboard or outdrive craft have fewer problems when turning but require a slightly different technique. Again, start by the right-hand bank with the helm to port (see Fig 22). Apply forward throttle and the boat will start to turn to port. If you leave the helm to port and apply reverse thrust as you approach the far bank, the boat will swing back to starboard, nullifying the turn. You should therefore smartly turn the wheel to starboard as the engine passes through neutral, which will have the effect of continuing the boat's turn to port when reverse is applied. This technique is so effective that these craft turn much tighter than their shaftdrive counterparts.

Twin-engined turns and bow-thrusters

Similarly, twin-engined boats will also turn tighter, by the technique of putting

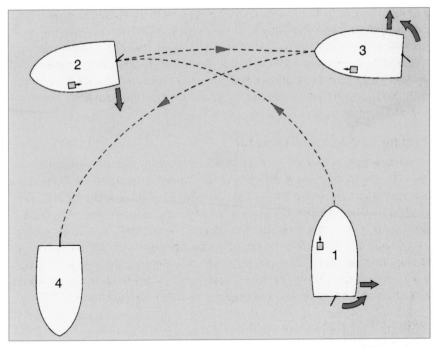

Fig 20 *Boat with right-hand prop doing a three-point turn to port. Paddlewheel effect counteracts this.*

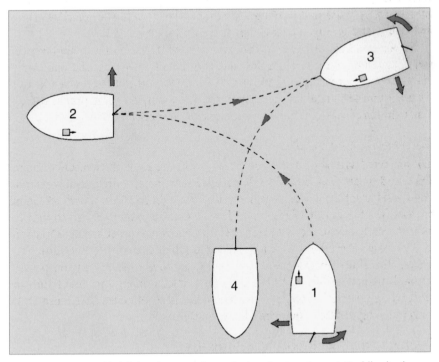

Fig 21 *Boat with left-hand prop doing a three-point turn to port. Paddlewheel effect assists.*

one engine ahead and one astern, though you should still turn the wheel hard over in the direction you wish to turn. There is also some benefit (or otherwise) from the paddlewheel effect but, in practice, this is minimal compared to the propeller thrusts and nil if the props rotate in opposite directions.

The lucky owners who have opted to install a bow-thruster now come into their own, being able to use the thruster to rotate the boat, the gears just keeping it in the middle of the channel.

Turning on narrow waterways

In some instances, particularly on canals, the width of the channel will only be a couple of feet more than the length of the boat. Here the to-and-fro technique is not a realistic approach. Instead, you should make the turn by holding the bow against one bank, and swing the stern around. If the bank is soft, you can push the bow into it. If it is firm, or a wall, it is advisable to put a crew member ashore with a fender down the gap. Again, with a soft bank, the bow will normally wedge into it, and not slide either way. With a firm bank, however, it may be necessary to take a line from the bow to a secure point, in the direction you are making the turn (see Fig 23).

To swing the stern round you can either use the engine, or pull it by hand. If using the engine, you put the helm hard over in the direction you are wanting to turn and put the engine in ahead. The propeller thrust over the rudder will push the stern round. The amount of throttle you need will vary depend-

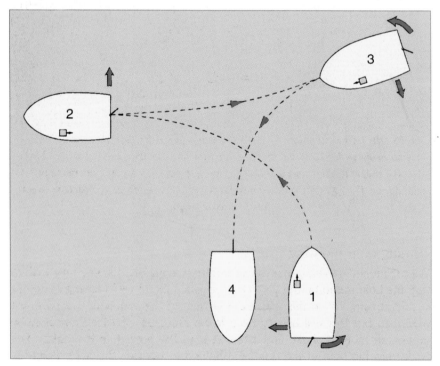

Fig 22 Outdrive boat turning to port. (It will turn equally effectively to starboard.)

ing on whether there is a wind blowing against the turn. Once you have turned through 90°, you should ease back on the throttle and the crew member on the bank can start to push the bow out; alternatively, this can be done on board with a pole. Then you either continue turning and straighten out or use reverse to pull yourself back from the bank.

If the water under the stern of the boat is shallow, you may find it better to put a crew member on the bank with a line to pull the stern round, rather than churning up the bottom and risking potential damage to the prop. At certain points along the canals you will find winding holes which are V-shaped broadened sections of the navigation in one bank (see Fig 24). These were designed to let 70ft (21m) barges turn, by putting their bow into the V, and driving the stern round. They are marked on the maps and guides but be aware that they may be shallow and overgrown with weeds.

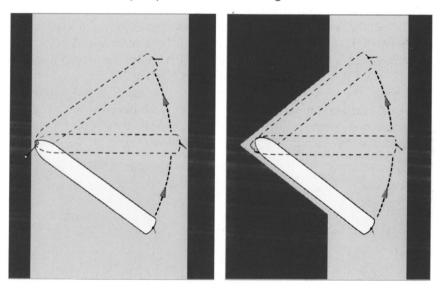

Fig 23 left: Turning in a river or canal that's only just wider than your boat. The bow will normally wedge itself in a soft bank, but the line should be used on a hard bank. Use the engine to drive the stern round if the water is deep enough; otherwise pull it with a rope. Fig 24 right: Winding hole for turning a narrowboat in a canal narrower than its overall length.

Turning on a mooring

We mentioned earlier, under the section on casting off, that you may wish to turn the boat round before you leave the mooring, to avoid having to do this in mid-stream. To do this you use a version of the technique we have just described but this will usually have to be modified because there may be other craft moored ahead and astern of you. The procedure is to take a line back from the bow of the boat to a bollard or cleat on the bank alongside amidships or farther aft. This stops you drifting down on the boat ahead (see

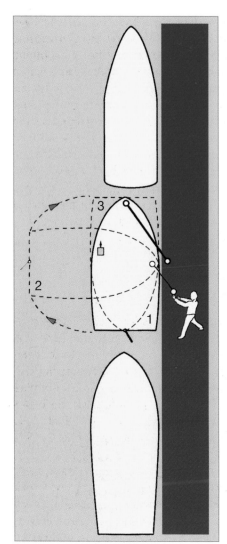
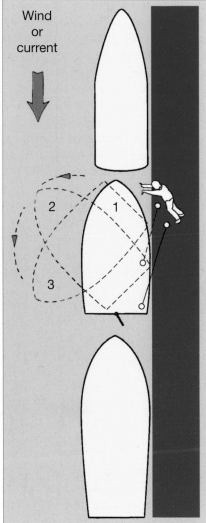

Wind
or
current

Fig 25 left: Turning a boat round in its own length with vessels moored ahead and
astern. Either drive the boat round with the helm hard over, and a fender at the bow,
or pull it round with ropes. Pull the bow along the bank as it turns.
Fig 26 right: If the boat is facing into wind or current when turning, push the bow out
and let the current take it round.

Fig 25). Then you let the stern line go, and allow the stern of the boat to
swing out. This can be assisted by applying ahead power and rudder, or can
be done with a pole. If you are using power, keep it as little as possible and, if
necessary, put a fender down to protect the bow.

As the stern swings out, past 45°, the bow should be pulled along the
bank. This can be done by someone on board taking up the line, but in practice it is usually easier to have one or more crew members ashore, walking

the bow round. As the stern passes through 90°, the bow should be halfway between the two adjacent craft; as it continues to swing, keep it moving along. This will prevent your boat from swinging down on the neighbouring craft. To pull the stern right in, the helmsman may have to throw a line ashore or, alternatively, you can prepare for this by running a long line from the far stern quarter up to the bow of the boat and on to the shore, before you let go. Finally, you should end up alongside the bank but pointing in the opposite direction.

Whenever you are turning your boat, take account of current and wind, and try to make them work with you rather than against. This may mean letting the bow swing out rather than the stern. In the example Fig 26, you should make sure that there is enough depth of water alongside the bank to clear the rudder and prop; if not, push the boat out slightly. You will not need to use the engine to turn the boat, as the wind will be doing that.

Reversing

This is the one manoeuvre guaranteed to sort the nautical men from the boys and to reduce the most composed skipper to tears. Start on the principle that reversing a boat is like backing a horse. Basically, it does not want to do it and needs coaxing all the way. If we go back to our principles of steering, the reasons for this become apparent. Firstly, in reverse there is no flow from the propeller over the rudder, because its thrust is all going forward. Secondly, the flow of water over the rudder from the movement astern is limited, so provides little steerage effect. Finally, you have the paddlewheel effect, trying to push the stern one way. So how do you cope with the situation?

Well, the answer is that you rely on the propeller to pull you backwards, and endeavour to keep the boat pointed in the right direction while still moving astern. In open water, you do this by engaging reverse followed by quick bursts of ahead throttle, with the helm over one way or the other. This may sound like a contradiction but, in fact, it does work. As an example, if you use enough reverse to get the boat moving, say, at 2mph backwards but the stern starts to swing off to port, then a quick burst of ahead, with the helm over to port, will swing the stern to starboard without stopping the progress backwards (see Fig 27). In calm conditions, the stern will always swing the same way when the boat is reversing, due to the paddlewheel effect; you can forestall that by starting off with the stern pointing slightly the wrong way before you engage reverse. Then you only have to make periodic corrections by using ahead thrust to keep it travelling straight.

If there is a wind blowing, it may also push the boat off course, possibly requiring a different correction but you will quickly gauge this at the time.

Some boats, particularly those with large rudders, and fine sections aft, may steer with the rudder once they have picked up enough speed in reverse but in most situations this cannot be relied on.

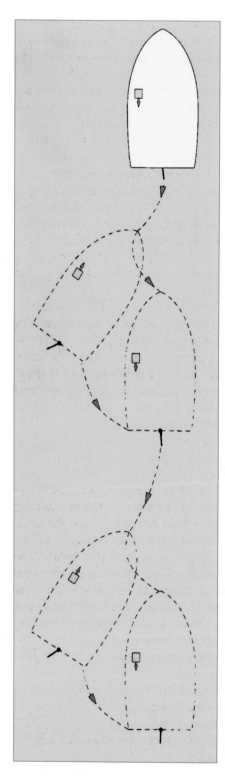

Fig 27 Reversing. Put the engine into astern with the helm amidships. The boat will travel backwards, and will tend to veer off one way or the other. Straighten it up with a quick burst of ahead with the helm over, but not enough to stop the overall movement backwards.

In narrow channels, especially canals, if you are faced with having to reverse a long way, another trick is to keep the stern pointing in the right direction by poling gently on the appropriate side. Then you just engage tick-over reverse and keep on course with the pole, either used from the stern or the bow. Alternatively, you can put someone ashore with a rope to keep the boat lined up. This requires that you have already worked out which way the boat is going to tend to swing or drift, because the crew member will only be able to pull one way. Again, in practice it will be either the paddlewheel effect or the wind which will be pushing you off course.

Also remember that the flow of water against the rudder will force it to one side or the other. Keep a firm grip on the wheel or tiller and try to keep it amidships. If it should start to turn, it can suddenly swing over. This is more of a problem with a tiller which will sweep across the aft deck with consider-able force and could cause an injury, or knock you overboard. Even with a wheel, it will make it difficult or impossible to straighten up the helm. If this should happen, put the engine briefly ahead to relieve the pressure on the rudder and straighten it up.

As with turning, outboard and outdrive boats have none of these problems in reverse. The directional thrust of the propeller means that you can point the stern whichever way you want it. All you have to do is remember that the helm has to be turned the opposite way to when it is in ahead. Of course, those insufferable people with their bow-thrusters can positively show off in reverse, with the thruster being used to keep the boat lined up in the same way as we have described with pole or rope.

Coming alongside

The last of the major boat-handling operations is bringing your boat along-side. Here you are trying to achieve two things: to get your craft to a suitable position in order to get a crew member or rope ashore, while at the same time avoiding a collision with the bank or wall. In general, your crew will be positioned at or near the bow; this is the part of the boat that needs to be close to the bank first. This means that you should approach at a shallow angle, usually around 30°. This has an additional benefit; if you are at all doubtful about the depth of water close to the bank, it is preferable to put your bow in first. This is normally the part with the least draught so less likely to touch the bottom. The rudder and prop then remain in deeper water, allowing you to pull yourself out if the water should prove to be too shallow for mooring.

Coming alongside brings into play many of the points you have learnt so far about handling your boat, especially preparation:

◆ **Crew briefing** Talk to your crew before you get in close and agree your plan of action.

◆ **Signals** Agree your system of signals so that the crew can keep you appraised of what they find as you get closer in.

◆ **Ropes** Make sure that the ropes are ready and coiled. This applies to the bow line that the crew member will use plus the stern line that you may have to throw to the crew.

◆ **Fenders** Check that the fenders are in place and at the right height.

◆ **Boathook** Check that the boathook is conveniently to hand.

As you approach, slow down as much as possible – sudden bursts of reverse indicate an amateur, though clearly if you have to stop quickly for any reason, do not worry about appearances – use as much power as is necessary. We have already recommended that you check that reverse is working before you get to the critical point – people may scoff at this caution but having had an engine that decided to start stalling as it went into reverse – just as we were piling up behind a shiny new cruiser waiting for the lock – I can assure you that it is not an experience that I would wish on anyone else!

Look around you to see what the current and wind are doing. Wherever possible you should aim to come alongside against the current as it will act as a brake and swing you in towards the bank. Look out for sudden currents in the vicinity of locks. If the sluice gates open just as you are approaching, this can cause a sudden flow of water. It may either drag you towards the lock if you are coming from upstream or push you away if you are coming from below. Clues to this are the actions of the lock-keeper or another crew opening the paddles. Coming from downstream, a burst of water from the bottom of the gates will show the same thing. Similarly, side flows can be experienced in the approach to a lock as water flows over a weir, or down a by-pass sluice.

The positive approach

As you come alongside, remember the paddlewheel effect. If you apply sudden reverse, the kick will either push the stern out or in, depending on the direction your prop turns. If it pushes your stern towards the bank, this will work in your favour as it will swing you in parallel to the edge. However, remember that at the same time the effect will be to push the bow out, just at the moment your crew was about to step ashore. The solution to this is to come in with enough way so that the boat swerves in bodily as it rotates, though not so fast that you hit the bank or wall too hard (see Fig 28). In this context, remember that you have got fenders down and that they are there for a purpose. They are not meant to be a substitute for good handling but they do allow you some leeway in how you come alongside. Better to be

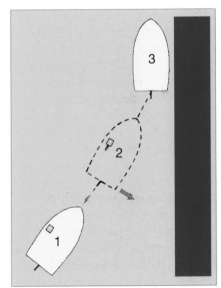

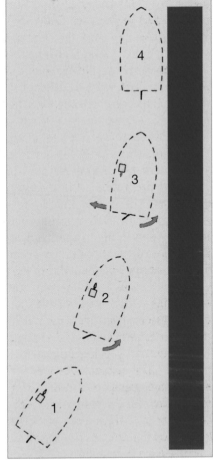

Fig 28 above: Coming alongside with left-hand prop. Approach at 30° with rudder amidships (1). As you apply reverse (2), the paddlewheel effect swings the stern in, and the boat stops parallel with the bank (3).

Fig 29 above right: Coming alongside with right-hand prop. Approach at 30° with engine at tickover ahead, helm amidships (1). Put helm to port (2) and (3). As the stern starts to swing in, apply reverse. The paddlewheel effect will balance the swing of the stern, and the boat will come alongside parallel (4).

there with a soft bump than drifting several feet away from the bank. This is particularly relevant if the wind is blowing you off; if you do not arrive firmly enough, you will never get there.

If the paddlewheel effect is tending to take you away from the wall, you should again allow for this by putting the wheel over at the last moment, before you go into reverse. This will start to swerve the stern in, just as the paddlewheel effect is throwing it out. If you have judged it right, the two will cancel out (see Fig 29).

Stepping ashore to make fast

If your crew are going to step ashore, you should take nearly all the way off the boat (slow down) with the engine before they do so. Otherwise, they are going to be jumping off a fast-moving boat, which can be dangerous. The crew should understand that they must not jump off until the boat has slowed down. Similarly, the crew should not suddenly make the rope fast as soon as they get ashore if the boat is still moving. This will bring it to a crashing stop which can be dangerous. The proper technique is to take a turn round a bollard, keeping hold of the end of the rope, and letting it slide through in a controlled way with the friction slowing the boat down, though preferably it should be the helmsman who stops the boat, with the engine.

Once the boat has stopped and the crew are ashore, you can quickly take stock of the situation. If you are coming into a potentially shallow bank, your stern should still be a couple of yards out in deep water. There are two ways of getting the stern in. If your crew quickly makes fast the bow line, they can then come back and catch the stern line that you throw to them. Alternatively, if you have practised the manoeuvre, you can use the bow line to drive yourself in. To do this, lead the line round a bollard alongside the shoulder of the boat and then make fast. Then, if you put the engine slowly ahead, with the helm away from the bank, the stern will gradually swing in.

Coming alongside in a lock

If you are coming into a broad lock, especially one with other boats already in it, you will have to come in parallel to the wall without swinging out. If you have a choice, you should opt for the side that allows your paddlewheel effect to pull the stern in towards the wall. Do not come in too fast as you will bump when you go into reverse. If you have no choice of sides and you know your stern will swing out, make sure that you and your crew are prepared for this to happen. This means that either they have to come quickly back to you as soon as they are ashore, to catch the stern line, or you have to be ready to pull the stern in yourself.

If you are coming into a lock that is full of water, you should be able to step off on to the wall with the stern line, having made sure that the engine is in neutral before you leave. Alternatively, you can try lassoing a bollard. This looks simple; in fact, it requires considerable practice but it is well worth it once perfected. If the lock is empty, you may be able to catch a chain by hand or with the boathook, or if the lock is narrow enough you can fend off from the far side.

In some cases it may not be possible for your crew to step ashore when you are coming into a lock. This may be because your boat is high off the water or your crew are not so nimble on their pins. If you enter an empty, deep lock your crew will have to lasso a bollard. This requires some practice and planning in advance. It also requires you to have stopped the boat with the engine, as otherwise the rope will be doing the braking, which can be dangerous.

The outdrive approach

If you have an outboard or outdrive, slight differences in technique are required. As soon as you engage reverse to stop, the stern of the boat swings in the direction the drive is pointing. This effect can be used to your advantage but must be borne in mind. For instance, if you come into a bank on the right-hand side at the 30° angle, you should turn the wheel slightly to starboard, just as you are going into reverse. Then, when reverse engages, the stern of the boat will swing in. Do not overdo this, as otherwise the bow will swing out at the same time.

Easy approaches with twin engines and bow-thrusters

Twin-engined boats will behave differently. There will be no paddlewheel effect as you engage reverse; altering the angle of the boat relative to the bank can be done by using the engines. Be aware that your props and rudders are positioned closer to the sides of the boat, and therefore more vulnerable to grounding on the bottom.

Of course, the last word is with the bow-thruster which is tailor-made for this situation. All you have to do is use the engine to stop the boat and the thruster to put the bow exactly where you or your crew want it. Be warned, however, that the sideways thrust can be sudden; make sure your crew are not poised to step ashore just when you hit the button.

Making fast

Making fast might seem a simple part of the boat-handling process, but it is essential to get it right if you are to have security and peace of mind when moored. We will discuss ropes and knots in the next section but here we will look at where, how and to what you should tie up.

The purposes of making fast are:

◆ To prevent your boat from drifting away.

◆ To protect the boat from damage.

◆ To stop your boat from damaging neighbouring craft.

◆ To ensure a peaceful night's sleep for everyone aboard.

We will look at the various factors that will enable you to ensure this, starting with where you should moor.

If there is a current it is preferable, but not essential, to tie up with your bows facing upstream. This will avoid pressure on the rudder from the water flow. It will also avoid flotsam and debris from drifting into the propeller and potentially damaging it or jamming it when you start off. It will also make casting off easier. The mooring may be empty when you arrive but other craft can later hem you in ahead and astern.

Try to avoid shallow water especially if there are rocks as it can not only damage the hull but will also give you a noisy night's sleep as the boat scrapes to and fro. Bear in mind that the water level may drop during the night, particularly if you are close to the top of a lock. However, mooring in shallow water may be unavoidable. You will usually find that the deepest part of your boat is aft. If this runs aground before you reach the bank, it is often possible to moor with your bow into the bank leaving the stern projecting out at a slight angle – clearly this should not be too extreme as it could impede the passage of other vessels. Also, in this case it will be essential that you moor with your bows upstream, to avoid the stern being forced further out. Remember that there will also be a 'flow' downstream from a lock, even on a canal, particularly if you are close to it. The stern should still be tied to the bank on a long line; it can sometimes be held from swinging in by using the boarding plank or pole. Alternatively, an anchor or mud-weight can be dropped over the 'off-shore' side of the stern and secured with a rope to prevent the stern swinging into the bank.

Boarding planks

A boarding plank is standard equipment on canal boats and can also be useful in some river situations. It enables you to get ashore from shallow moorings when you are unable to moor the boat right alongside. Its construction is worth a short mention here. The plank should obviously be strong enough to take the weight of the heaviest crew member, bearing in mind that they may also be jumping down on to it. It must not flex significantly, otherwise this may worry the less confident of your party; 8in x 2in x 8ft (20cm x 5cm x 2.5m) is a suitable dimension if made from solid timber, reducing the thickness to 1½in (38mm) if you use plywood.

It is essential that the top surface has a good non-slip finish as it may be wet and, when positioned, may slope upwards or downwards. The best non-slip coating is sanded paint or one of the proprietary rubber deck coverings. Some people use cross-battens but these can be distracting underfoot and can cause you to trip. The underside should have rubber strips at each end. These will prevent the board from damaging the deck, stop it slipping off and give you a quieter night. It will also protect the deck when the board is stowed. Two carrying handles from a hardware shop fitted on each edge will make it easier to pick up and deploy. They will also give you securing points to tie the board in place on steep banks, or where there is a lot of movement of the boat. Otherwise, large holes drilled near the ends will serve the same purpose.

Mooring pins

There are a variety of options as to where you may tie up. Permanent moorings will have bollards, rings or posts. If another craft is already using one of these, do not wrap your line over theirs, or make it difficult for them to untie. If the mooring has no fixed points, then you will have to use your own. These

*A boarding plank enables you to moor in shallow water, where you cannot get
the boat right into the bank, yet still get onboard easily.*

are variously called mooring spikes or pins. They consist of steel bars with pointed ends, 15–30in (40–75cm) long, and ½–¾in (12–20mm) diameter, depending on the size of boat they have to secure. A galvanised finish will prevent rust which will discolour both your hands and the rope. Preferably, they should have an eye or loop welded to the top. This will stop the rope from slipping off. It will also give you a purchase with which to pull or twist the pin out of the ground.

The pin is hammered into the ground at an angle of 20–30° away from the direction of pull. This will help prevent it from being pulled out and will also stop the rope slipping off the top. Hammer it down as far as it will easily go, to give the maximum grip. Keep the rope as low down as possible to reduce the leverage effect which may pull out the pin.

It is good practice to put a cover over the tops of the pins. This will help to make them visible to anyone walking down the towpath at night. It will also soften the blow to ankle or shin if a pin is not seen. White plastic washing-up liquid bottles with their tops cut off serve both purposes admirably. When removing a pin, twist it first to break the grip of the soil, then pull it out, twisting at the same time. If a pin will not move, putting another one crossways through the eye will give you extra leverage to both twist and pull.

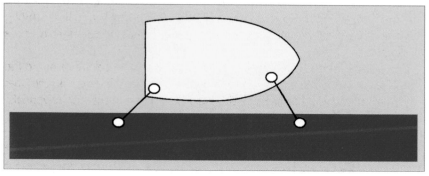

Fig 30 When mooring on non-tidal rivers or canals, two lines will normally be sufficient at 30–45° to prevent the boat moving fore-and-aft or outwards.

Mooring pins should preferably be put in on the same side of the towpath as the boat to avoid ropes stretched across the path. In some cases this will not be possible because of insufficient width of bank. Do not put pins in too close to the edge, as the constant working will gradually break up the bank. In these cases, the lines will have to lead across the path. Leave them slack enough so that they lie along the ground and tie a white rag to the middle of them.

Mooring lines

Under most conditions, two lines will normally be sufficient when tying up on non-tidal rivers or canals. They should be taken from the bow and stern, preferably at an angle of 30–45° (see Fig 30). This will prevent movement of

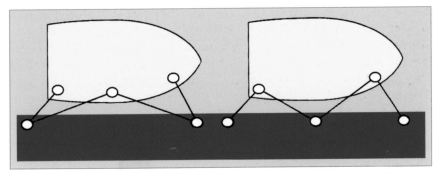

Fig 31 For greater security, two extra lines (springs) can be used. These can either be taken from a central cleat in the boat to the same bollards ashore, or from the same cleats to a central bollard ashore.

the boat both outwards and fore-and-aft. In some cases it will not be possible to achieve this angle but the boat may then surge ahead and astern. Even on a canal this can be a problem, as passing boats will suck your vessel first one way then the other.

Do not tie the lines too tight, otherwise the constant working on the pins will pull them out, while the boat will snatch every time another craft goes by. The boat will then rub up and down the bank, damaging the hull or scuffing the fenders. Leave enough slack for a couple of inches of free movement in all directions.

The best technique is to double the line back from the bollard or pin to the boat. This halves the strain on the rope. It also positions the knots on the boat which is both neater and reduces the likelihood of being cast off by vandals. At the same time, it allows you to let the line go from the boat when casting off without stepping ashore.

When leaving the boat for an extended period or when moored on a fast moving or busy river, two more lines should be taken from the boat for greater security. These are known as springs. They run at shallow angles to the bank, and prevent the boat from surging fore-and-aft, as well as spreading the load by doubling the number of lines. They can either run from the same two pins or bollards on the bank to a point amidships on the boat or from the bow and stern of the boat to one or more additional mooring points on the bank (see Fig 31). The advantage of the latter arrangement is that you have increased the number of pins on the bank, thereby spreading the load and reducing your dependence on just two points. For ultimate security from vandals, a padlocked chain which fixes the boat to a bankside ring or bollard is worth consideration.

So far we have assumed you are tying up permanently, or for an extended period of an hour or more. However, there will be occasions, particularly when waiting for a lock, when you will only need a temporary attachment. Here it is often possible to use a single point mooring with a line or lines taken to a point on the bank alongside amidships. This has the benefit that

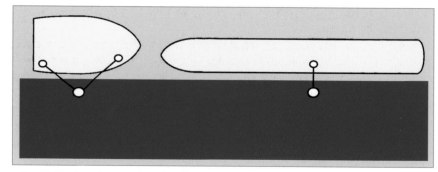

Fig 32 Single point moorings for short stops, using the bow and stern lines on a short craft, or a single central line on a long narrowboat.

only one person need tend the line(s), allowing the rest of the crew to go ahead and work the lock. On small craft up to 20ft (6m), the existing bow and stern lines can be used for this purpose. On a narrowboat, a single line taken from amidships is preferable. This line is made fast to a strong point on the cabin top – either the handrail or a purposely fixed cleat, sited so it can serve either side of the boat (see Fig 32). The line should be long enough that it can be led forward or aft, with enough spare to allow it to be thrown ashore.

The line can be thrown by the helmsman to a crew member who has already got ashore from the bow. If he is adept at the manoeuvre, the helmsman can step ashore himself with it, having first brought the boat to rest using the engine and checked that the gear is in neutral. When casting off, coil the rope neatly in one hand, step aboard while pushing the boat gently off at the same time. Then work your way aft and pull clear. Always start the engine before casting this line off.

If you anticipate that the water levels are going to rise or fall due to rain, tides, or lowering of the pound (a level length between locks), you should leave enough slack in the lines to allow for this. In this situation, longer lines will give you more movement allowance. A long line run at a shallow angle will have more adjustment potential and capacity to stretch than a short one run at 90° but will hold the boat just as securely. This is due partly to the geometry of the arrangement and partly due to the flexibility of the rope. All ropes have a certain degree of stretch as we will see in the next section. This can be up to a maximum of 30% under extreme load but the actual amount will be proportional to the original length. Thus a 3ft (1m) rope stretched by 10% will only give you 3in (76mm) of movement. A 10ft (3m) rope on the other hand will give you 1ft (30cm) of stretch under the same load. In addition to this, the geometry of the situation shows that if a short line (say 3ft (1m) in length) is tied amidships at 90° to the boat, the rope has got to stretch 33% if the water level drops 1ft (30cm). If the line is 10ft (3m) long, still at 90° to the boat, the stretch will be only 10%. If, however, the same line is taken from the bow or stern of the boat at 60°, for the same drop in water level, the extension will only be 1in (25mm), or

1%. In practice, a 33% extension is likely to break either the rope or the cleats on the boat.

Except in emergencies, do not tie up to trees. Quite apart from direct damage, the bark will gradually be worn away, eventually killing them.

For ultimate safety, you can use the anchor. Put it out upstream, and make sure it has held. Then if your ropes should break loose, the boat will still be attached. In areas that are prone to vandalism, the same technique can be used but in this case, put the anchor out over the side of the bow away from the bank, so it will not be seen. Then, again, if your lines should be let go, the boat will not drift far.

Ropes

'By his ropes ye shall know the measure of the sailor'. The old saying, coined in the era of sailing craft, is just as appropriate to the modern motorboat. The condition of the boat's ropes will give you much evidence as to the general care and condition of the craft and the attitude of its skipper.

Whole books have been written on the subject of knots and ropes. Here we will confine ourselves to the basic ropecraft required for a motorboat on inland waterways which mainly relate to mooring and making fast.

By the very nature of their use, craft on rivers and canals will be constantly tied up and cast off, yet it is surprising how little attention many owners pay to either their mooring ropes or their crew's understanding of them. Correct lines, in good condition, will make a pleasure out of this part of boat handling and earn you the thanks of all the crew.

All too often, mooring lines will be neglected and poorly suited for their purpose. It is somehow assumed that they will last for ever but this is not the case. Man-made fibres, which are the norm these days, will harden with age and exposure to ultraviolet light and ultimately lose their strength. Hard lines are difficult to handle, coil and throw; they are stiff to make knots with and can cause painful bruising to fingers and knuckles.

Ropes with cut or frayed sections are even worse; they will be weak and might break at a critical moment. Similar comments apply to knots in the line. These will get increasingly tighter, making them impossible to undo. They will weaken the line, and can cause it to jam when pulled quickly round a cleat or ring.

At the same time, the actual type of rope you use is important. Some will be easier to handle and better suited to repeated tying up, as in locks; however, they may be more expensive. Cheaper ropes can be used but they will be hard on the hands. The best solution, therefore, is to have two sets of lines for the boat. For your permanent mooring you can use one set, and either leave them at the mooring or take them with you as a back-up. If these lines should harden or get dirty with age, it is not a problem, as you will not be handling them often. They can also be cut to exactly the right length for your mooring, avoiding the problem of having lots of spare line lying around. You can then invest in a new set of soft, easily handled lines for use when out on the waterway. These can be stored when not in use and will therefore remain clean and flexible.

Rope comes in various types and specifications which we will briefly look at here. The three materials most commonly used are nylon, polyester and polypropylene and each has its own benefits and disadvantages.

Nylon

Nylon is the strongest material. It also stretches the most. This might appear a disadvantage but, in fact, it gives it greater shock-absorbing properties which is useful for a mooring rope. It is available in either three-strand, braided or plaited forms. (See Rope construction opposite.) It is usually only available in white. It will tend to harden with age and exposure to sunlight.

Polyester

Polyester is almost as strong as nylon but it has far less stretch. It can be supplied in either three-strand or braided forms and is also available pre-stretched. It is mainly used for halyards and sheets on sailing boats, where the resistance to stretch is essential. However, in its matt finish braided form, it is good to handle and therefore especially suitable for mooring lines which are used frequently. In this respect, buy the non pre-stretched forms. It remains softer and better to handle with age.

Polypropylene

Polypropylene is the cheapest. It is also the weakest of the three. It is usually blue in colour, and comes in three-strand form only. Its one advantage is that it floats. It hardens rapidly with age and exposure to the sun and when it does, the strands start to break and fray. They then form sharp, hard splinters which can cause painful injuries to your hands. It is popular with hire-boat companies because of its price, and also, because of its buoyancy, it is less likely to be sucked into the propeller if left hanging over the side when the boat is underway. However, we would not recommend it for the private owner except possibly for permanent moorings for light craft or as a spare line.

Rope construction

Modern rope comes in a variety of different forms of construction or 'lays'. Three-strand is the most familiar form. It actually consists of many hundreds of strands but these are bundled into three main strands which are then twisted to form the rope. This is the style formerly used for making all natural ropes and is still the commonest form for man-made fibre ropes. Because of the twisting of the strands, it has the greatest amount of stretch. It is best suited for permanent mooring lines, but can also be used for repeated tying up, though it will become hard to handle with age.

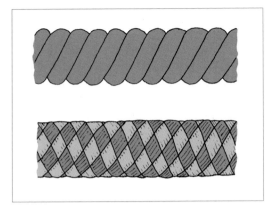

Fig 33 Rope construction:
laid (top) and braided rope.

Braided or plaited rope consists of multiple strands, usually 8 or 16, woven into a plaited form. It can be solid all the way through or can form the outer sheath to an inner core. This inner core can be three-strand, plaited or continuous parallel filaments. The outer sheath can either be matt or shiny depending on the application. The outer sheath does not contribute significantly to the strength, but it does make the rope easier to handle. It was designed originally for the sheets or sail-handling ropes on sailing boats but also makes excellent rope for lines used for repeated mooring. In this respect, the matt finish gives the best grip. It remains soft and flexible with age. Also, the outer sheath protects the inner load-carrying core from abrasion and cuts. Braided lines are also available in several colours, allowing you to colour-co-ordinate your lines with your boat or identify lines for different purposes.

Plaited lines are usually polyester but one form, sometimes known by a trade name of Octoplait, is an 8-plait nylon line. It was originally devised for anchor lines due to its high stretch and because it does not kink. Some people use it for mooring lines as it is slightly easier to coil and more flexible but it is not so easy to grip as matt braidline.

Obviously the different types and materials have different prices but think twice before buying on price alone. On a river or canal, your lines will be in continuous use and their overall cost, in comparison with the rest of your boating expenses, will be comparatively low. As an example, for 12mm* rope, the comparative prices in 2005 were:

Polypropylene	90p per metre
Three-strand nylon	£2.50 per metre
Matt braidline	£3.40 per metre
Octoplait	£3.15 per metre

* Most rope today is sized by its diameter in millimetres. In times past, it was sized by its circumference in inches and the old habit sometimes dies hard. If you should encounter the old system, divide the circumference by three to give the approximate modern equivalent. Thus 1½in rope is the same as today's 12mm.

Sizes and lengths

The diameter of the rope you choose for your lines governs its ultimate strength. This obviously relates to the size of your boat, but diameter also affects its handling qualities. If it is too thin you cannot easily grip it; too thick and it will be too heavy to handle. As a general guide, for a boat up to 20ft (6m), 10mm will be suitable for general mooring lines. Any thinner and it will be hard to grip. Between 20–30ft (6–9m), you should use 12mm. From 30–40ft (9–12m), 12mm will be suitable for a light boat but for heavier craft you should go up to 14mm. Above 40ft (12m) you should use 14mm or 18mm.

Length is another important consideration. If it is too short, you will not be able to reach the top of a lock but if it is too long, the coil will become unwieldy to handle or throw. In practice, the best length will depend on whether you are using the line for temporary holding in a lock and short-term

If you are worried about security, you can use a length of anchor chain,
possibly padlocked, to reinforce your rope mooring lines.

mooring or whether it is needed for longer stops. Again, you should consider carrying more than one line to achieve both requirements. For your bow and stern lines which are in continual use, you must have enough length to reach up to the bollard and back down to the boat on the deepest lock you are likely to encounter. In practice, this means a minimum of 20ft (6m), but, except for the smallest craft, we would recommend 25–30ft (7.6–9m). In addition to this, for boats over 20ft (6m) you should carry one or, preferably, two more lines for springs if you should need them.

Finally, all boats should have the capability of putting together one really long line, up to 50–60ft (15–18m), for emergencies. On smaller craft this can be achieved by tying together your two spare spring lines but for maximum safety, on boats over 30ft (9m), there should be one line set aside for this purpose, readily accessible in case it is needed. An occasion might occur, such as engine failure either on your boat or another craft, when it is drifting towards a weir or possibly you may need it to haul yourself across to a better mooring in the teeth of a strong wind.

All the above points apply to craft used on canals and non-tidal rivers. If you are venturing out into the tideway or commercial waterways such as the Severn or Trent, you will need at least two 60ft (18m) lines to deal with deeper locks or exposed moorings with a high rise and fall of tide.

Knots

It is essential that all your crew are confident in rope handling and making fast. Out of the many thousands of knots that have been derived through the ages, a minimum basic selection will deal with most of the situations you will encounter. It is more useful for the crew to understand these, and be able to tie the correct one immediately, than filling their heads with obscure examples.

All the main rope manufacturers print booklets of simple knots, so make sure you have some drawings on board with a handy length of thin line to practise with.

Round turn and two half hitches

The simplest, and most useful, knot of all in mooring situations is the round turn and two half hitches. This can be used to make fast to a bollard or ring and will also attach the fenders to their eyes or loops. It is simple both to make and release and can be used either at the end of the rope or, with caution, in the middle. The form of it is shown in Fig 34, but the important thing to remember is that it must go twice round the bollard or ring. In fact, for the layman, the name 'round-turn' is confusing, as it implies just round the bollard and back. It would be better described as two round turns because while this is strictly not correct in knotting terms, it gets the message over. If you only go round half a turn, the knot will slip.

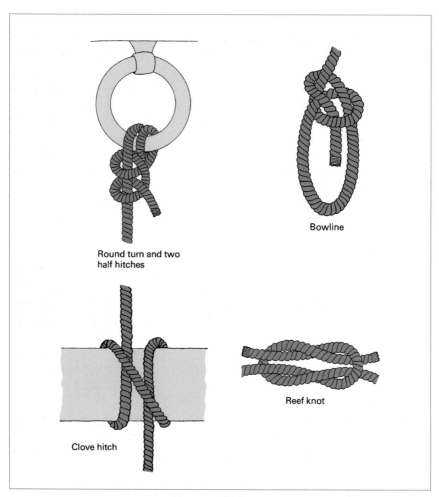

Round turn and two
half hitches

Bowline

Clove hitch

Reef knot

Fig 34 Useful knots.

Similarly, it is essential that you apply both of the half hitches as, again, one will slip. The second hitch can be applied with a loop of line, known as a bight, for quick-release situations, but not for longer stops.

If your mooring line is long, and you are needing to make a quick knot, pulling the whole length through twice or more will take too much time. In this instance, it is permissible to use a loop for the round turns as well but this can leave you with a lot of knitting round the bollard and should be sorted out at your leisure when the boat is securely moored.

For light-duty, temporary applications such as tying fenders quickly to the rail, the second half hitch can be omitted, allowing the line to be adjusted quickly to suit the height of the dock but the second hitch should be added for long-term security. For quick release, again, the hitch can be made with a loop.

The bowline

The second essential knot is the bowline. This is used for making a loop or eye that will not slip but can be untied easily. No matter how much load is put on it, the loop will not close up but it can be easily released when the load is taken off. For this reason, it is the only knot used by climbers for tying a rope round themselves. On boats, it can be used for putting an eye in a mooring rope to enable it to be quickly put over a cleat or bollard on board. Another good use is for securely joining two ropes – a bowline is tied in the end of each – the second one through the first. This is important to remember if, for instance, you have to tow someone off an obstruction; the mooring lines of each craft can be quickly used to make a longer line. The bowline is not the easiest knot to tie and needs some practice. Quick methods are sometimes described but they need regular use if you are to remember them.

Clove hitches and reef knots

Other common knots you may encounter include the clove hitch and reef knot but they need to be used with caution. The clove hitch is sometimes used for mooring round a post or bollard. It can slip or unwind, however, and should therefore be secured with a half-hitch. The reef knot is familiar to most people, and can be used for joining two ropes together but should only be used when they are the same size and construction and then only for light loads. In practice, it is a knot best reserved for parcels and shoe-laces.

Splicing rope

Splicing is the technique of joining two lengths of rope together without a knot by unlaying the rope ends, then laying them back up round each other as in Fig 35. Its most useful application on river boats is to put a smooth eye

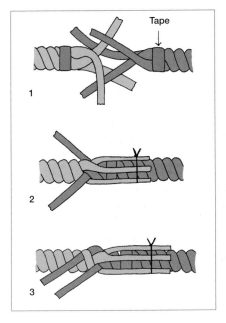

Fig 35 A short splice – used for joining two ropes.
(1) Use tape or twine to stop the ropes unlaying. Put the rope strands together so that opposites lie between each other.
(2) Tie down one set of strands and remove the tape from the other rope.
(3) Tuck each free strand under the laid strand in front of it. Do three tucks for each strand. Then take off twine and tape and repeat with the other rope. Heat seal the ends.

in the end of a rope (see Fig 36). Here it can be used on one end of the mooring line where it attaches to the boat, making a smooth neat loop to go round the cleat. It can also be used on one end of a fender line to make a neat attachment to the fender. Do not use it on the working end of lines as it will complicate the tying of knots and can jam if the rope is pulled quickly off a cleat. The only exception to this rule is for your permanent mooring lines which can be made to length with an eye spliced in one end.

Rope handling

The principal requirements for rope handling are coiling and throwing. Coiling is done to keep the line neat and ready for use. In theory, plaited lines should be coiled in a figure-of-eight but this makes them impossible to throw and, in practice, loops are best. Always coil a rope starting from the fixed end and work your way to the free end. This will allow any kinks to work their way out. Shake the loose end to remove kinks and, if necessary, give a twist of the wrist to keep the loops flat. Keep all the loops the same size, by stretching your arm out for the same distance each time – you will find this easier to do than it sounds. Always make the coils in a clockwise direction – for three-strand rope, this is essential, and it is a good habit to get into. To stop the coil unravelling, a couple of hitches round the body of it will suffice, though for a better finish, take a loop through the head of the coil then pass the free end through this loop. Hang the coil over a cleat or bollard to keep it off the deck and ready for use.

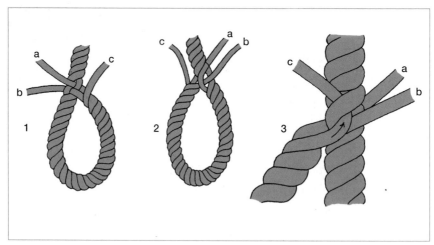

Fig 36 Eye splice. This splice is used to put a permanent eye in a rope. (1) Use a splicing tool to tuck strand (a) under the chosen strand on the standing part of the rope, and strand (b) under the adjacent left-hand strand. (2) Turn the splice over. (3) Tuck strand (c) from right to left under the strand adjacent to the one used for strand (b). Repeat until three tucks have been done. Heat seal the ends.

When you come to throw a rope you should first coil it as described, to ensure it has no knots and kinks in it. Even if the rope looks coiled and neat, you will find that experienced crew will always unravel it and re-coil it while they are waiting for the boat to approach the mooring, just as a double check. To throw a line, a right-handed person should hold the fixed end of the line in their left hand, then throw the coil with the right, with a round-arm motion. Do not throw the line straight at the receiver – aim it to one side or, for a long throw, over their head – a heavy line can be painful in the face. If the line is longer than needed, break the coil in two, and hold the fixed half in your left hand while throwing the other half with your right. This avoids too much line hitting the receiver. The same technique should also be used when you need to throw the whole of a long line over a long distance. Again, hold the fixed half of the coil in your left hand while throwing the other half with your right; when the first half is in mid-flight, let go with your left hand.

Warning! Before throwing any line, make sure that one end is fixed to the

In manned locks, the keeper or his assistant will often take your ropes when you are travelling upstream. However, you must be prepared to lasso a bollard yourself, so always have the rope neatly coiled.

boat. This may sound amusing but throwing unattached ropes is not an unusual occurrence, as anyone who has spent some time on the rivers will tell you!

Maintenance

Finally, your ropes should receive a certain amount of attention at the end of every season. Modern synthetic fibres do not rot, so they can be stored wet or damp but they will harden with age; they will also gradually lose their strength due to grit working its way into the strands. At the end of the year, take them off the boat and wash them in a bucket of warm water with some detergent. Then rinse them; this will flush out any grit or dirt. It will also make the rope more pleasant to use and improve its appearance. For the ultimate luxury treatment try putting them in a pillow case and cleaning them in your washing machine – you will be impressed with their transformation!

Check for any chafing or cuts; superficial chafes of the strands or outer braid can be tolerated but need to be checked on. Most of the constant wear will occur at or near the boat end of the rope; if there is any chafe here, the rope can be turned round end-for-end, putting the chafe at the landward end where it will not normally be taking any strain. However, if in doubt, renew the rope, and keep the old one as a spare. For permanent mooring lines that have a consistent chafing point, such as where they run over the corner of the deck, a sleeve of clear plastic hose will help to protect them.

5 | Locks, Bridges and Tunnels

Locks

Locks are an integral part of nearly all our navigable waterways. On a river that runs continuously downhill to the sea, the locks and their associated weirs hold up the flow in steps. This increases the depth of water in each section, thus allowing boats to navigate. At the same time, they reduce the speed of flow of the water which also assists navigation upstream. The principle of the weir has been in use on rivers such as the Thames for many centuries. It was used originally to produce a head of water to drive watermills but, at the same time, it assisted navigation, enabling boats to travel upstream, even in times of low water. It is now used in water management and flood prevention schemes.

Originally, boats were allowed to pass through the weir simply by opening a section of it and letting the boat flow through the gap when travelling down-stream, or hauling it up against the flow when going upriver. The principle of the lock with its gates at each end was possibly first invented by the Chinese or subsequently by Leonardo da Vinci in the 15th century. It was further developed for river use in the 17th and 18th centuries. Locks greatly simplified the process of passing through the weir and removed much of the friction between boat crews and mill owners, who hated to let precious water go to waste when the weir was opened! At the same time, the lock made possible the second man-made inland waterway – the canal.

In a canal, there is generally no natural direction of flow. The water between locks, known as a *pound*, is stationary and level. Hence, the lock can either raise or lower the water; this allows the canal to travel up and down hills, across the country, with its route governed only by the centres of trade that it joins, rather than the intervening geography. The canals were mostly developed in the late 18th and early 19th centuries, at a time when roads in England were little more than tracks. All goods previously had to be carried on horses or in carts; canals allowed the transport of large quantities of raw materials, and finished products, thus enabling the industrial revolution to take place. In their heyday, canals reached nearly all parts of England and Wales with separate systems in Scotland. Their commercial demise came with the development of the railway which did the same job, only faster.

However, thankfully, much of the original system still remains, its principal use today being for pleasure purposes.

The principle of a lock

Locks come in a huge range of shapes and sizes, but the principle of their operation remains the same. Every lock has a set of watertight gates and a set of opening sluices at each end to let the water in and out. These sluices, known as paddles on the canals, can either be set in the gates themselves, or in the sides of the chamber, but the principle of operation remains the same.

Let us look at a boat coming upstream on a river or uphill on a canal. When it arrives, the lock may be either empty or full. If it is full, it first has to be emptied. This is done by opening the bottom sluices, after first making sure that the top ones are closed. When the lock has emptied, the bottom gates are opened and the boat enters the chamber. The bottom sluices are then closed and the top ones opened, allowing the water to fill the chamber and the boat to rise. When the lock is full, the top gates are opened, and the boat leaves.

Going downstream or downhill, the process is reversed. If the lock is empty when the boat arrives, the bottom sluices must be closed then the top ones opened and the chamber filled. Once it is full, the top gates are opened and the boat sails in. The top gates and sluices are then closed and the bottom sluices opened. The water runs out; when the chamber is empty, the gates can be opened and the boat leaves.

At no stage must both sets of sluices be left open at the same time, otherwise the water will run straight through, emptying the pound above. Even on a river, with a steady flow of water, the levels can be reduced by this situation and, in any case, considerable scouring of the bottom of the lock can take place. Similarly, both sets of gates must be closed whenever any sluices are opened.

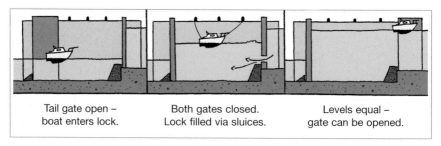

| Tail gate open –
boat enters lock. | Both gates closed.
Lock filled via sluices. | Levels equal –
gate can be opened. |

Fig 37 The principle of lock operation with an upstream bound boat.

Lock gates and sluices

Lock gates come in several different forms. The commonest is a pair of hinged gates which close together in a V with the point facing upstream or uphill on a canal. The reason for the V is that the pressure of water will

always tend to close the gates; the tighter they are closed, the less they leak.
Some narrow locks may replace one of the pairs of gates with a single hinged gate closing against a frame. This allows one person to operate the gate without changing sides on the lock. Hinged gates can either be manually opened and closed by pushing on a balance beam projecting either side of the lock or they can be mechanically operated, usually by electrically powered hydraulic rams.

Alternative forms of gate include the guillotine type, which is raised vertically in a frame by a chain tackle. When it is lowered, it makes a seal with the bottom of the chamber to keep the water in. Other types are the half-cylindrical gates, favoured on coastal marinas, where the gates seal by meeting in the middle. They have the advantage that they can withstand some pressure from either side, useful in tidal situations. They also do away with the need for sluices, with the water being allowed in by partially opening the doors, but this requires a qualified operator on hand at all times, otherwise the flow of water could be uncontrolled and dangerous.

Similar variations occur with the paddles or sluices. The original sluices in weirs were paddle-shaped boards, hence the name, supported in vertical side-frames. They were raised by means of crow-bars, and wedged open or

Lock gates come in different shapes and sizes. Narrow locks can have single gates or double. These are double bottom gates, with a single top gate in the distance.

shut. The next development, devised for the canals and still in use today, used a rack-and-pinion system. A handle was turned, rotating the pinion or gear-wheel, and lifting the toothed rack which was attached to the paddle below. This paddle was a square board that closed off an opening, either in the door or in a duct set in the side of the lock. Other systems for raising the paddle include worm-and-bevel wheels, used on some canals, or simple capstans and chains, as used on the upper reaches of the Thames. In the latter case, a balance weight reduces the effort required to lift the paddle.

When using a rack-and-pinion lock paddle, make sure you engage the pawl in the teeth of the rack, to prevent it from dropping.

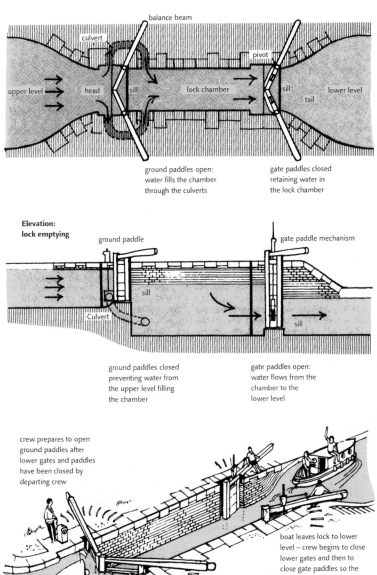

balance beam

culvert

pivot

upper level · head · sill · lock chamber · sill · lower level

tail

ground paddles open:
water fills the chamber
through the culverts

gate paddles closed
retaining water in
the lock chamber

**Elevation:
lock emptying**

ground paddle

gate paddle mechanism

sill

Culvert

sill

ground paddles closed
preventing water from
the upper level filling
the chamber

gate paddles open:
water flows from the
chamber to the
lower level

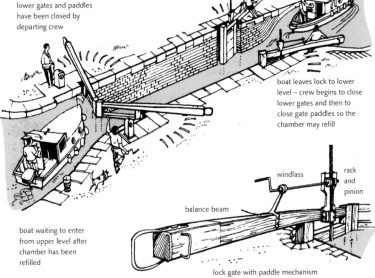

crew prepares to open
ground paddles after
lower gates and paddles
have been closed by
departing crew

boat leaves lock to lower
level – crew begins to close
lower gates and then to
close gate paddles so the
chamber may refill

rack
and
pinion

windlass

balance beam

boat waiting to enter
from upper level after
chamber has been
refilled

lock gate with paddle mechanism

Fig 38 *The design and mechanism of a manually
operated narrow canal lock.* © *Nicholson. Reproduced with permission.*

Hydraulically operated sluices use a hydraulic ram to raise the paddle, this being driven either by a manually turned hydraulic pump or an electrically driven pump.

The winding gear for paddles is extremely robust, some of it nearly as old as the system itself; it can, however, gradually get stiff or damaged through lack of maintenance, or misuse. Each boat carries its own windlasses or winch handles to operate the gear; it is essential that the size of the square in the end of this is the correct one for the canal you are on, or damage and injury may well result. Most spindles are tapered and it is essential to get the handle positioned correctly before applying any load. When you are winding, be sure that your knuckles are clear of the post or any of the mechanism. If you cannot overcome the initial friction and water pressure to get the handle moving, take it off and move it round so that you can apply an upwards pull rather than a downwards push. This will allow you to apply more force and run less risk of injury should you slip.

Before raising the paddle, make sure you apply the pawl or safety clip. When it is up, take the handle off. If you leave it on and the pawl slips, it could be thrown off, or strike you or someone standing close by. To lower a paddle, do not just let it drop, as the mechanism will be damaged. Instead you should wind it down, taking care not to let go of the windlass and avoiding trapping your fingers in the pawl. The cheapest windlass is a simple bent steel round bar which is favoured by most hire-boat companies. However, over the course of a week, the constant friction of the metal on your hands will quickly blister or cut them. A much more sophisticated version has a rotating plastic sleeve on the handle, which avoids wear on the skin.

The simplest sluices are set in the top gates of the lock but they can cause considerable turbulence in the water when they are opened. The next development was to let the water in through ducts set in the side of the lock wall, near the top gate, known as ground paddles, which cause less turbulence; the most sophisticated system uses a line of outlet ducts along the length of the lock which causes minimum disturbance of the water and boats. Some locks use a combination of gate paddles and ground paddles. The lower paddles are usually set in the gates.

Using a river lock

We will now look in detail at some of the practical aspects of passing through locks. Because there can be considerable differences in size and technique for river and canal locks, we will look at the two separately, starting with those on a river.

It must be remembered that, on a river, a lock will always be associated with a weir. The lock may be actually part of the weir, usually at one end, or it may be some distance away, approached down a channel, or lock cut. In either case, there will be a flow of water leading to and from the weir. This flow may be considerable, especially in times of flood, but at all times it must be taken account of. Approaching from upstream, you should keep well away

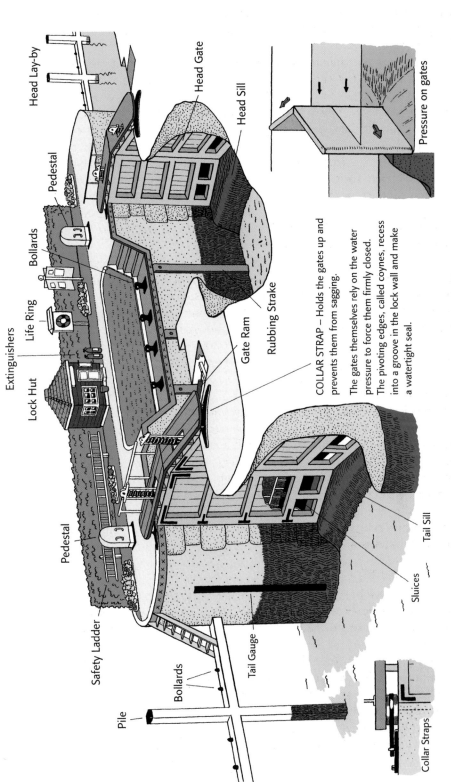

Head Lay-by

Pedestal

Head Gate

Head Sill

Bollards

Life Ring

Extinguishers

Lock Hut

Pedestal

Safety Ladder

Bollards

Pile

Tail Gauge

Gate Ram

Rubbing Strake

COLLAR STRAP – Holds the gates up and prevents them from sagging.

The gates themselves rely on the water pressure to force them firmly closed. The pivoting edges, called coynes, recess into a groove in the lock wall and make a watertight seal.

Pressure on gates

Tail Sill

Sluices

Collar Straps

Fig 39 Simplified diagram of an electro-hydraulic river lock. © Jake Kavanagh.

from the weir at all times. If you get too close, the flow may carry you down on to the weir or even over it, if you have a small craft, with serious risk of injury or drowning. Even away from the weir, the water flow may draw you to one side of the channel; this has to be allowed for in your approach to the lock.

Approaching from downstream, there is no risk of being carried over the weir but, even so, its flow (usually entering the river at an angle) can push your boat to one side. Again, this can spoil your approach to the lock at a crucial moment or can throw you against moored craft or the bank. Keep your eye open for a sideways flow of water ahead, usually indicated by swirls, bubbles or foam; counteract it by steering slightly into the flow. The final sting in the tail of the weirstream is that it can cause an eddy, just downstream of the lock, that can actually pull you towards the lock at the last moment. Even canal locks can have overspills that cause a sideways flow of water just below the lock and catch out the unwary.

On some rivers, particularly the Thames, the locks are manned and all you have to do is wait for the lock to be opened. On others you have to operate the lock yourself but, in both cases, you should pull into the side and tie up while waiting. The reason for this is that it prevents your boat swirling about as the lock is emptied. It also allows more boats to wait securely. If other boats are waiting in front, you should obviously form an orderly queue. If there is any doubt whether a boat ahead is waiting, you should pull up alongside and ask. You are not permitted to tie up in the lock approach except when waiting to go through but some people still insist on doing it. Inconsiderate mooring may clog up the waiting area causing some confusion.

Once you have tied up and the keeper has seen you, you should await his instruction if it is a manned lock. If it is unmanned, or there is no keeper in sight, you should walk up to the lock. If someone else is working their own boat through, ask them if they want any help but, above all, do not touch any sluices or gates without being asked. If there is a sudden flow of water at a time when they are not expecting it, it can cause their boat to go out of control or be damaged.

If there is no one in sight, then you will have to operate the lock yourself. Before you do this, check whether any boat is approaching from upstream. If the lock is full and a boat is approaching, then the rules say you have to wait and let them through first. This not only saves wasting water but also speeds up the time taken by boats passing through. It will save time if you walk up and open the gates for the other boat but do not open the bottom sluices unless asked. If the lock is empty then you have right of way.

We have already made the point about checking the top sluices before you open the bottom ones but this should be repeated here. On some locks, it is easy to see if the top sluices are shut but on others you may have to walk up and check. Even if they are only slightly open, the lock will be much slower to empty and may never empty enough for you to open the gates. Once you have ensured that the top sluices are shut you can then open the bottom

Learn to perfect the art of lassoing a bollard, holding the free end of the line, and throwing the middle portion.

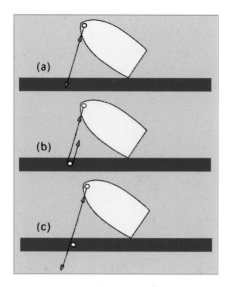

Fig 40 Taking a turn. How taking a turn
of rope round a bollard or cleat reduces
the load on the end.
(a) Direct-pull.
(b) Half a turn round a bollard reduces the
load by up to one third.
(c) A complete turn round the bollard
reduces the load by up to one half.

sluices to empty the lock. When it is completely empty, you can open the
gates. Do not try to force them too early, as even an inch or so of difference in
the water heights will make it difficult to open the gates and can damage any
opening mechanism. Once the gates are open, close the bottom sluices. Do it
straightaway and you will not forget. When lowering hand-operated sluices,
do not let them suddenly drop as this can damage them.

You can now drive your boat into the lock. With a manned lock, the keeper
will tell you when to enter and which side to go. Obey his instructions at all
times and acknowledge that you have understood them. You will be expected
to look after the ropes yourself in a lock. The keeper may help you if you are
having difficulty, or if he has time, but do not expect this automatically.

To make the boat secure in the lock, you must pass lines from the bow and
stern up round whatever bollards or posts are provided, then back down to
the boat. If you are travelling alone then you should take a single line from a
point amidships. You might be able to lasso the bollard from on board the
boat, otherwise you will need assistance from the shore. If you have crew you
can put someone ashore on to the lock wall to take the lines. Care must be
taken when doing this, as walls can be high and slippery; if anyone falls in
they can be trapped between boat and wall. Ladders are provided in some
locks and it is your job as skipper to position the boat suitably alongside
them. Make sure the boat is stationary before anyone climbs off. Some locks
have steps set into their sides but beware that these will be slippery and
often covered in weed.

Once your boat is secured alongside, you may have to move it up the lock.
If anyone is behind you, you will have to do this and it is in any case good
practice. Unless the lock is full of boats, do not get too close to the top gates
as the flow of water here can be very confused as the lock fills.

It is important that your bow and stern lines are not made fast but are each held by a crew member. This is because, as the lock fills, the boat rises and the lines have to be progressively shortened or taken in. If this is not done, the boat may surge forwards and backwards or can drift out across the lock, either damaging itself or other craft. On larger craft, in order to reduce the load on the free end of the rope (the one being held by the crew) it should be taken back round a cleat on the boat. The reason why this is so is not immediately clear to a newcomer, but is to do with friction, and is a principle that will apply in other situations. It is called taking a turn.

To understand it in more detail, consider the three situations in Fig 40. In (a) the crew member stands on the bank holding the end of the rope. If the boat should pull away with a force of say 100lb (45kg) the crew will have to apply the same 100lb (45kg) of force to resist it. If the rope is taken half round a bollard as in (b), the force required to resist a pull of 100lb (45kg) will be reduced to about 75lb (3kg). Take the line another half turn round the bollard (c) or back down to a cleat on the boat, and the force required will be further reduced to 50lb (22kg) or less. Incidentally, this explains the importance of the round turn in the knot of a round turn and two half hitches.

Note that the free end is not made fast to the cleat but is held by the crew; it can then be progressively shortened. The same principle applies when going down a lock, only here the line is paid out as the boat falls but the friction of the turns around the cleats allows immediate control if required.

Once the lock has filled, wait for the signal from the keeper, then leave. If other boats are alongside you, make clear which of you is to go out first – do not both try to move at the same time or you will jam together. Getting away

When leaving a lock, the crew should coil the bow line and leave it neat and ready for use. This 30-year-old Freeman 22 was a very successful river cruiser and is still popular today.

from the wall will be easier if the foredeck crew gives a slight push away when you signal – not too hard, or you will drift across the lock or hit neighbouring craft.

When in a lock, you should put fenders down to protect your boat from the wall, and other craft alongside you. It is then usually deemed the best form to pull these fenders in when you have left the lock but, in practice, many craft leave them down all the time. The choice here is yours but bear in mind, before you pull the fenders in, that they may be green and dirty from the wall.

Travelling downstream is usually less of a problem; it is easier to get your lines round the bollards and there is no turbulence in the chamber as it empties, but you must still keep your wits about you. The first thing to remember is to keep your boat far enough down the lock so that the rudder does not catch on the *sill* (or *cill*) of the top gates as the water drops. The extent of the sill is usually indicated by a painted line on the wall. Secondly, it is vital that you pay the lines out steadily as the water falls but always keep some tension on the end. Again, take the free end round a cleat on deck but be sure that it does not jam on the line already there. If this should happen, or if someone should have mistakenly made the line fast, the line will gradually start to take the weight of the boat as the water drops. When this happens, the increased tension will make the line impossible to undo even if you should get to it in time. You are now in a potentially dangerous situation. As the water drops further, either the line will break, or the cleat will be torn out of the deck; in both cases bystanders or crew could possibly be injured.

If you see that this is about to happen, the first thing to do is to make sure that everyone stands well clear of the rope. Shout at them as loudly as you can to ensure they get the message. Then signal to the lock-keeper, or whoever is manning the lower sluices, to close them immediately. This will stabilise the situation. They will then have to go back up to the top end of the lock and open the sluices here. The rising water will gradually take the tension off the rope which can then be undone. Do not indulge in any heroics. Don't try to cut the rope as, under extreme tension, it can whip back and injure you, or may pull the cleat out just as you approach. Remember, a nylon rope can stretch by up to 40% before it breaks, and the spring in this could cause serious injury.

Once the lock is empty, you can prepare to leave. To do this, you will have to pull the ropes from around the bollards. Make sure that there are no kinks or loops in the free end as it goes up the wall, or it may jam. If you are the helmsman, make sure that both lines are back on board before you engage gear; see that the ends are not dangling overboard where they may be sucked into the prop. When you have left, make sure that all gates and paddles are closed, unless there are boats waiting to enter, or the lock has other instructions in place.

On the Thames, you are required to turn your engine off while made fast in a lock. The reason for this is mainly to reduce the risk of fire on board in a crowded lock; it also removes the temptation for drivers to try and use the engine to stop the boat moving backwards and forwards. Even on other waterways, where you are allowed to leave your engine running, it is usually preferable to use ropes rather than the engine to stop the boat surging. Otherwise, in a crowded lock, you will have everyone moving around in different directions, and running into each other.

Finally, as you leave, wave your thanks to the lock-keeper. They may seem rather official in their uniforms on occasion, but remember that at all times, they are in charge. On a busy summer's day this can bring considerable responsibility, as craft from 10ft to 100ft mill about, with their skippers' experience ranging from expert to complete novice. Obey their instructions, offer to help if it seems appropriate and remember, they have seen it all before!

Canal locks

Locks on canals require different procedures to those on rivers. First, you will nearly always have to operate the sluices and gates yourself. Second, the lock may only be as wide as your boat or, at the most, double the width. Let us look at a narrow-beam lock first. The width of the locks on the narrow canals is approximately 7ft (2.13m), though as built they were originally between 7ft 1in and 7ft 3in. The original barges were 7ft wide but today most craft which are designed to use canals will have been made to a maximum beam of 6ft 10in (2.08m) giving you one or, at most, two inches of clearance either side. When you approach a lock from downhill, assuming the gate is not open, you should pull into the side to let one or more crew members ashore. The boat should, ideally, be made fast at this time as the surge of water from an emptying lock can cause it to drift away. If the helmsman is alone on the boat, the easiest way he can control it is by using an amidships line rather than bow and stern lines but, again, making it fast is still a good idea.

If the lock is empty, all the crew have to do is to open the gates. Having done this, they should check to see that the paddles are right down. If the lock is full, you should first check to see that no other boat is approaching from upstream. If any other craft is in sight, the rules are that you let them go through the lock first. This not only conserves water but, overall, it saves everyone time. Then empty the lock by raising the lower paddles. Check while doing this that the top paddles are not open. They should not be, as all crews should leave them down but some are lazy, or in a hurry. The top paddles may be just open slightly; you will not notice this until you realise that the lock will not quite empty.

Once the lock is empty and the gates are open, the helmsman can bring the boat in. For many people, this is the trickiest manoeuvre on the canals but, in practice, it should be easy. Approach slowly, with the engine in forward gear. Line up your boat as straight as you can while you are well away from the lock; do this by sighting down one side if it helps. At this point, you have to think back to the handling section where we said that, at slow speeds, a boat will only steer if the engine is in forward gear with a flow of water going over the rudder. If you drop into neutral, you will lose nearly all your steerage way. Even worse, if you go into reverse, the boat will sheer to one side or the other as the paddlewheel effect takes over. To avoid this, keep the engine in tickover all the way into the lock. If you think this is bringing you in too fast, go into neutral as you approach but remember always to go into ahead to steer. It takes some initial courage to do this, as the natural reaction is to reach for the 'brakes' if you seem to be going off course but, in practice, it is easier to drive your way in than hesitate at the entrance. Beware of any side-flow from the overflow spill below the lock, which will push you to one side at the crucial moment. There is not much you can do to stop this except to steer slightly up towards it.

Once in the lock, you can use the engine to bring the boat to a stop. Do not use ropes to do this. In fact, under most circumstances, you should not need to use ropes at all in a narrow lock, provided there is someone at the helm. Assuming your craft is less than 70ft (21m) long (the length of narrow locks), you will have to decide where to place it in the lock. To do this, you have to bear in mind that, as the top paddles are opened, there will be an initial surge of water down the lock, followed by a surge back forward, particularly at the top end. Therefore, do not place yourself too near the lower gates, as you will be driven back down on to them. If you should find this happening, a quick burst of ahead should save the crunch. Equally, if you are too close to the top gates, you will be sucked forward, often with more force than the engine can overcome. The best place therefore is about 6ft (1.8m) away from the lower gates for a 45ft (13.7m) boat or larger, or farther forward for smaller craft. Even so, be alert to the boat surging. The amount of this initial surging can be reduced by opening the top paddles slowly, or only opening one at a time. However, as soon as the lock is about half full, open the paddles fully, or you will take too long in going through.

As we have said before, in these circumstances do not open the paddles for another boat unless they ask you to, as you can cause damage to the craft if you open them faster than its crew is expecting.

As the boat rises, make sure that it does not jam underneath anything. Risk areas here are the rudder or tiller jamming underneath the frame of the lower gate, or under the walkway across them. Also, the bow may jam under the frame of the top gate though, in practice, it should not be near either of these.

As the lock gets close to full, do not let your boat surge up to the top gate. Even worse, do not use the engine to try to force the gate open early. You may see a few 'experts' practising this technique. Be assured, they are only displaying their ignorance and arrogance, and causing damage and premature wear to gates, hinges and gear. A gate will only open when it is ready; no amount of pushing will hasten this moment. Occasionally, if the lower gates are leaking too badly, the water level inside and outside the lock will never equalise and the gate will prove impossible to open. Under these circumstances, get as many people pushing on the beam as possible but if

Narrow canal locks are only inches wider than your boat. Sight along one side of the boat to line yourself up, and keep the engine in tickover ahead until you are right in, to maintain steerage way.

you do not have enough volunteers available then, and only then, is it permissible to bring the bow of the boat gently up to the gate, with a fender taking the pressure, and apply gradual ahead thrust while others are pushing on the beam. This action should only be used as a last resort.

Once you have left the lock, be sure to lower the paddles, and close the gates, to help conserve precious water.

When coming down through a lock, the principle is reversed. When you tie up, you should still be aware of the fact that there will be a flow of water, as the lock fills, that could pull you towards it. When the lock is open, drive in and stop. As you get more experienced you will find that the helmsman can step off and close the gate behind him, allowing the crew to walk to the other end of the lock in advance. When you are in the lock, make sure that the stern of the boat is well clear of the sill. If, by misfortune, you should get the rudder hung up on the sill, immediately shout to the crew to close the lower paddles. If you do not do this, the boat will tip down by the head as the water level drops and could fill up with water through the front cockpit.

To refloat the boat, the crew should come back and open the top paddles to let the water level rise; be cautious when doing this, in case you flood the boat from the stern. Beware of the boat catching on any other projections in the lock as it falls, including the tiller catching on the top of the wall. As you leave the lock, you will have to pick up the crew. It is often possible to do this just alongside the bottom gate where there are steps leading down; this saves coming into the bank later. If no other boat is coming through, close the gates and lower the paddles.

If your boat is over 40ft (12m) or so, you will normally always have a narrow lock to yourself. Smaller craft can share a lock, thus saving both time and water. In this case you will have to be even more vigilant to avoid damage when the boats surge to and fro and should take more care when opening the top paddles.

Locks on broad canals are generally 14ft (4.2m) wide. They can take two narrowboats side by side and, wherever possible, you should try and share, particularly in times of water shortage. The second crew will also make locking through quicker. On some of the major flights in the middle of dry summers, you have to wait till there is a second boat to lock through with. If yours is the only boat in a broad lock, you will have to take lines ashore when locking up, to avoid the boat being swung about. Again, a single line from amidships is a better system than bow and stern lines, provided that there is a handy bollard. If there is only one boat in the lock when locking up, open the paddle in the gate on the same side as the boat first. Because of the angle of the gate, the water from this tends to flow across the lock in front of your boat, with the reflected wash from the far wall pinning your craft to the nearside wall. Once this circular flow of water is established, or when the lock is about half full, you can start to open the second paddle. If you open the wrong side first, or both paddles at the same time, your boat will tend to be driven away from the wall, and can swing around uncontrollably. When locking down in a broad lock, be careful not to get the bow fender hooked under the bottom gate or the stern caught on the sill.

Techniques for faster locking

Although you are probably in no hurry, it makes sense to get through locks as quickly and efficiently as possible. This is especially true on the major flights of locks, where up to 30 or more can be closely spaced together. The amount of time taken through the locks depends on the number of crew. You will move comparatively slowly with two, however clever you are. Three will make a considerable difference, while four is probably the best number.

The secret of rapid progress is having someone ahead preparing the next lock; either emptying or filling it in readiness for your arrival. If another boat arrives at the lock from the other direction then you should not turn the lock against them, ie empty or fill it to your advantage. If the lock is already in your favour, then they should not turn it against you. In practice, you should not work more than one lock ahead of your boat, otherwise the water you release will be wasted. Also, you should not open the bottom paddles of the lock ahead until the top paddles of the lower lock are open, for the same reason.

Everyone can help on the waterways, but small children should be supervised and non-swimmers should always wear lifejackets.

Once you have got a system going, you can either let the same person work ahead, or alternate with another crew member. The technique varies depending on whether you are on a broad or narrow canal. On a narrow canal, one person can close both the bottom gates behind the boat, without having to walk all the way round the lock. On a wide lock it is quicker to have someone already operating both gates, with a third crew ready to open the top paddles. The third person then walks on to the next lock, leaving the other two to open and close the top gates. There are certain things that you must not do when working fast through a set of locks:

◆ Do not use the flow of water from the top paddles to close the bottom gates.

◆ Do not use the boat to push open the gates.

◆ Do not leave paddles or gates open behind you, unless another boat is approaching.

If you are working up a flight of narrow locks with another boat following behind you and they are short of crew, you can help them considerably by opening the paddles in the bottom gates of the lock you have just left, so that it will be empty when they arrive. If, however, you are going to do this, check with them that they are going all the way up and make sure that there is no boat approaching from the other direction. Also, only open the paddles when they have got their top gate paddles open otherwise the water in the lock will be wasted over the by-pass weir.

Bridges

A bridge requires a certain amount of care in its navigation – you first have to decide whether it is high enough for your boat to pass underneath. On a narrow canal, the main difficulty is squeezing through without hitting the sides. This is because the bridge builders wasted no extra brickwork or labour in making them any wider than necessary and, consequently, made them only a few inches wider than the beam of the barges. They may appear wide but that is because they include the towpath; the actual water channel is a tight fit. Again, as with entering a lock, you can only steer your way through if the engine is in ahead, so slow down gradually well in advance. Line yourself up on one side of the channel (preferably not the one that is overgrown with weeds) and simply drive through. If you allow a gap of three inches from one side, you know that the other side will be clear. It can be daunting the first time you do this, but it becomes much easier with practice.

Oncoming vessels

On a straight stretch you can see if another boat is approaching from the opposite direction. The rules say that the boat nearest to the bridge has the right of way. If you are in doubt, slow down and call the other boat through. If, however, the bridge is on a bend (and by Murphy's Law many of them seem to be) then you should sound your horn and listen for a reply. Otherwise, be prepared for a nerve-wracking trip. Position a crew member forward as a look-out. A simple system of hand signals will give you advance warning of oncoming vessels or a clear passage.

Clearance under canal bridges

Height under canal bridges is not normally a problem for narrowboats as they are built low enough to clear them but this does not include items on the roof. Chimneys, plant pots, windscreens and the like should be taken off on stretches with low bridges or moved to the centre of the roof where there is generally more height. Make sure that all the crew are off the roof – it may be a pleasant place to sunbathe but you might end up with more than sunburn! For more information on bridge clearance, see later in this section.

Lift bridges

Problems with height can occur under lift bridges. There are still a few of these on the system; they are always marked on the guide-book or map. Just to confuse you, some of them may have been removed but still appear on the map. They were built in the early days of the canals to link little-used areas, such as outlying fields, though some may have roads going over them. They are often left in the down position, meaning you have to raise them to pass under. The technique is to slow down and put one or more crew members ashore – some bridges require considerable weight or strength to operate them. The crew then run up the towpath and pull or wind the bridge open (remember to take a windlass with you unless you know which type it is) while the boat passes underneath.

It is essential for the crew to keep the bridge fully up at this stage and for you to keep the boat on the side of the channel away from the sloping side. If you do not, the forward corner of the cabin will be the first part to hit the bridge, and it will stop the boat dead. Some hire fleets, in areas with many lift bridges, have deflector bars welded from the bow up to the port and starboard corners of the cabin, to reduce the risk of damage, but these can make getting in and out of the boat awkward at other times. Any crew on board should keep well down in the cockpit on the side of the boat away from the bridge. If another craft is in sight, it is polite to keep the bridge open and let them through – hopefully they will do the same for you one day.

Some lift bridges are mechanically operated. To do this, you will have to have a BW key. This is the standard British Waterways key that opens gates, padlocks and sanitary stations. It can be bought at any British Waterways depot, and it is essential that you have at least one on board, preferably with a spare.

Mechanically operated bridges are usually on roads, which can be busy. For this reason, you should always send a responsible crew member ahead to one of these, preferably someone with enough authority to handle the complaints from motorists! The operating instructions are explained next to the bridge and include some system for stopping the traffic – either flashing lights or a bar. Read the instructions carefully, and be sure you understand them before starting the cycle. This will avoid any more delay than necessary to motorists. Use your common sense and if a car is in sight, let them across first. Also, if another boat is approaching, wait until they are close enough to pass through with you.

Swing bridges

Swing bridges fall into the same category, except that they move horizontally rather than vertically. Some just require pushing round. Others need to be lifted on to their bearings by winding them up with a windlass before they can be turned. In either case, they will often need two people to open them, particularly if the bearings have become worn or damaged.

Clearance under river bridges

If you are in any doubt as to the height and clearance of your boat, you will have to gauge whether it will pass under a bridge. The method for doing this is straightforward, and shown in Fig 41 (overleaf). Position yourself so that your eye is at the same level as the highest point in your boat. Then, keeping in this position, look at the bridge.

If your eyeline is above the lowest point of the bridge, all you will see is the face of the brickwork, concrete or iron, and you will not pass underneath it.

If your eye is below the lowest point, you will see the face of the bridge with the shadow or dark crescent of its underside and should clear it. If you are in any doubt, slowly stand up – you will then see the point where the shadow disappears – this is the height of the bridge. Practise this, even on bridges that you are sure you will clear, and you will quickly get the hang of it (see Fig 42).

Always remember, when approaching arched bridges, that it is the outside edge of the cabin top that will probably hit first. So do your sighting along this line. If you are still in doubt, you can approach the bridge slowly and hand your way through, though this is easier done when travelling upstream. Also remember that on a light boat, the weight of the crew can make a crucial difference. If they are forward then the bow will be lower in the water. In a really tight situation, you can use this to your advantage by moving crew forward or aft as you pass under, lowering each end of the boat in turn. This manoeuvre should, however, be used with care and not when other boats are passing, as their wash can throw out your calculation.

Lift bridges are found on some canals. Clearance under them is restricted, and they require particular care when negotiating, to avoid damaging the boat or injuring crew.

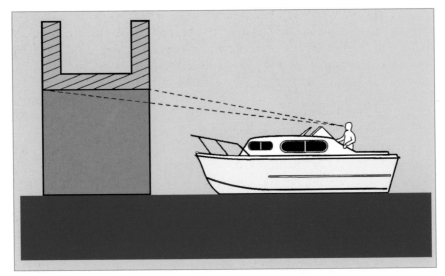

Fig 41 *Gauging whether your boat will pass under a bridge.*

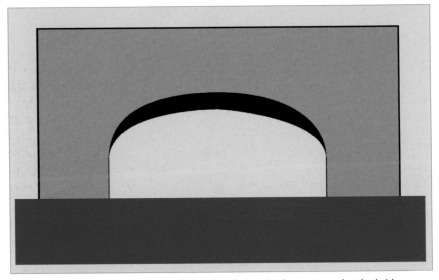

Fig 42 *The view from eye level showing if there is clearance under the bridge.*

Where there is only one arch, or only one in use, the rules of the road say that vessels travelling upstream give way to those coming down. This is because, with the current against you, a position can be held with the engine in tickover ahead and still maintain steerage way. With the current behind you, however, you cannot easily stop and may be carried down on to the bridge if you have to give way. Where there is more than one arch in use, take the right-hand one, unless signs indicate otherwise.

Some bridges will have height gauges alongside them with a scale that is uncovered as the water level drops. If you know the clearance of your boat then you can check whether you have room. Use these with caution, however, as they might be set to the centre of the arch which may not be the critical part of your boat. In the brochure or handbook, the height of your boat above the water may be described as bridge clearance, or it may be called air draught; this sounds odd but is self-explanatory when you think about it.

Most boats designed for rivers with low bridges will be able to reduce their air draught by lowering the mast, screens and canopy. Remember to do this, especially in wet weather when everything may be raised.

Finally, on really low river bridges, there is an extra technique you can employ to get through but it is one that requires skill, nerves and practice. As you approach the bridge you fully open the throttle at the point of passage. Extra suction from the propeller literally sucks the water out of the channel under the bridge, taking the boat down with it; you could gain anything up to three or four inches. On the Norfolk Broads, the pilots at Wroxham and Potter Heigham bridges employ this technique; it is remarkable to see the size of boat that they can get through. However, don't try this if you are a beginner.

Tunnels

Tunnels are another fascinating feature of canals. They were built to negotiate large hills and their construction, in an age that had little more than spade, pick and gunpowder for excavating, was nothing short of miraculous. Their length can vary from a few hundred yards up to several thousand; the now derelict Standedge Tunnel was the longest, being a staggering 5698 yards (5208m), or nearly 3¼ miles (5.2km) long. Even today, the longest navigable tunnels, Blisworth and Dudley, are still over 3000 yards (2743m) long, or 1¾ miles (2.8km), and can take over half an hour to navigate. While you are doing this, spare a thought for the original bargees, who often had to 'leg' their way through – lying on their backs on the top of the boat, or on planks, and 'walking' their way through the tunnel.

Tunnels require a certain technique for their navigation. There are narrow tunnels, wide enough for just one boat to pass, and also broad tunnels, where two narrowboats can pass each other. At first, a tunnel might appear alarming, but you will quickly discover that they have a fascination of their own and are perfectly safe if you observe the rules.

Headlights and safety precautions

Certain basic principles apply to all tunnels. Your boat must be fitted with a spotlight or headlight forward, and this must be on at all times. Do not aim it straight ahead, as it will be ineffective and dazzle an oncoming boat. Instead, angle it down and to the right, shining slightly ahead of the boat. It will then illuminate the side of the tunnel, giving you a reference point to steer by. Make sure that you have a powerful torch handy, in case the bulb in the headlight should blow. Do not show a bright light at the stern, as this will confuse boats following behind.

Before entering the tunnel, turn some lights on in the cabin, and open the curtains; light will then shine through the windows, on to the tunnel wall, making it easier to hold your position in the centre of the channel. The lights will also help you to move safely inside the boat. Do not let the lights shine directly at the helmsman, or they will obscure his vision.

Clear all loose items off the roof before entering a tunnel, or secure them in place to avoid objects being swept back into the helmsman's face; fold down any windscreens. Obviously, no crew should be on the roof; they should be safely in the cabin or cockpit and briefed not to try to touch the tunnel walls. Make sure that children and pets are safe. Do check engine temperature, oil pressure, cooling water and fuel gauge before entering a tunnel – you do not want to break down! Extinguish all naked flames – cookers and heaters.

Tunnels are wet places; you will frequently encounter drips or even streams of water from the roof. The first you will know about these is a flood of cold water down your neck, so put on waterproofs before you enter. Also remove maps, books and papers from the cockpit or roof.

Navigating in tunnels

Some narrow tunnels will have a traffic light system, or set times for passage in either direction. Most do not, however. In these cases, as you approach the tunnel, you must look carefully ahead for oncoming craft. In short tunnels, an oncoming vessel will partially block out the light from the far end but, in most cases, it is their headlight that you will see. If you cannot see a headlight, then turn on your own before entering. If you are unsure whether there is a boat in the tunnel, approach closely, then turn off your engine and listen. You should be able to hear the other boat's engine, but bear in mind that it may be going in the same direction as yourself. It is quite acceptable to follow another boat through, unless you have passed any allotted time for entering. If in doubt, wait until you are quite sure that no other craft is coming towards you.

When travelling through a narrow canal, you have to be aware that the restricted width, and sometimes shallower water, will tend to slow your boat down. Do not open the throttle to compensate for this, as it will only make matters worse. In fact, you should actually throttle down to 3mph maximum which will help your steering. If you get it exactly right, you can steer the boat in a dead straight line down the middle of the channel. In practice, however, the boat will tend to veer gradually to one side or the other. If it gets too close to a wall, the suction will keep it stuck there, and you will bump along the edge. To get yourself off, throttle back slightly, and wait for the boat to sheer away. Do not push off with your hands unless the boat has come to rest. If you should get into a situation where you are zig-zagging from wall to wall, throttle back and start again straight. Some narrow tunnels will have a towpath running alongside them. It is possible, but not advisable, to walk

Tunnels are among the fascinating features on our canals. Some are wide enough for two boats to pass, some only wide enough for one boat. Chirk Tunnel here on the Llangollen Canal is unusual in having a tow-path for horses.

along the towpath. The risks are holes, puddles and projecting masonry; there is the danger that, if you fall in, the boat will crush you.

If you look behind you, you may be alarmed to see sparks coming from the exhaust. This is nothing to worry about, as it is probably happening all the time but you only notice it in the dark. Obviously, if there are too many, then you should have the engine or the exhaust system checked over.

In wide tunnels, boats can travel in both directions, and therefore will occasionally have to pass each other. This is the most nerve-wracking experience in a tunnel. You will have plenty of warning as it will probably take 10 minutes or more for the approaching craft to reach you. As you get closer, you should slow down to tickover speed. Do not stop altogether as you will lose steerage way. Make sure that your headlight is pointing down and to the right and move gradually over to that side of the tunnel. Then you simply have to keep a straight course. If something should go wrong and the boats are about to collide, it is vital that you do not let your crew fend off at the bow, as they could be injured. Instead, hold on tight, and let steel and brick take the crunch!

The only exception to this rule is if you are on a glassfibre cruiser. These are vulnerable and will come off worse in a collision with a steel craft. In this case, you may feel it prudent to come to a complete stop and pull yourself over to the right-hand side, or at least travel hard up against the wall at minimum speed.

Breakdowns

If you should have the misfortune to break down in a tunnel and there is a towpath, you should start to haul yourself through. Send someone ahead and behind with torches to warn approaching craft or flash your light. In a narrow tunnel, a vessel behind can slowly push you through, though you will have to be careful that they do not press against your rudder. In a wide canal, again flash your light to warn approaching craft and ask them to tow you out.

6 | *Dealing with Problems*

Running aground

Everybody runs aground at some stage. It may be just a minor stick on the side of a canal, or a major grounding, but you should know how to deal with it, or how to help someone else in this situation. On canals, the commonest running aground situation is when you pass an oncoming boat and veer off to one side. Here, the speed at which you were travelling before you went aground governs the degree of difficulty in getting off. This is one reason why you should slow down when passing other craft. Most boats are deepest at the stern and most canals and rivers are deepest away from the bank, so the first priority should be to get your stern out away from the bank. You can try putting the engine gently astern – this may pull you off, but usually, all it will do is to churn up the bottom, and possibly drag stones or branches into the prop. Instead, give a gentle shove out from the bank with pole or boathook.

Most boats will usually have a long pole plus a shorter boathook. Keep the pole at the forward end of the boat, where the crew are better able to handle it and the boathook next to the helm. With the stern out in clear water, you can try to pull the boat off with the engine in reverse. If this does not work, try pushing the bow out with the pole. When wielding a pole, there are certain rules to remember. Make sure that the end is firmly located against the bank before starting to push. Try to avoid pushing against trees, stone or concrete, as the pole can slip. Keep the end of the pole to one side of your body when you push, as it can injure you if you slip. Push along the line of the pole rather than using it as a lever.

If you are still stuck, do not try to drive yourself off with the engine in ahead, as this will just make your hull more embedded. Instead, work out where the boat is touching on the bottom and try to use the crew weight to help it off. You will normally be stuck hardest on the side closest to the bank, so get the crew all over to the other side to heel the boat that way, possibly rocking at the same time to loosen the grip. If you are stuck at the bow, get the crew aft, and vice versa. If all this fails, you will have to wait for another boat to come along and pull you off.

When pulling a boat off, certain rules have to be followed. Always try to pull them off in the opposite direction to the one in which they went aground. If this does not work, pull them sideways from the opposite end they are stuck to try to lever them off. Tie the two boats together with the strongest line available fastened to the strongest point on each craft. Do not tie on to handrails or stanchions and definitely do not pull off with someone holding on to the end. Make sure that the line is secured with a knot that will not slip but can be quickly undone. Work out the direction of pull and clear anything off both decks along that line, including crew. Try to line your boat up along the direction of pull, as otherwise you will just swing your own boat round. Make sure that your own craft remains out in deep water, especially the stern. Ensure that both crews understand what is going to happen before applying power, and agree whether the stuck boat should use his own engine or pole to assist.

Your own boat will have more pulling power in ahead than astern but, on the other hand, it is sometimes easier to keep straight in reverse; also, your prop will be clear in deeper water. If you are pulling off in reverse, make the line fast to your most forward bollard or cleat. If you are pulling off in ahead, use the cleat that is farthest aft. This will reduce any tendency for the boat to swing when you apply power. Again, make sure that all the crew on the grounded boat are positioned at the opposite end to the one which is stuck and, if necessary, put some of your own crew aboard to add weight.

On a narrow canal, you may be able to get a line on to the other bank but you will rarely be able to get enough pulling effect on this to be of much help. In theory, you can take the anchor out and pull yourself off but, in practice, this will not help much.

You may run aground in the pound between two locks, especially on a flight at times of low water supply or when there are a lot of boats moving. In this case, when the uphill lock is opened, you will get a surge of water that may be enough to lift you off. Be aware of this and be prepared for it when it comes. Similarly, when the downhill lock is filled, the level in the pound will drop and if it is already shallow, you should make sure that you are clear of the bank, or you will run aground just when you wanted to cast off and enter the lock.

On a river, similar principles apply, but you will also have to take account of the current. This will usually have the effect of driving the boat harder on to the bottom, but it can be used to give a twisting effect and help to get it off. On some rivers, the shallow water may not be close to the bank. This can occur on bends particularly, where the shallows will run out in a spit from the inside of the bend. These may be marked but not always, so you should always give them a wide berth.

If you are unsure about the depth of water round a grounded boat, use the boathook or pole to work your way round it steadily, checking the depths. This will give you an idea of the best direction of pull, bearing in mind that the deepest part of the boat is usually at the stern, under the rudder or prop.

Anchoring

Unlike a sea-going boat, an inland cruiser will rarely have to anchor, and then usually only in an emergency, rather than for mooring. However, your boat must still be equipped with an anchor which is ready for use, and you must understand when and how to use it. You may have to use an anchor if your engine should fail and your boat is close to a weir or other hazard.

Types of anchor

The anchor should be large enough and of a suitable type to hold the boat. The commonest forms today are the Danforth or spade type, which has flat triangular blades; the CQR or plough, which has a plough-shaped blade; the Bruce, with a rounded claw-shaped blade, and the grapnel, which has four folding blades. The traditional type of anchor, known as the Fisherman, is rarely used, as its holding power is much less than a modern type of the same weight. Arguments over the relative merits of the modern types rage endlessly in the yachting press but for river use, the first three can be assumed to be equally efficient. The more important criterion is ease of stowage; in this respect, the spade type usually takes up the least space.

The only other type of anchor you will encounter is the mud-weight used on the Norfolk Broads. It is simply a large conical cast-iron weight which is

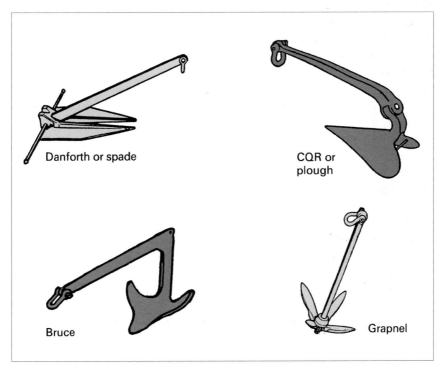

Danforth or spade

CQR or plough

Bruce

Grapnel

Fig 43 Common types of anchor.

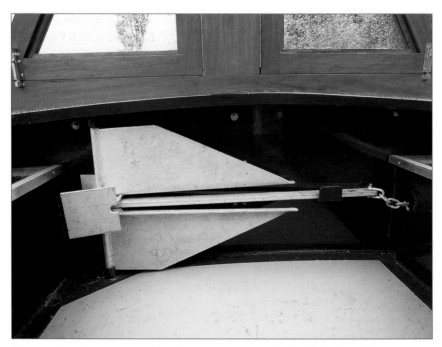

You may have to use your anchor in an emergency, so it should be stowed in readiness.

used mainly for mooring at night in the middle of a Broad – an experience that no one should miss.

The size of the anchor is important; it is relative to the size and weight of the boat and the strength of the current in the rivers you use. Anchors are measured by their weight. Precise figures for suitability are not easy to give and will vary according to the weight of your boat and its length, as well as the river strength. A general guide is that it should be at least as heavy in pounds as the length of the boat in feet. For sea-going craft different criteria apply; also, you should carry two anchors for extra security.

Cable and chain

The anchor should have its own permanent cable, coiled and ready for use. Sea-going craft use chain for this purpose but rope will be suitable for river use; you should, however, have a length of chain, 6–12ft (2–4m) long at the anchor end of the line. The weight of this will keep the pull on the anchor horizontal, helping it to grip; it will also avoid chafing of the rope on the bottom. Diameter and length of line will vary according to the boat and river but, as a general guide, rope length should be at least five times the depth of the water. Assume 12–15ft (3.6–4.5m) as the maximum depth of a non-tidal river, though on some rivers this can increase in time of flood. Regarding diameter, for up to a 20lb (9kg) anchor you should use 10mm line, 20–40lb (9–18kg) you should use 12mm line. Above 40lb (18kg) use 14mm line.

The waters you are likely to be cruising will have a bearing on these figures; strong-flowing, tidal rivers such as the Severn or Trent need heavier equipment and longer lines. In all cases, therefore, it is wise to check with the relevant river authority for their recommendation.

When you are anchoring, let sufficient line out to allow the anchor to bed in. This usually means at least five times the depth of the water. If in doubt, let out too much rather than too little.

Anchor stowage

On most craft the anchor is stowed on the foredeck with the cable stowed in a locker. On some vessels, particularly narrowboats, it is stowed at the stern. Here, it will be immediately to hand for the helmsman, who will usually be the first person aware of an emergency. It also means that the anchor and line can be stored inside the boat, reducing the risk of theft. While it may seem strange to anchor a boat by the stern, provided that there is a suitable point for fastening, it makes no difference. Make sure that the end of the anchor line is permanently attached to a strong point on the boat. In an emergency, it is all too easy to throw anchor and line overboard, without first checking whether it is attached!

Towing

There will be an occasion when you will be called upon to tow another boat, or be towed yourself. If you are the towing boat, the best arrangement is for you to take a line from the other craft. This will then give you full control of the situation, enabling you to lengthen or shorten the tow as required, or cast it off. However, the lines of the boat in difficulties may be inadequate or too short in which case you should pass them your own line. If you do this, make sure you can release your end, even under strain – if for instance you use one of your mooring lines which is looped round a cleat, take it off and retie it first. Make sure that both ends of the line are attached to strong points on either boat, and can be led clear of any obstructions when the tow is taken up. Over the short distances that are likely to be involved, you will not normally have to bother with anti-chafe protection, but this could occur on longer tows in heavy weather.

Use the heaviest line available and do not tow too fast – the strains on cleats can be considerable. Keep the towing line short enough so that the boat behind does not swing around too far, but long enough so that it keeps clear of your boat if you have to slow down suddenly. When you know you are coming to a stop, do this gradually, allowing the boat behind to drift up alongside. Remember that if the towed boat has a broken-down engine, it will have no way of stopping.

When you need to manoeuvre in confined spaces, or with other craft around you, shorten the line to reduce the swing. In this situation, it may be better to tow alongside, taking lines from the bow and stern of each craft with a row of fenders in between. Remember that your boat will then be steering and braking for both. Turning in the direction of the boat alongside will be easy, but turning the other way will be slow. Under the International Collision Regulations, you should show the correct visual signals when towing but, in practice, there are few people on most inland waterways who would recognise these. Accordingly, you should take extra care and be aware that other boat users may not understand that you have a boat in tow. On waterways used by commercial or sea-going traffic, the correct signals must be shown. At night you must definitely show the correct lights, but this is a situation you should avoid, except in an emergency, or if you are sufficiently experienced.

Note also that many hire companies forbid their craft to tow or be towed, for insurance reasons. The only exception to this would be in an emergency, to pull a vessel away from a hazard.

Man overboard

If you or one of your crew fall off your boat, mostly it will merely be inconvenient, wet and amusing. Sometimes, however, life could be at risk. It is essential, therefore, that everyone aboard knows what to do in this situation. On most of our canals, the depths are less than 3ft (1m) – waist deep on most adults. However, it is another matter for children which is why they

The lifebuoy should be kept ready to hand, when the boat is underway, for the helmsman to use in an emergency.

should wear lifejackets at all times. Also, locks will be much deeper, up to 12ft (4m) when full.

The following procedure should be carried out whenever a man-overboard incident occurs:

- If someone falls off the boat shout 'man overboard'. Never mind how dramatic or hackneyed this sounds, it will be immediately understood.

- The helmsman should immediately put the engine into neutral to stop the boat and avoid any risk of injury to the person in the water from the prop.

- As soon as the victim is located, you should throw a lifebuoy to them. Every craft should have at least one of these; it should be mounted close to the helm, ready for use. At sea there should be a line attached to the lifebuoy but inland there is a danger that it could get tangled, and the victim is unlikely to drift far away.

- Do not throw the lifebuoy straight at the person in the water. The round belts are hard and will cause a nasty knock; even the soft horse-shoe buoys are heavy.

- Point continuously at the victim, calling out their position to the helmsman. If you are in rough water or it is dark, the casualty could soon be lost to view.

- Once it is certain that the victim has reached the belt, the helmsman can set about recovering them. By this time they will probably be astern. Do not reverse up to them or you will run the risk of injuring them with the prop. Go ahead and turn, coming up to the victim from downwind or downstream. On a narrow canal it will not be possible to turn so you have to reverse very carefully.

- The next priority is to get a rope round the casualty, to stop them sinking or drifting away.

- If they have been injured when going overboard, and are unconscious or unable to help themselves, you should consider putting an able-bodied adult over the side, with a lifejacket on, but only if this does not deplete the crew on board. At all times you should reassure the casualty.

Continued overleaf

◆ Now you will have to get them back on board. This will be harder than it sounds. The weight of water in their clothing will make even children difficult to lift, and adults virtually impossible unaided. If your boat has a bathing platform, this can be used to help them aboard.

◆ If you have enough strong people on board to lift the casualty, then do so, otherwise you can launch the tender or hail a smaller passing boat.

◆ Alternatively, you can drive your boat slowly towards the bank following the casualty (at the bow) into shallow water so that they can scramble ashore if they are able. On most rivers and canals, the bank will be close by and this will be the most effective solution. Do not allow the boat to drift in sideways, as this could trap the person underneath; also keep them clear of the prop.

If someone falls into a lock, this calls for different actions. If the lock is filling or emptying, the first priority is to drop all the paddles. This will reduce the risk of injury from the turbulence or moving boats. At the same time, ensure that the boat does not crush the victim against the gate or wall. The lifebuoy will give some protection but you should quickly drop extra fenders from the other side or a large round fender that many boats have near the bow.

Once the water flow has stabilised, it is often very difficult, however, to get the victim back on board; it may be easiest to shepherd them to the ladder or steps. If they are injured or distressed, an adult should go in with them, wearing a lifejacket. In a part-filled narrow lock where the boat is blocking access to the steps and you cannot recover the casualty, then you should secure them with a rope, let the remainder of the water slowly out of the lock and drift the boat to the step outside the lock.

The best way to prepare yourself and your crew for a man-overboard situation is to practise it in advance. Use an inflated lifejacket as the victim and follow all the steps through – it is a worthwhile exercise that could save a life one day.

Clearing the prop

One of the hazards of both rivers and canals is the amount of debris that can get caught round the prop, bringing you to a complete stop. Some of this debris is natural, such as weeds and branches, but most is man-made. The most common (and problematical) of the latter is the ubiquitous plastic bag. This varies according to where you are travelling, ranging from carrier bags in built-up areas to heavy-duty polythene bags used by farmers for fertilisers. To these can be added ropes, traffic cones, car tyres and supermarket trolleys – the latter having now replaced the old bedstead in urban canals.

You will know when you have got a small bag or bundle of weed round the prop because the boat will gradually slow down and the engine note sounds strained. This may also be accompanied by black smoke from the exhaust. At the same time, the steering may go slack as the flow of water over the rudder ceases. The engine may continue to run like this for some time and eventually free itself but, more usually, it will need help. The first tactic is to drop into neutral, then gently into reverse. Ease the engine forwards and backwards once or twice at tickover and the less tenacious debris will usually work its way free.

More dramatic will be a rope, bucket or piece of wood in the prop which will bring it to a stop with a bang, usually stalling the engine in the process. If this happens, put the gear-lever into neutral and restart the engine. Then gently nudge it quickly in and out of reverse to try to shake the debris free. If

Clearing the prop. It is often easiest, particularly on an outboard or outdrive boat, to pull yourself to the side of the waterway, and work from the bank.

this does not work, then more direct action is required. First, you should try to get the boat to the bank to allow you to get to work.

Before carrying out any work on the prop, ensure the engine cannot be started, preferably by removing the key, and putting it in your own pocket. The next step depends on whether your boat has a weed-hatch or not. This, as the name implies, is a square trap set in the bottom of the hull above the propeller. The trunk of the hatch extends above the waterline, so that when you unbolt or unclamp the top hatch, no water enters the boat. You can then look down on the prop. Surprisingly, however dirty the river or canal, the water here will be remarkably clear, allowing you to see what is causing the problem. You can then either free off whatever is jammed with your hands, or if it is tightly wound plastic or rope, you can cut it clear. The best implement for this is a serrated blade such as bread-knife or hacksaw but, whichever you use, take care not to score the shaft or prop.

Every steel narrowboat is fitted with a weed-hatch but, strangely, GRP cruisers have not followed the trend even though it would be fairly simple to mould it in when the boat is being built. Without a weed-hatch you will have to attack the blockage round the prop with the boathook from the bank, or, as a final resort, send someone into the water to remove it.

Props on outboard engines are fairly easy to access; all you have to do is tilt the engine and all will be revealed. Unfortunately, this does not immediately solve your problems because it may be difficult to reach the prop from on board. One solution is to push the bow of the boat out so the stern swings towards the bank, allowing you to get at the prop from the land. On the smallest craft you can even lift the whole of the stern of the boat by holding the motor leg, bringing the prop right up on to the bank. In theory, outdrives enjoy the same ability of access to the prop but, in practice, this is not always so. Because of the position in which they are mounted on the transom, they often do not break the surface, even when completely tilted up, but they will at least come most of the way. This will allow you to reach over the stern or get at the prop from the bank or a dinghy.

One device which is strongly recommended for solving the problem of fouled props is known, appropriately, as the weed-cutter. Designed originally in the USA, where weeds may be more of a problem, it consists of a set of stainless-steel cutting blades clamped round the propeller shaft ahead of the prop. The blades rotate with the prop, slicing through anything that could get caught round the boss. Although they will not deal with solid items wedged in the blades, they handle everything else, from weed and rope to plastic bags and even thin wire. We have had one fitted to our narrowboat for four years and have had no problems. Occasionally we know when we have hit a bag because the engine note changes; eventually it picks up and a trail of shredded polythene shows that the cutter has done its job. A particularly tenacious bag may require a couple of quick reverses to dislodge it. Weed-cutters will also deal with the occasional rope that gets sucked into their jaws, with anything up to 12mm line being chewed up and shredded.

Water pollution

Before you jump into the river to clear your prop bear in mind the risks to health from pollution. Even apparently clean-looking water may be polluted by sewage, industrial effluent and toxic fertilisers. Prolonged contact of the skin with polluted water can cause rashes and infections, while swallowing it can cause stomach upsets. To this has to be added a problem called Weil's disease. This is an infection carried by rats and transmitted by water. It can cause severe flu-like symptoms, paralysis and even death. Its main route into the blood-stream is via the skin, so if you have any cuts or abrasions, they should be protected before putting your hands into the water; it is best to wear industrial rubber gloves. If you experience symptoms two weeks or so after contact with water, go to a doctor immediately and tell them you have been in contact with stagnant water.

Travelling at night

As a general rule we recommend you try not to have to travel on the waterways at night. The chances of damage to your boat and injury to crew members is increased, and you have to be experienced and your craft properly equipped. However, circumstances may require you to navigate in darkness, so you need to know what to expect.

Travelling on the waterways at night is one of the most magical experiences, but your crew and craft must be properly prepared.

Navigation Lights

Motorboat with separate

Motorboat with combined
port and starboard bow light

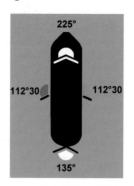

Arcs of visibility of lights

Motor vessel with mast light forward

The text below explains which boats have which lights.
Drawings reproduced from The Adlard Coles Book of EuroRegs for Inland
Waterways, by kind permission of Marian Martin.

First, your boat needs to have the correct navigation lights. In this respect you must understand that the headlight, or tunnel light, on the front of a narrowboat is not a night-time navigation light. It is for passage through tunnels only. It must not be used in open waters, as you will blind oncoming craft.

Correct lights include a red light on the port (left) side of the boat, and a corresponding green light to starboard. These must be positioned to show ahead, and slightly aft of the beam. If you buy proper nav lights, and fit them correctly, they will comply with this requirement. Small craft can use a combined red and green light at the bow. The definition of 'small' varies. On the Thames it is 23ft (7m). On International Waterways, surprisingly, it is now 64ft (20m). You need a white steaming light showing ahead, and a white stern light showing aft. The precise size, height and positioning of these lights will vary with the size of your craft, and whether it is sail or power. The waterway you are on should be able to supply you with the requirements, or the *RYA Inland Helmsman's Handbook* has them.

In addition to these basic lights, there is a huge range of lights and shapes that you might encounter other vessels carrying, and you should familiarise yourself with these from the *RYA Handbook*, especially if you are travelling on a river where you might meet commercial craft, or on Continental waterways.

Before you cast off at night, you must ensure that all the guides, maps, torches and equipment you might need are readily to hand, and that ropes are coiled neatly out of the way so no one will trip over them. Turn off all unnecessary lights on board, or dim them, to preserve your night vision, and stress to all crew members that they should not switch them back on.

Everyone on deck should be wearing a lifejacket, regardless of whether they can swim. If you fall overboard, you may bang your head, and will drown before you can be found. Be careful that nobody on deck obscures any of your nav lights. It is all too easy for a carelessly draped coat to cover a light.

Drive at a reduced speed, and instruct everyone aboard to keep a sharp lookout all round, particularly on rivers. Always pass on the correct side of oncoming craft. You will learn to gauge the position and direction of oncoming or overtaking craft by their lights you can see. If a craft is approaching dead ahead, you will see both its red and green. As it passes to your port, the green will go out, and the red will remain.

Do not drive at night if you are tired, or have been drinking. Your reactions and judgement will be impaired.

Take care, and enjoy one of the most magical experiences afloat as you drift along under the stars.

7 | *Maintenance and Repair*

No matter what type of craft you own, however large or small, cheap or expensive, the key to enjoyable, trouble-free boating is to keep it well maintained and repaired. You go afloat for pleasure, but there is no pleasure in an engine that won't start, a warm fridge or taps that won't deliver water. At the same time, badly maintained gas or fuel systems can be dangerous or even fatal.

The majority of maintenance work on an inland waterways boat is well within the capabilities of an averagely competent DIY person, and many people do most of their routine maintenance themselves. It is part of the fun of boat-owning, and also saves money. At the same time, you are better placed to effect running repairs should something break down, if you have at least an idea of how it all works. Some areas are best left to the professionals but, again, it is a good thing if you understand what is involved, as it puts you in a better position when discussing what needs doing and agreeing prices with the boatyard.

Most maintenance work is best done during the winter period, when the boat is out of commission. Some work is better done at the end of the season; some at the beginning of the next one. The two operations are called, respectively, laying-up and fitting-out. In practice, many items overlap between the two, and natural inertia usually pushes many of them round to the end of winter rather than the beginning. The drawback of allowing this to happen is that everyone does the same, so that suppliers and boat-yards become overloaded just when you want them. A little pre-planning will avoid some of these problems. At the same time, it is generally true that the weather is better at the beginning of winter than at the end. Boats are cold and bleak places to work in, so November is usually a better bet than February.

There are other areas of maintenance and repair which are specific to each boat and its equipment, but the following gives you the basic groundwork for most inland waterways craft.

Engines

The engine is usually the most expensive single piece of equipment on board. It should therefore get the most attention.

Outboard motors

If possible, the outboard should be taken home and stored for the winter. This makes it easier to work on, reduces corrosion, and protects it from theft. You should be able to lift off an engine weighing up to 6hp on your own. Up to 15hp can be managed by two people, provided you take care. Above this, and you will need three people, or assistance from a yard, but it will probably not be worth the effort. When lifting even a small outboard off the transom, tie a strong line round it which is made fast to a point on the boat. This will at least enable you to recover it if it should drop overboard. The line can also aid a helper to get a purchase for lifting. Make sure you have left enough slack in the safety line to allow the outboard to be lifted on to the pontoon or bank.

Ideally, before you remove the engine, you should start it up and let it run, to check that everything is in order, or note any problems that might need treatment. Check that it ticks over smoothly, goes easily in and out of gear, and that there is a good flow of water from the cooling outlet. Then disconnect the fuel line, electrical harness and control cables before starting to slacken the clamps. Coil them up and tie them together to prevent them dangling and catching. Undo any security bolts – all engines over 5hp should be bolted as well as clamped to the transom for safety. If the clamps have seized, do not force them. Apply penetrating oil and come back in 10 minutes; these can be expensive items to replace if they should shear or break. Make a point of greasing them as part of future routine maintenance.

When transporting the engine, do not let the powerhead lie below the height of the prop, or water can run up the exhaust into the cylinders. Four-strokes will have an instruction as to which side you lay them down. This is to prevent the lubricating oil in their sump from running out, or into the cylinders.

Once you have got the engine home, or if you are leaving it on the boat, you have to decide which work you do now, and which you leave till next year. For preference, it should all be done now, as it prevents corrosion taking place over the winter. At the very least, you should carry out the basic winterising procedure now.

Stand the unit upright to work on it, preferably clamped to a vice or the bench. The first job is to flush out the cooling water system. This is essential if the boat has been used in salt water, as it reduces corrosion, but it is also useful on river boats, as silt and sludge can accumulate in the passageways. To flush the system, use a hose to force water up from the cooling water intakes. To assist this, rubber 'muffs' can be bought, which clamp round the leg and the openings. Alternatively, for smaller engines, you can stand them in a dustbin of water, and start them up. Clear out any weed or growth from the intake first. If you run the engine up, check that there is a good flow of water from the outlet, indicating that the pump is working well.

Next, you should drain the fuel system. The easiest way to do this is to run the engine with the fuel line disconnected, or the fuel tap off. If you are clever, you can spray a carburettor cleaner or rust inhibitor into the intake, as the engine gradually dies. This protects the carburettor and coats the inside of the cylinders. Remove and clean the fuel filter.

Now remove the spark plugs and check them for signs of any problems. Burnt or badly blackened plugs indicate problems that you should have professionally checked. The ideal colour is a light tan or brown, with no oil. Even if they look in good condition, fit a new set of plugs every season. It is the cheapest form of preventative maintenance, and will go a long way to ensuring easy starting and smooth running. If the old plugs look good, keep them as spares. Set the gaps according to the maker's handbook. While the plugs are out, spray the inside of the cylinder with a rust inhibitor, then loosely refit the plugs. Tie a label on to the throttle to remind you next season that the plugs are not tight.

At this point you will realise that you might as well finish the whole job. This includes checking the gearbox oil. To do this, undo the filler plug in the lower unit, and top up with the correct grade oil – not engine oil. Depending on the maker's instructions, you should periodically drain and replace the gear oil. When you do this, look at the condition of oil that comes out. A milky-white colour indicates that water is getting in, and the rear seal will need professionally replacing. Check that the prop is secure. Check for damaged or bent blades. Slight damage or nicks round the leading edge can be filed smooth. Bent blades can be straightened, but it is better to replace the prop, keeping the old one as a spare. Check for nylon fishing line jammed into the rubber seal ahead of the prop. If this has been badly damaged, it will have to be replaced.

Most modern ignition systems are sealed electronic units, which require no maintenance. Older engines had magneto, or points and a coil. It is usually only possible to get at the points by removing the fly-wheel – a professional job. If in doubt about the engine's performance, take it to the local dealer for that make for a full service. This will include tuning the carburettor, usually beyond the scope of an amateur. It is wise to have a full service at least every two years, to pick up any problems. Four-stroke outboards will need their sump oil renewing, according to the maker's recommendations.

The next stage of winterising is to grease all the moving parts of the engine. These will usually be indicated in the handbook, and will have grease nipples. Use a waterproof grease, preferably one designed for outboard applications. Remember to grease the clamp screws.

Check the fuel installation – tank, hose and primer bulb – for chafing, damage or leaks. If in doubt about the condition of any of these, replace them; the safety of you and your crew may be at risk if you ignore faults.

At the beginning of the season, clear the inhibitor out of the cylinders, and tighten the plugs.

Inboard engines

Inboard engines will be either petrol or diesel. They can be directly cooled, with water from the river passing round the block itself, or indirectly cooled, with the river water passing through a heat-exchanger, and a sealed-circuit cooling the block. These two systems are sometimes called raw-water and fresh-water cooling, respectively. A third system, which is used on most narrowboats, is keel or tank cooling, where water in a closed-circuit system passes through a tank welded to the inside of the hull. Finally, some engines are air-cooled.

Many of the maintenance procedures are common to all inboards. First you need to winterise the cooling system. For raw-water cooling, this involves turning off the seacock, then draining the water from the block and pipes to prevent it from freezing. With indirect cooling, the closed-circuit system should have anti-freeze in it to prevent freezing. Check that this has not been diluted by topping up during the season; then drain the raw-water side of the circuit. For keel-cooling systems, check the anti-freeze. Owners of air-cooled engines can relax at this stage.

With the piping drained, open up the water-pump, and check the impeller. If in doubt, fit a new one; take the opportunity of clearing out the inlet strainer. Tie a label on the throttle to remind you, next season, that the system is drained and turned off.

The fuel system is next on the list. With a petrol engine, you should check very closely for leaks, as these can be difficult to detect during operation, but can cause an explosive build-up of fumes in the bilge. It is especially important to check the rubber diaphragm in the fuel lift pump, and in the carburettor if it has one; these can perish, but only leak when the tank is filled right up. This is thought to have been the cause of explosions on petrol-powered boats a few years back. If you have any doubt about your own capabilities in this area, have the system checked professionally and, in any case, have this done every second or third year. Diesel systems should also be checked for leaks, though these will usually manifest themselves in drips, or air in the fuel lines. Clean or replace the filters on both systems.

Next, you should clean the air filter. Then, with a petrol engine, you should spray a cleaning agent into the carburettor. With a diesel, you should clean or check the injectors. This used to mean removing them, and sending them to a specialist. However, lately it has been possible to buy cleaning additives that you put in the fuel, and these do an excellent job. For routine maintenance the additive is diluted as instructed by the manufacturer, and will clean the injectors as you drive. If black smoke is visible when the engine is running, you use the additive neat, filling the fuel filter bowl with it, and running the engine until the smoking stops. If the injectors are badly worn or damaged, they should be removed and serviced. The additive will also clean the injector pump at the same time. On a petrol engine, clean or replace the spark plugs, and check the contact-breaker points.

On either type of engine, the oil and filter should be changed, preferably at the end of the season. Otherwise, all the impurities, water and acids that have collected in the oil during the season will corrode the vital running surfaces inside the unit over the winter period. It is essential that you use the

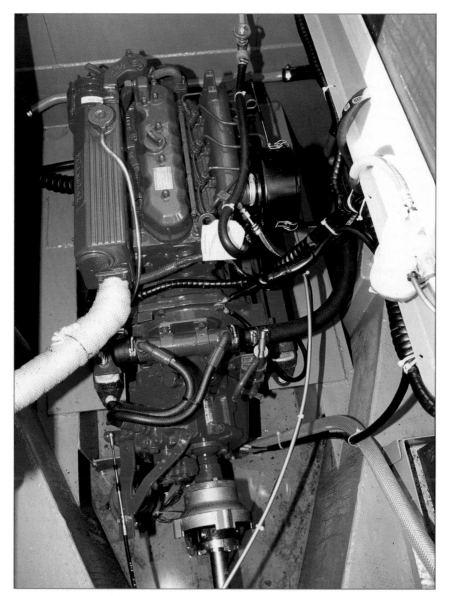

A typical narrowboat engine installation, with a keel cooled diesel and dry exhaust. Also visible are the prop shaft and coupling.

correct type and grade of marine oil. Do not use oil which is sold for road vehicles; this will be designed for engines running at much higher temperatures, and will not have the correct structure or additives in it. The maker's handbook will tell you how much oil to use. Give some thought as to how you are going to collect and dispose of the old oil. It is easiest to collect it in old cans; keep last year's empty cans for this purpose. It should then be disposed of at the local authority or marina disposal point. Do not put the cans in the dustbin or general skip, and under no circumstances pour the oil down the drain – it will flow into your river at some point, having killed all the wildlife en route. Most boat engines will have a hand-pump fitted to get the oil out, as it will be impossible to get under the sump. Alternatively, you can buy electric extractor pumps that you insert down the dipstick hole. Run the engine for a few minutes to warm the oil and make it flow more easily, but do not do the job at the end of a long run, as the oil will be very hot.

The gearbox oil should be checked, but does not usually have to be changed except at extended intervals. This is because it does not carry all the combustion impurities that engine oil contains and does not get so hot. If you have to top it up, make sure you use the correct lubricant – sometimes Automatic Transmission Fluid (ATF) as recommended by the manufacturer.

Now check the engine over for general leaks. Try to keep the unit clean at all times, as not only will this make it easier to detect problems or leaks, but it will make it much more pleasant to work on. Check the mounting and coupling bolts – these can gradually work loose, with potentially disastrous results. Check the stern-gland, and tighten as necessary. Do not overtighten; the conventional gland contains greased packing, and this requires a certain amount of water to prevent it overheating or drying out. An occasional drip while the boat is underway is permissible. To stop these drips becoming a puddle of water swilling around the bilge, a washing-up bowl underneath will catch the worst. If there is already water in the bilge with a film of oil on it, do not pump this out into the river or canal. Not only is this illegal, but it will destroy the plant and animal life; use one of the proprietary bilge-cleaner solutions to turn the oil into an emulsion. Then either pump it into containers with a hand-pump, or operate the bilge-pump and catch the fluid as it comes out of the outlet pipe. Alternatively, you can use a specially designed oil absorbing pad or blanket.

Some boats may be fitted with one of the modern patent non-drip glands. Instead of using gland-packing, these consist of two watertight discs that spin against one another, and are held together by pressure from rubber bellows. One disc is clamped to the shaft, the other to the sterntube. The discs are usually stainless steel and graphite; all you have to check is that the rubber has not perished, and look for signs of wear on the mating surfaces.

The sterntube may either have a rubber cutless bearing in its outer end, which will be water-lubricated, or a white-metal bearing that needs grease. In the case of the latter, refill the greaser and give it a turn. You should, of course, be giving this a regular turn, every day, while the boat is being used.

Onboard electrics

Electrical systems serve two functions, first to start the engine, second to run the domestic services – lights, pumps, fridge etc. On small boats, one battery will serve both purposes, but on larger craft the systems are usually divided into two. The purpose of this is to ensure that you have a separate battery to start the engine if your domestic batteries become run down.

Batteries are the heart of the electrical system and should be looked after with care. They will let you down if they are not maintained, and are expensive to replace. Routine maintenance of batteries involves checking the level of the electrolyte (acid) inside, and topping up as required. This should be done at least once a month, but more frequently in hot weather, or if the boat is being used a lot. Check each cell, using distilled or deionised water, top up to 1/2in (13mm) below the filler, or 1/2in (13mm) above the plates. Do not overfill; if large amounts of water are required, suspect an overcharging fault, and have the system checked. Low-maintenance batteries will also need topping up, though not so frequently, while sealed maintenance-free batteries should need none at all. Keep the tops of the batteries clean and dry, and check that the terminals are secure.

At the end of the season, repeat the process, then decide how you are going to maintain the batteries over the winter. All batteries lose their charge slowly, even if they are not connected. This self-discharge is accelerated by damp and dirt on the battery top – which encourages a minute current to flow – but will still occur on a clean battery. Over the six-month winter period, the battery will discharge to the point where it could be permanently damaged, or its capacity reduced. Therefore, you have to arrange to charge them up at least once, preferably twice, during this period. This can either be done by taking a charger down to the boat – if mains supply is available – and leaving it on overnight. Otherwise, you have to take the batteries home. Even if your engine is not yet winterised, it is not worth trying to charge your batteries by running the engine at tickover as you will not get much charge from the alternator at low rpm.

Low-maintenance batteries have also got a low self-discharge, and may not need boosting, but you must not take this for granted. To check the state of charge of the batteries, the traditional piece of equipment is the hydrometer. This can be bought from any car accessory shop, and shows the specific gravity of the acid. The acid in a fully charged battery will have a specific gravity of 1260–1280. Fully discharged it will be 1100–1120; halfway between will be half-charged. Check all the cells in each battery, and note the readings. Each cell should be within 10–20 points of each other. Any greater variation will indicate a faulty cell, which will mean a new battery. When taking specific gravities, do not let the acid drip on anything else. Wear rubber gloves, and, ideally, protect your eyes. Alternatively, the modern way is to use a digital voltmeter, available cheaply from electrical stores. Fully charged, with no loads on it, and the engine stopped, a 12V battery should show 12.6–12.8V. Fully discharged it will show 11.6–11.8V. Maintenance-free batteries can only be checked by looking into the light indicators sited in their tops or with a voltmeter.

Undo the terminals and check for corrosion. Clean any deposits off with a wire brush, then replace the terminals and coat them with Vaseline® or

Pressure washers can be bought or hired to make lighter work of cleaning weed growth and mud from the hull.

silicone grease. Then check the rest of the wiring and circuits on board for loose connections or corrosion.

The hull

The underwater hull can obviously only be properly checked when the boat is out of the water. Unless you have reason to suspect a problem, this does not have to be done every year, but you should do it preferably every second year, or definitely every third. Otherwise, small problems can build up into a major breakdown.

With the boat out of the water, you should check both the hull and the stern gear. To enable you to do this, you should first clean off any weed, slime or encrustation. By far the best way to do this is with a pressure washer. These can be hired, either from boatyards or hire shops. Scraping by hand is laborious and lengthy.

With a glassfibre boat, check for damage underwater, particularly along the keel and the chine. Any damage should be repaired with gelcoat or mat, depending on how serious it is. You can deal with small scratches yourself. Larger cracks or holes should be professionally mended. Look for blisters under the gelcoat, which could indicate osmosis. If you find any, call in an expert. Finally, put on another coat of antifouling. Suitable grades for inland waterways are available. Check that the type you choose is compatible with the antifouling that is already on. Some types have to be applied just before launching while others are designed to be left out of water; if in doubt, call in a yard.

With a steel boat, check for rust or pitting, particularly round the waterline. Light rust can be wire-brushed, primed and painted. Serious rust or pits may indicate a problem and should be professionally inspected. The steel hull can then be painted; two or possibly three coats of bitumastic are the best covering. Antifouling is not used with bitumastic.

Check the anodes. These are blocks of magnesium alloy, bolted to the hull at the bow and stern; their purpose is to prevent electrolytic corrosion of the steel plate and the bronze stern gear. These sacrificial anodes corrode in place of the metal of the hull and prop, thereby giving protection. They should be replaced every second or third year; if they are more than half wasted away, replace them. If they are not wasting away, suspect a fault, and have them checked. Glassfibre boats used only on rivers, not the sea, will often not have anodes. However, check whether they are needed by looking at the stern gear.

Checking stern gear

Signs of electrolytic corrosion are when the golden bronze of the propeller turns pink, either all over, or in spots. Scrape off any paint, weed or encrustation to check this. The other check is to tap the prop with a coin. If it is in good condition, it will ring like a bell. If it is electrolysed, it will give a dull click. If in doubt, tap your neighbour's prop and note any difference.

Check the rest of the stern gear. If the prop is damaged, nicks and dents in the leading edge should be filed smooth. Bent blades should be professionally straightened by taking the prop off and sending it to one of the specialists. If you do not do this, vibration and premature bearing wear will occur. Check the bearing for wear by lifting the shaft up and down. It should not move significantly. If it does, call in an expert. Similarly, the rudder should not move in its bearing, nor should it have any free movement either way. Check the prop nut for corrosion, and replace if necessary. Check the split pin. You cannot check the shaft without breaking the gearbox coupling and sliding it back. Unless it is old, or you suspect wear, only do this every 4–5 years. The prop can be polished after it has been cleaned. It will not do much for performance, but you will enjoy looking at it!

Whenever you are working near the propeller on any boat, ensure that the engine is immobilised and cannot be started.

Outdrives

If your boat has an outdrive, this should be checked and serviced. Precise procedures will vary from make to make, but general points include checking

All boats should be lifted from the water every two years, or definitely every three, for inspection and fresh coats of bottom paint.

the rubber bellows for chafing, perishing or wear. Check the anode, and replace if necessary. Touch up any damaged parts of the casing. Check the prop and nut, and check the control cable for corrosion or wear. Have someone operate the tilt while you watch. Then have them turn the steering fully to the left and right. Anti-foul, using only the correct grade for aluminium.

Above the water – the topsides

Whether the boat is in or out of the water, check the hull above the waterline for damage, and repair as necessary. If you ignore scratches or holes in a glassfibre boat, you will get water in the laminate, while damage on a steel hull will go rusty. Check the guardrails, cleats, fender eyes and any other deck fittings for security, and tighten or refit as necessary. Loose fittings will leak, and cause rot or mildew inside the boat, quite apart from possibly failing under load. Check the ropes, fenders, boathooks, anchor and so on, for damage or wear. Check any canopies and awnings for the beginnings of chafing, and protect them wherever possible, as replacing covers is expensive. Check the navigation lights, and other electrical fittings for corrosion or loose connections.

The interior

One of the main priorities for interior maintenance is to prevent condensation and mildew. Condensation occurs if the boat is tightly closed, with no ventilation. It will cause mildew, rot, and a general damp feeling throughout the craft. Your boat should already have adequate permanent ventilation in the form of door and roof vents. If it does not, you should have these installed. They are also mandatory on some waterways, where you have open-flame gas equipment (such as a cooker), to prevent the build-up of carbon monoxide. Otherwise, leaving strategic windows partly open will provide a flow of air, though be sure that they do not let in rain, or increase any security risk. Condensation can also be reduced by installing a de-humidifier on board. This will need a mains electricity supply to run, though it only consumes about 50W. In operation, the de-humidifier draws the damp air inside the boat over a cooling plate, on which the moisture condenses out, to be collected. They are extremely effective, reducing condensation, dampness, mildew and rot. Ventilation on the boat needs to be carefully adjusted, however, so that the de-humidifier does not suck in damp air from outside the boat.

Other areas affected by dampness are the furnishings and fabrics – particularly cushions and mattresses. The best solution is to take them home at the end of the season. If you cannot do this, stand them on edge, to allow as much air circulation as possible. Take bedding, coats and wet weather gear home or they will go mouldy and musty. Open doors, lockers and drawers for the same reason. Remove any food that is not in tins. Not only will this go off, but it can attract animals, bugs and birds. Wedge the fridge door open, or you will be rewarded with a musty, mouldy smell for the next season.

Empty the drinks cabinet, as you don't want to refresh any casual thieves. What you do with other stealable equipment is a subject in its own right. By

The weed-hatch on a narrowboat allows you to clear the prop. This one is slightly unusual in reaching right up to the stern-deck.

and large, it is impossible to make a boat completely thief-proof. There are too many windows and doors. Even on a marina, night-time in winter provides a cloak for most clandestine operations. A burglar alarm is one possibility, but the rate of accidental triggering is high, and the chances of anyone being near enough to hear it are low. The best solution is to remove all items that are easily stolen and, more importantly, easily sold. These include radios, generators and expensive tools. Write your post code on other equipment with an ultraviolet marker pen and, just as importantly, note down any serial numbers. It is surprising how much equipment the police do recover, but often they are unable to identify it for return to its owners.

Domestic equipment

The first priority is to drain the fresh-water system to prevent it from freezing. Good boats will have drain taps in the line at the lowest points. Otherwise, the process is to turn the water off at the tank, then run the pump for a few minutes with all the taps open; this will blow as much water as possible out of the system. Then look for the low points in the lines, and crack open the joints here. Don't forget to drain the shower head and mixer unit, plus the hot water heater or calorifier. Leave the taps open and, with luck, you will avoid frozen pipes and equipment damage. Make a note of what you have done and where all the joints are broken, so that you can tighten them all up next season.

The water tank itself should be cleaned out and sterilised every year. This prevents any build-up of bacteria, or bad-tasting water. This operation can be done at either end of the year, but is probably best at the start of a new season. The precise technique depends on which product you are using. Many of those you will find in the chandlery consist of powder and tablets. The powder is dissolved in warm water and poured into the tank. The tank should be about a quarter full; this avoids having to use too much powder, and waiting too long for the tank to empty. Add the required amount of powder in half-a-dozen batches, following it with a couple of saucepans of water each time to spread it through the tank. Then run each tap in turn until the water coming out has a soapy feel. This ensures that you have got the cleaning solution through the whole system. Leave it to brew for an hour or so, depending on how badly affected the water was, before running all the water out of the tank. Rinse out with some clean water, running it through each tap till it comes out fresh, and then refill. Occasionally, through the season, drop a couple of tablets into the tank to keep the water sweet. If you still have problems with a taint to the drinking water, you can fit a filter into the line, or, more simply, use one of the domestic jug-filters that are now commonly available.

The gas system was mentioned earlier, and we have emphasised the importance of safety. Gas is heavier than air; any leak will collect in the bilge, forming a potentially explosive mixture. Detectors are on the market that can warn of a build-up of gas, but it is more important to ensure that the system is sound in the first place. To this end, any work should be done by a CORGI-registered fitter. You should have the appliances serviced annually or bi-annually. We recommend that you fit one of the Gaslow gauges at the supply to warn of any leaks. The gas-bottle locker should be adequately ventilated, with drain holes in its bottom, and should be sited outside the accommodation.

8 | *Trailer Boating*

Many people take to the waterways in trailable boats. The reasons are economy, convenience and the flexibility to cover areas that other craft cannot reach. Trailer boats bring their own advantages, but some have their own problems and techniques.

Some people trail their boats to and from every trip, keeping them at home in between times. The advantages are no mooring or marina costs, and the ability to choose a new cruising ground every time. Other craft are left on their trailers at boatyards or parks by the water, only being launched when required. A third category – usually the largest craft – are only towed at the beginning and end of the year, being left on a mooring for the season. This still gives you the benefit of storage at home over the winter, but avoids the hassle of launching on every trip.

Trailers and tow vehicles

The size of boat you can tow depends on the size, or weight, of your car, and whether the trailer has brakes or not. With an unbraked trailer, the combined weight of the boat and trailer must be less than half the weight of the towing vehicle, and a maximum of 750kg. In practice, this restricts unbraked trailers to runabouts and dayboats, usually no more than 14–15ft (4.2–4.5m) or so in length.

For a braked trailer, there is no specific legal maximum weight, but a practical guide is that the weight of boat and trailer should not exceed the unladen weight of the towing vehicle. You must ensure that you have enough power to be able to pull the boat up the slipway, and maintain a comfortable speed on the road. You must be careful to avoid overloading the car's suspension and brakes. Most vehicle manufacturers quote maximum towing weights for each of their models and, in practice, if you were to exceed these limits, you might find your insurance would not cover you if you were involved in an accident.

To give you an idea of what these figures mean: a small family car, such as an Astra, has a kerb weight of 840kg and maximum recommended towing weights of 750–1000kg depending on engine size. A Vectra weighs 1000kg, and can tow from 1000–1200kg, depending on engine size. A Volvo 760 weighs 1400kg, and can tow 1500kg. Four-wheel drive vehicles such as the

Range Rover will usually have a maximum recommended towing weight of around double their own weight. In fact, for the Range Rover the figures are 1900kg vehicle weight and 3900kg towing weight. A Daihatsu Four Trak has figures of 1500kg and 3500kg respectively.

To relate these to boat and trailer weights, a 14ft (4.2m) runabout with small outboard will weigh around 400kg on an unbraked trailer. A 16–18ft (4.8–5.4m) outboard-powered cruiser will weigh around 1000kg on a two-wheel braked trailer. The 23ft (7m) Wilderness Beaver on a four-wheel trailer will weigh around 1350kg with normal cruising gear on board.

Rear-wheel drive cars will give better traction when pulling up a slipway than front-wheel drive models, while four-wheel drive gives the best grip of all.

An automatic gearbox is better for towing than a manual for three reasons: it avoids frequent gear-changes, necessary when towing an extra load on the roads; it gives you far better control on the slipway, with no need to operate hand-brake and clutch, and no chance of stalling; it also gives you more pull at slow speeds and up hills because of the torque converter. Similarly, pulling away at junctions is simpler, while crawling along in motorway traffic queues is totally relaxed.

Slipways

For practical purposes, the size of boat you can tow is as much restricted by how easy it is to launch as its overall weight. Bear in mind that not all slipways are equally good for launching. At their simplest, slipways can be gravel slopes on the edge of the river. Often, these coincide with old ferry locations. They will be suitable for dayboats and smaller cruisers, up to 16ft (4.8m), but larger boats can be difficult to launch. The problem comes not just with launching, but with recovery; the towing vehicle may be unable to get enough grip to pull the trailer up the slope.

Concrete public slipways will give a better surface, but sometimes the water will not be deep enough at their outer end to float your boat off. The best slips are usually those used by boatyards. They will be deep and steep, with enough depth to float the boat off, and a good surface to get a grip. There will also be space available to park the boat and trailer securely which is often a problem with public slips.

Towing tips

Towing a boat on the road is not difficult, but it does require different techniques, and a lot of concentration. Before you even get underway, it is important that the boat is loaded correctly. This means that it should be in the right position on the trailer to give the correct nose-weight. Nose-weight, or

The towing vehicle must be appropriate for the weight of the boat and trailer. This 16ft cruiser can be towed by a family car, but the 4WD makes it even easier.

the downward load that the trailer exerts on the hitch, is important if the boat is to tow well. If it is too light, the trailer will snake at maximum speed. Snaking, as its name implies, is when the trailer starts to swerve from side to side behind the car. If it is not controlled, it can dangerously affect the handling of the car. The onset of snaking is usually caused by a sudden swerve or braking of the towing vehicle, or by the passing of a large lorry or coach. It is affected by incorrectly adjusted tyre pressures, but the principal cause is nose-weight. Maximum nose-weight figures will be given in the handbook by the vehicle manufacturer, but these are usually in the range 110–220lb (50–100kg). Adjust the position of the boat on the trailer to give as high a figure as permissible, and measure this with a set of bathroom scales under the jockey wheel. If it is correctly set, you should be able to drive up to the maximum speed allowed with confidence.

You will have to increase the tyre pressures of the towing vehicle, particularly at the rear. The maker's handbook will give precise figures, and it is essential that you adhere to these. Remember to reduce them when you are not towing. Also carry a spare wheel for the trailer.

Speed limits for trailers vary from country to country. In the UK they are 50mph on single-carriageway roads, assuming no lower limit is in force, and 60mph on motorways and dual-carriageway roads. If you should decide to travel farther afield and take your trailer and boat abroad, you should check the various regulations for the countries you are planning to pass through. The trailer manufacturer Indespension produces an excellent manual that covers this and all other aspects of trailing. Additionally, the RYA will advise on regulations including the necessary paperwork you will require.

Preparation

Make sure you adjust the nose-weight of the trailer with the engine on the transom, and all movable gear in its normal stowed position. If you put in extra gear, stow it as close to the axle as possible. Fix all loose equipment securely in place. This especially applies to the fuel tank.

Fix the engine securely in place. If you have to drive with it tilted up, do not leave the weight supported only on the tilt mechanism, as this will put considerable strain on it. Chock it up with blocks, or make a permanent support. Cover the propeller and skeg with an orange PVC bag. This is necessary for legal reasons, as the propeller is classed as a dangerous projection and has to be covered. It also helps visibility, and prevents the car behind running into the engine.

Lash the boat down with webbing straps that have ratchet end fittings. These are quicker, neater and safer than ropes, which will always work loose. Pad the gunwale of the boat where the webbing passes over it, as it can chafe; also the dye can run out of the webbing if it gets wet. Two straps will provide 'belt-and-braces' protection, and give you peace of mind, especially at night. The same applies at the bow. Do not rely solely on a winch, as this can slip. Instead, tie the front of the boat down to the trailer with several turns of rope through the bow eye. This will act as a back-up, and will also prevent the boat from riding forwards and up if you should suddenly brake.

It is always best if the driver takes the responsibility for checking the lashings and ropes, as he is ultimately responsible for the load. This also applies to connecting up the hitch. Make sure that the hitch has securely locked into place on the ball, and that the breakaway chain or wire is attached. In the case of a braked trailer, the purpose of the breakaway chain is to apply the brake should the hitch break or come apart. With an unbraked trailer, the chain should keep the trailer attached to the car, and should be short enough to keep the nose off the road.

Lighting boards

Most trailers will have removable lighting boards. The lighting regulations are complex, and beyond the scope of this book, but your trailer manufacturer will be able to advise you. The regulations usually relate to the length and width of the trailer and its load; a reputable manufacturer will supply the trailer with a board with the correct lighting configuration. Make sure the board is securely attached. A trailer will bounce about considerably, particularly when it is empty and the board can easily come adrift. Every time the board is removed (and every time you set off) check that all the lights are working. Do this with someone standing behind as you operate brakes, indicators and running lights. Lighting connections have a hard life, with the towing socket often immersed when you launch the boat, so it is essential, both for legal and safety reasons, that you know all the lights are working.

Driving techniques for towing

Driving a tow vehicle takes some getting used to; it is often prudent to have a few trial runs with an unloaded trailer, starting in an empty car park to get the feel of how it responds. When pulling away, the important thing to remember is to take a large enough swing around parked cars or obstructions ahead of you. Otherwise the trailer will drag across the corner. This particularly applies when travelling through towns, and passing parked cars, and when manoeuvring in a petrol station, or motorway service station. It is all too easy to forget the trailer behind and go for the usual gap, with expensive consequences.

Most modern cars have wing mirrors that will give you sufficient vision behind. However, if your mirrors are inadequate, or the boat is wider than the car, extension mirrors as used by caravan owners will do the job.

Similarly, when turning sharp corners, make sure that you leave enough clearance so that the trailer does not drag across the kerb. At the same time, remember that the outside rear corner of the trailer, usually the lighting board, or the back of the boat, will swing out in the other direction.

Reversing is a special delight of its own. The first thing to remember is that you have to turn the wheel the opposite way you would expect, if you want the trailer to start to turn. You then have to straighten the wheel up to continue the turn, or the rig will jack-knife. Again, practising in any empty car park with no pressure is much better than trying to learn on a crowded slipway on a busy summer afternoon.

Launching

Launching and recovery have their own techniques and your boat and trailer will probably have their own peculiarities. If it is your first time, choose a quiet slipway at mid-week or an off-season weekend. Do not spoil your first major outing with dramas on the slipway.

The main priority is to think through what is going to happen; make sure that everyone knows what they are expected to do, and take things slowly and carefully. Before you get to the top of the slipway, undo all the lashings except the winch strap, and take off the lighting board. Remove the outboard bag and any chocks, and make sure that the bung is fitted in the boat. Tie the bow and stern lines to their cleats, and put on any fenders required. Check that the winch ratchet works freely, and make sure that whoever is to release it knows how it works. Check that the engine is tilted up enough to avoid catching on the slipway as you go down. If you need to move the boat away from the slip immediately, make sure that the engine is ready to start. Connect and prime the fuel line, check that the battery is connected and the ignition key is in place. Give the key a quick blip to check that the engine is going to turn over. However, do not start the engine out of the water, as you will overheat it and burn out the water-pump impeller. Someone may have to get their feet wet so either put on a pair of boots, or roll up your trousers in advance. It is wise to invest in a pair of waders if your boat is difficult to launch.

Back the boat slowly to the top of the slipway, and straighten it up as you go down. If space at the top of the slip is severely congested, it may be simpler to unhitch the trailer and manoeuvre it into position by hand, but make sure you reconnect it to the car before it gets to the slope. Back down until the trailer is in the water, and the car has nearly reached it. Then, if you have a winch, carefully release the ratchet. Keep tight hold of the handle as you do this, as the boat may still be pulling on it. Do not release the winch any earlier, or you may launch your boat down the concrete.

Next, back the rig further into the water, until the boat floats off. You may have to help it off by pushing the bow, preferably with a rocking motion. You can back the car down the slip until the exhaust reaches the water, but do not let the engine stop or you could suck water into it. Beware of filling the boot if you go too far! Also, if you get the brakes wet, do not then leave the car in the park all day with the hand-brake applied, as it can seize on.

If you still cannot get the trailer far enough into the water for the boat to float off, you should consider disconnecting it, and pushing the trailer farther out on the end of a rope. However, be careful when doing this. Always put the hand-brake on when disconnecting the trailer, and take a turn of the rope round the towing hitch, to prevent the trailer from running away. Let it down slowly, keeping tension on the rope. Be aware that, when the boat starts to move back along the trailer, the front of the trailer will lift as the weight comes off it. Keep well clear at this point, or have someone apply downward force.

Some of the modern trailers that use multiple rollers rather than solid side-supports or bunks will prove easier for launching and recovering the boat, as it will roll on and off easily.

It is usually a good idea to start the engine while the boat is still on the trailer but in the water. This will allow you to warm it up ready for departure, and check any problems. Make sure, however, that the engine is deep enough for the cooling water intakes to be submerged, and that the prop is clear of the trailer and the bottom. With experience, you can use reverse on the engine to pull the boat off but, again, be sure that the prop is immersed, and that the engine will not hit the bottom as the boat comes off. If in doubt, tilt the motor partly up, while still keeping the intakes submerged.

Recovery

Recovering the boat may appear to be the reverse procedure of launching, but there are differences. First, the car must have enough traction or grip to pull the boat and trailer up the slipway. So make sure that there is solid

Launching and recovering this 18ft Wilderness Beaver is made simple by a purpose-built trailer.

ground under the tyres. In theory, a front-wheel drive car will be able to go farther down than its rear-wheel drive counterpart, but in practice this is usually offset by the fact that the rear-wheel drive vehicle will have more potential grip. The reason for this is somewhat complex, caused by a phenomenon called weight transfer. As the drive is taken up, the car tends to sit down at the rear, and lift up at the front. This puts more weight, and hence grip, on the rear wheels and reduces it on the front. Also, the nose-weight of the trailer tends to put more pressure on the rear tyres, and lift the front ones. If you have serious lack of grip with a front-wheel drive car, it also helps if someone presses down on the bonnet over the wheels to increase the weight, but this is risky, as the person can slide off; they should always keep to one side rather than ahead of the car.

If the trailer has a winch, it is unnecessary to reverse far into the water when recovering a boat, as you do not have to float it on. This will usually allow you to keep the car far enough up the slipway to keep a good grip. However, if this is still not enough, or you are without a winch, then you will have to unhitch the trailer and push it out into the water. Using a strong rope, take a turn round the tow-hitch if the slipway has a slope. At least 12mm rope should be used, preferably doubled to reduce the stretch. Keep the length required as short as possible while still keeping the car wheels on solid ground. As you winch or lift the boat on, remember that the front of the trailer will lift when the weight first comes on.

In normal circumstances, however, you should be able to recover the boat with the trailer still connected to the car. In this situation, guide the boat to the back of the trailer, keeping it central and straight. Clever crews can do this by using the boat's engine, but this requires practice otherwise you will damage the bow. It is simpler, if wetter, to have someone in the water, or work from the side of the slipway. With a winch, run the strap or wire out, with the ratchet off, then hook it on to the bow eye. Engage the ratchet, and winch the boat up. As it comes up, make sure it keeps central and straight. With some boat/trailer combinations this is easy. With others, you may have to devise some means of side supports or markers to keep lined up. As the wire comes in, make sure it winds neatly round the drum. The modern webbing strap systems are safer, stronger and neater than the old wires, but can still run off centre as they go round. If this should happen, reverse the ratchet and back off the strap, as it will be crushed, and eventually damaged, if it folds up. Remember to tilt the engine before the boat gets too far up the trailer, to stop it grounding.

Once the boat is right up to the correct forward position on the trailer, it is a good idea to take a turn of rope quickly round the bow eye as a safety measure. You are then ready to tow it up the slip. For safety's sake and to lessen the weight make sure that all the crew are out of the boat when you are doing this. Ensure that no ropes are dangling over the side, as they can get trapped under the wheels. As the boat comes out of the water, someone should be watching underneath from behind to make sure that it is sitting central and square. A certain amount of misalignment can usually be adjusted on level ground, by two or three strong people putting their shoulders under the hull, and bouncing the boat across, but it is better to get it right in the first place. When the boat is still on the slope, remove the bung and let any water drain out – it is surprising how much weight a few gallons of water add to the rig, especially if it is sloshing from side to side.

As soon as you are on level ground, lash the boat down securely for the return trip. While doing this, you should check that all the side-supports or bunks on the trailer are securely tightened and making even contact along the length of the hull. They may have worked loose on the outward journey, or been strained as the boat was launched or recovered. With some boats, particularly those with round-bilge hulls, you may have to drop the rear side-supports when launching and recovering. If so, be careful that the legs do not project too far down and catch on the slipway or kerb; remember to raise them before setting off.

Finally, fit the lighting board, check the lights, and prepare to leave. If the lighting socket on the car has been dunked in the water, it will appreciate a quick dry with a piece of tissue and a squirt of WD-40 to reduce the risk of a failure on the motorway or in the dark.

Trailer maintenance

If your boat's trailer has performed satisfactorily throughout this season, the temptation is always to leave well alone, and hope that it will do the same next year. In some cases, you will be lucky and it will but, more likely, you could face costly and potentially dangerous breakdowns.

The maintenance necessary to keep your investment safe and sound is not complicated, and can be carried out by any owner. However, if you are in any doubt about your capabilities, your local trailer centre can easily do the work for you. As with all maintenance work, we tend to put it off for as long as possible, but most of the jobs are better done before winter if they are to be effective. So, set aside a day before the frosts set in, and you will be able to set out confidently on next year's trips.

We still tend to think of a trailer purely in terms of its boat-carrying function but, first and foremost, it must be remembered that this is a vehicle travelling on roads and its safety, road-worthiness and legality are the first priorities. Modern powerful cars allow us to tow bigger boats at faster speeds, while the motorway systems in the UK and Europe encourage you to undertake longer and more ambitious trips. These put ever-increasing demands on the trailer and require it to be maintained to the highest standard. The consequences of breakdowns are not just inconvenient, they can endanger the lives of yourself and other road-users, so the first area to tackle is the running gear.

Tyres

The obvious starting point for any trailer are the tyres. Treat these like a car tyre, and inspect for damage or wear. The comparatively short journeys mean that tread wear is unlikely to be a major problem, but it can still occur if you have badly aligned wheels, or a binding brake; so check using the normal tread depth criteria for your car. It may sound obvious, but if the trailer is new to you, just confirm that all tyres are the same pattern: either radial or cross-ply. Regardless of the tyres on the towing vehicle, trailer tyres can be either pattern, but those on each axle must be the same, and all four must be the same on double-axle trailers.

Damage to the tyre walls is likely to be common; it is caused by clipping kerbs on the road, or walls and steps around the launch site, so inspect for this on both the outer and inner walls. Also check that the tyre has not been fouling the mudguard or its fixings. Suspensions will flex considerably when travelling over bumps at speed, and what appears adequate clearance at rest could be insufficient underway.

Check the tyre pressures against the manufacturer's recommendations. Any significant variation could indicate a slow puncture or defective valve. Check for grease on the tyre from the bearings and remove stones from the tread.

A modern Roller Coaster trailer from Indespension. Features include pivoting rollers for easy recovery; braked hubs; winch with strap, hook and telescopic post; hand-brake; telescopic coupling and adjustable jockey wheel.

If the boat is not going to be moved throughout the winter, you should jack the trailer up to relieve the load on the tyres and suspension, or rotate the wheels periodically. This will prevent the tyres from perishing in one position.

Brakes

Serious wear of the brake-linings will be unlikely in normal use, but if they have been binding, this could be increased. Remove the wheel and check for wear on the linings; also look for excessive lining dust inside the drum, and clean this out carefully. Check for grease inside the drum from the bearings. If grease is on the linings, the only answer is to replace them as, even if they appear clean, the ingrained grease will migrate to the surface when they are applied and get hot. Always replace both shoes in the drum and both sets of shoes on an axle all at the same time, otherwise uneven braking will occur. Check the brake adjustment, both at the drums and in the actuating linkage. To do this, replace the wheel then start with the drums first. Tighten up the adjuster one click at a time, spinning the wheel each time, until the brakes lock on to the drum. Then back-off the adjuster two clicks. Repeat this on the other wheel.

Having adjusted each drum equally, move to the actuating linkage. Check first for any wear or rust and grease each moving part, including the nipple on the outer cable casings where fitted. Check adjusting nuts and lock nuts. Lightly grease the threads on the adjusters to prevent corrosion. Adjust the linkage to take up any slack in the cable or rods with the hand-brake released. For precise instructions on adjusting and setting up the particular brakes on your trailer, refer to the manufacturer's manual. If in doubt, ask the dealer to set up the brakes correctly.

Bearings

These are the major moving parts on any trailer, yet are usually treated as out of sight, out of mind. They should be packed with grease, but continuous immersion in water, particularly sea water, will dilute this, wash it out, and reduce its effectiveness. Bearings should be checked for wear with the wheel in place and the trailer jacked up. To do this, spin the wheel, and listen for roughness, or rattles, having first checked that the brake shoes are clear of the drum. Then, hold the wheel top and bottom, and rock it gently to and fro. If the bearings are correctly adjusted, there should be just the slightest movement. Any more than this indicates wear or mis-adjustment.

With the wheel off, check the bearings. If the trailer has been lightly used and the grease looks good, plus there is no sign of rust on the bearing, add more grease as necessary to fill the housing, then replace the wheel. Do not overpack the housing, as the grease will be forced out into the brake-drums. If there is little grease or it looks discoloured, you should replace it with fresh grease. Check the bearings, if there are signs of rust in these, they should be replaced. This is the cheapest form of preventative maintenance you can apply, and one that will ensure trouble-free towing next year. If the old bearings are only slightly rusted, they can be packed up and carried as spares in the event of an emergency.

Check the split pin holding the castellated nut; replace it if it looks worn or damaged. The precise tightening sequence for the bearing depends on its type. Most trailer bearings are of the taper type. To adjust these, tighten the castellated nut while spinning the wheel, until a clear resistance to motion is felt. Then loosen off the nut just enough to release the resistance and insert the split pin. At this point you should feel no end-play. Ball race bearings should be tightened enough to ensure that the inner races are seated against the centre spacer, then the split pin inserted in the nut.

Suspensions

Most suspensions will be of either the sealed rubber block type, such as made by Indespension, or leaf springs. Check fixing bolts for all types, and check for loose movement in the nylon bushes at the end of the sealed unit type. Check for broken springs in the leaf type, and check that both wheels are not leaning in or out, or that one wheel is lower than the other. In either of the latter cases, replacement may be necessary; you should check with your stockist. In general, suspension units are reliable and long lasting, and will rarely need replacing.

If the boat is going to be left on its trailer over the winter, the rubber block type of suspension can slowly distort; it is beneficial to jack the trailer up partly or completely to relieve the load. Make sure that it is left securely chocked up on blocks. This also acts as an effective deterrent to the opportunist thief, but not the professional, who will bring along a jack. Remove a wheel to beat him!

Tow-hitch

This simple and reliable piece of equipment is the key link between car and trailer and needs routine attention. Check for damage to the components, and for free movement of these. Check the securing bolts. Turn it over through 180° and check the lock in the ball. Grease this together with the other moving parts. Check that there is no movement of the hitch when on the ball. If there is, you should replace the head. If the trailer is being left out in the open, spray the hitch with rust-proofer, then cover loosely with a polythene carrier bag to keep off the rain, but maintain air flow to prevent condensation. Check the brake actuater and the hand-brake, particularly the release pawl, and grease the latter.

While you are at this end of the trailer, take the opportunity to check the nose-weight of the rig with the boat in its normal position. If you have moved equipment on board during the season, or fitted a new engine, you may have altered the hitch load, and possibly seriously affected the handling on the road. The recommended minimum is a 110lb (50kg) nose-weight, more if your vehicle will allow it. The owner's manual will give you the maximum figure for your car, and the bathroom scales will confirm the weight. Put the scales under the jockey wheel with a board to spread the load.

Jockey wheel

The jockey wheel is subjected to a continuous bombardment from road dirt, and is then dunked in the water at every launch. Consequently, the interior thread gradually rusts up, unseen and unnoticed, until it finally seizes. To avoid this, unwind the thread completely, remove the inner section, then clean and grease both parts. Spin the wheel to check that it turns freely, and grease if necessary. Jockey wheels have a habit of dropping down every now and then as you are driving along the road; a quick burst at 60mph usually destroys the simple bearing, so check this, and replace it now.

Lights

The lighting board is best removed after every time you use it. While it is off, check the glass lenses, and the bulbs and connectors inside. Check the cable for damage and chafe. Wrap any sections that have started to chafe with insulating tape. Check the multi-pin plug for damage. Clean the contacts inside, and spray with de-ruster. You can buy an ingenious abrasive probe, with male and female adaptors, to clean the contacts thoroughly, otherwise emery paper will do. The same treatment applies to the socket on the car. Check the reflectors on the trailer for damage.

Chassis

Most modern trailers will have a galvanised frame. Check this for major damage, such as distortion or bending, and for minor chips and knocks. The latter can be touched up to prevent rusting. Unless yours is an old trailer, corrosion inside the box sections is unlikely. However, any sign of rust in here means that you should have the trailer professionally inspected. Check all the nuts and bolts of the chassis and axle assembly for tightness. Then inspect the rollers and side-supports for damage and free movement. Make sure that the supports are still snugly fitting the hull of the boat. During the course of a year's towing these can gradually work their way down, allowing the boat to rock on the keel.

Winch and straps

Check the winch for damage and free operation, and grease the moving parts. Pay particular attention to the ratchet and pawl, which can be easily damaged. Unwind the rope, wire or strap completely, and check for damage or chafe. A frayed wire or rope should be replaced, and this might be the opportunity to replace the winch with a model that will take a nylon webbing strap. This system is far superior to the other two.

At the same time, check your hold-down straps for damage or chafe. The modern ratchet strap is by far the best system to use here, being strong and positive, but you should still check them over. It is also a good idea to wash the webbing in warm soapy water. During the course of the year, road grit and sea salt will be embedded in the straps, reducing their life, and risking damage to the finish of the boat.

Tow-bar

The tow-bar is held on to the car by surprisingly few bolts; these should be checked, together with those securing the ball-hitch. The latter should give no trouble, but it is still worth checking, particularly if you have had a rear end shunt, or have backed into a wall. While you are here, check the wiring to the tow-hitch for damage, and check that the repeater light or buzzer is working.

9 | *Inland Waterways of Great Britain*

aving decided on your boat, you now want to know where you can take it. In this chapter we list the principal navigable waterways of Great Britain and give a brief entry on each one.

We describe what you can expect to find in each waterway, and the principal restrictions on size of boat that can navigate it – length, beam, draught and height. However, we should stress that this information is for general guidance only. If you should decide to navigate any particular waterway, you should consult a more detailed guide or map, or contact the telephone number given. Also, the navigable status of some waterways may have changed by the time you read this book. Restoration projects are opening or extending some waterways, while closures are restricting others, so up-to-date information should be sought before setting out, or making detailed plans for a cruise.

Because the canal system was originally developed before metric measurement was introduced into Britain, dimensions for canals and narrowboats are always given in Imperial measurements. In this section, therefore, metric equivalents are inappropriate and will not be given.

History of the system

Before describing our inland waterways of today, it will be useful to have a brief look at the history of the system. This makes a fascinating story in its own right, and charts the development of our modern industrialised nation.

The rivers of Great Britain have been used for transporting goods and materials for a thousand years, and our principal cities have grown up on their banks. However, with a river nature dictates where you can carry these goods, and navigation is subject to floods or drought. Two hundred years ago, roads were not the smooth, wide, flat highways that we know today. They were little more than cart tracks – bumpy, rutted and narrow, and virtually impassable in winter. The heaviest load was limited to no more than a ton, and delicate goods were likely to be damaged before they reached their destination.

The breakthrough came with the canals. These could be dug in any direction, almost regardless of the terrain, thus linking the new centres of prosperity, industry and raw materials. They allowed carriage of loads up to 20 or 30 tons, at a steady, predictable speed, with little or no damage to the goods. An excellent example of this were the canals servicing the potteries of the Midlands, such as Wedgwood. The canal allowed the delivery of the huge quantities of clay required for pottery production and enabled the delicate finished products to be carried undamaged to the markets of Manchester, Bath, London, and all the other major cities of the day.

The golden age of canal building was the last part of the 18th century and the beginning of the 19th century. Entrepreneurs, speculators and local communities scrambled to dig their own canals. The skilled engineers who designed and constructed them, including Telford, Brindley and Rennie, were in huge demand as towns vied to be included in the network. A canal was like a motorway of today, bringing population, employment and prosperity. However, the canal was restricted by one thing, its speed, and its maximum dimensions. When they were first built, the only motive power was the horse. The maximum load this could comfortably pull, at 2–3mph, was deemed to be around 35 tons. Thus the standard sized barge was developed, measuring 70ft long and 7ft wide. Once the dimensions were fixed, locks and bridges were built to match this specification, and most new canals had to follow suit if they were to link with the rest of the system.

No sooner had the canal age blossomed than it was overtaken by another technical development. The advent of steam power was followed by the discovery that if you put your cart on rails, then the amount of goods they could carry, and their speed, increased tenfold. The railway had arrived.

Many of the same engineers turned their skills to developing this new form of transport; often parallel to the routes they had chosen 20 years earlier for the canals. Trains could travel at the remarkable speed of 30mph and more. The load they could carry was limited only by the number of trucks you could add on behind the engine; also the railway had no locks to slow traffic down. Unlike canals, it did not freeze up in winter, and it could be used just as easily at night. The future of the canal network for commercial purposes was doomed to slow but eventual decay.

The canals struggled on into the 20th century, with schemes to double the width of the locks giving some of them a new lease of life, but the final blow was delivered by the development of the motor vehicle. Most of the waterway system was nationalised in 1948, but, by this time, less than a third of the original canals were still navigable, and many of these were in a decrepit state of repair. In fact, it is surprising that so many of them still survived, but the tenacity of the canal is due mainly to the complex Act of Parliament needed to set it up. Once a navigation has been established, it is an involved process to close it down. Most of the railway companies had solved this problem by the simple expedient of buying the near moribund canals and providing only token maintenance to comply with the Act. The other contributing factor was the sheer quality of the original design and workmanship which is a tribute to the skills of the early engineers. Simple engineering and construction techniques outlasted the men that built and operated them.

The late 1940s were a watershed for the canals. As their commercial use declined, a small band of pioneering private boaters started to take trips on them. These enthusiasts established the principle that a canal can be used for pleasure purposes. They banded together to form the Inland Waterways Association (IWA), a body dedicated to the preservation and use of our navigable waterways. Their struggle to keep navigation open and to expand their use is a fascinating story, well documented in a number of books.

Today, most boats using canals are pleasure craft, creating a thriving holiday and leisure industry. At the same time, modern enthusiasts have taken up the cause of re-opening derelict waterways. This reached its first peak in the 1970s, with many of the rivers and canals open today owing their present life to these devotees. Now a second wave of restorations has been funded by cash from the Heritage Lottery Fund, and the Millennium Commission. Details of these projects are included at the end of this section, but most canals have their own societies, with details available from the IWA.

The development of pleasure boating on our major rivers followed a slightly different course. As early as the 1890s, the Thames was alive with boats on summer weekends and ironically, it was the train that contributed much to this. By taking the working people of London quickly and cheaply out of the city, it promoted the expansion of such riverside venues as Maidenhead and Henley. This popularity has continued to this day, though the boats are more likely to be cruisers with accommodation for weekend stays or longer.

The other key area for pleasure boating was the Norfolk Broads. These wide, placid rivers and lakes proved perfect to enable novices to take to the water, and a thriving hire-cruiser industry grew up between the wars. Nelson first learnt to sail here, and it is true to say that probably more of his countrymen have followed his steps here than on any other part of our system. Their remoteness from the rest of the network means that the Broads are more populated by hire-craft than private boats, but they are still a beautiful area to cruise.

When the canals were built, some were joined with existing rivers, and today much of the system is still linked. However, some of the key canals are narrow ones which means that you can only cover the whole of the network with a narrow-beam craft. With a boat wider than 7ft you will normally be restricted to one waterway or part of the system, unless you travel out and round by sea. This does not usually prove to be a problem, as the continually changing nature of a river means that many people spend their entire boating life in one area. Bridge height also governs the waters you can travel, which is why we have included this in the details of the waterways that follow.

You will also find that several of the Northern Waterways have locks that

Whilst the canals were initially built for commercial cargo carrying, they are now almost exclusively used for pleasure boats. But modern owners still wish to remember the heritage of the waterways. This is a replica of the original boatman's cabin, built in a modern narrowboat and decorated with traditional roses and castles paintings.

are only 62ft long, meaning that to completely cover the whole network, you will need a narrowboat that is no longer than 62ft.

In the following pages we have covered the waterways that are open to full navigation. There are many more that are under restoration, or partly open, and for full details of these, we recommend *Inland Waterways of Great Britain* by Jane Cumberlidge.

Quick reference list of waterways

Some river systems, and river and canal navigations, have been grouped together.

r = river
n = narrow canal (7ft beam)
b = broad canal (over 7ft beam)
i = isolated from network

England and Wales

Aire & Calder Navigation, **b**
Ancholme, **r**
Ashby-de-la-Zouch Canal, **n**
Ashton Canal, **n**
Avon, Warwickshire, **r**
Basingstoke Canal, **b**
Birmingham Canal Navigations (BCN), **n**
Bridgewater Canal, **b**
Bridgwater & Taunton Canal, **b**, **i**
Calder & Hebble Canal, **b**
Cam, **r**
Chelmer & Blackwater Navigation, **r**, **i**
Chesterfield Canal, **b**
Coventry Canal, **n**
Dee, **r**
Derwent, **r**
Exeter Ship Canal, **b**
Fossdyke & Witham Navigation, **b**
Gloucester & Sharpness Canal, **b**
Grand Union Canal, **b**
Grand Western Canal, **n**
Huddersfield Canal, **n**, **b**
Idle, **r**
Kennet & Avon Navigation, **r**, **b**
Lancaster Canal, **b**, **i**
Lee & Stort, **r**
Leeds & Liverpool Canal, **b**
Llangollen Canal, **n**
Macclesfield Canal, **n**
Manchester Ship Canal, **b**
Medway, **r**, **i**
Middle Level Navigations, **b**

Monmouth & Brecon Canal, **b**, **i**
Montgomery Canal, **n**
Nene, **r**
Norfolk & Suffolk Broads, **r**, **i**
Ouse, Great, **r**
Ouse, Yorkshire, **r**
Oxford Canal, **n**
Peak Forest Canal, **n**
Regent's Canal, **b**
Rochdale Canal, **b**
Severn, **r**
Sheffield & South Yorkshire Navigation, **b**
Shropshire Union Canal, **n**
Staffordshire & Worcestershire Canal, **n**
Stourbridge Canal, **n**
Stratford-upon-Avon Canal, **n**
Thames, **r**
Trent, **r**
Trent & Mersey Canal, **n**
Wey, **r**
Worcester & Birmingham Canal, **n**

Scotland

Caledonian Canal, **b**, **i**
Crinan Canal **b**, **i**
Forth and Clyde Canal, **b**, **i**
Union Canal, **b**, **i**

Ireland

Ballinamoore & Ballyconnell Canal, **b**
Barrow, **r**
Grand Canal, **b**
Lough Erne and River, **r**
Royal Canal, **b**
Shannon, **r**

The principal Inland Waterways of England, Wales and Scotland

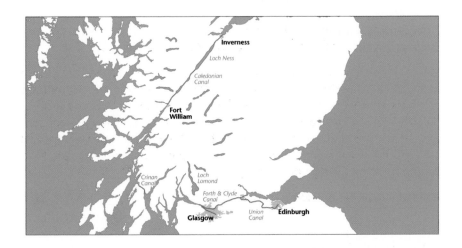

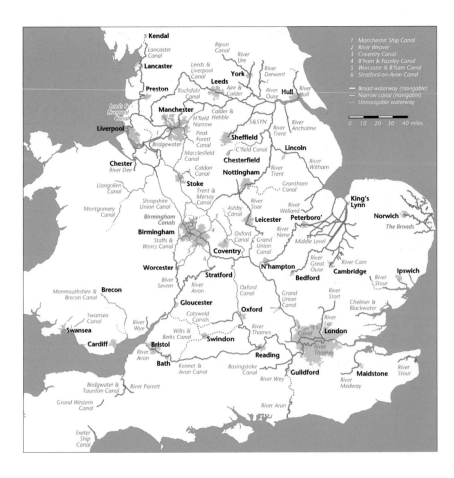

AIRE & CALDER NAVIGATION

Length: 41 miles, from Goole to Wakefield
Locks: 17
Maximum dimensions of vessel:
Length: 140ft *Beam*: 17ft 8in *Draught*: 6ft 10in *Height*: 12ft 2in

Still in commercial use, this waterway is part of the system of canals and rivers that links north-east centres of industry, and forms our only significant commercial network. Large barges and tugs can be met on these waterways, but they can still be navigated by private craft provided you are equipped with VHF radio, and use reasonable caution. They provide an essential link between the eastern end of the Leeds & Liverpool Canal and the rest of the system from the Trent southwards.

Contact: 01977 554351.

RIVER ANCHOLME

Length: 19 miles, from South Ferriby to Bishopbridge
Locks: 1
Maximum dimensions of vessel:
Length: 50ft *Beam*: 12ft *Draught*: 3–6ft *Height*: 11ft 6in

A short stretch of river, running from the south side of the River Humber, and used mainly for drainage purposes. Unnavigable in times of flood.

Contact: 01522 512927.

ASHBY CANAL

Length: 22 miles from Marston to Snarestone
Locks: 1
Maximum dimensions of vessel:
Length: 70ft *Beam*: 7ft *Draught*: 2ft 6in *Height*: 6ft 6in

Running from the Coventry Canal with only one lock – at the entrance – this canal passes through pleasant countryside that includes Bosworth Field. Originally it extended to Moira, and there are plans to extend it this far again.

Contact: 01283 790236.

ASHTON CANAL

Length: 6¼ miles
Locks: 18
Maximum dimensions of vessel:
Length: 70ft *Beam*: 7ft *Draught*: 2ft 9in *Height*: 6ft 9in

This short canal links Manchester with the derelict Huddersfield Canal (being restored), and the Peak Forest Canal. It forms a key part of the Cheshire Ring, and was re-opened as a result of one of the earliest voluntary restoration projects in the 1970s. A special key is required for the gate padlocks.

Contact: 0161 819 5847.

RIVER AVON

Length: 44 miles, from Stratford to Tewkesbury
Locks: 17
Maximum dimensions of vessel:
Length: 70ft *Beam*: 12ft 6in *Draught*: 3ft *Height*: 6ft

Another fine example of a voluntary restoration project, or in fact two separate projects, the river navigation is one of the oldest in the country, but much of it had fallen derelict by the 1940s. The Lower Avon was re-opened in 1964, then the Upper Avon was re-opened by the Queen Mother in 1974. It now forms part of the Warwickshire Ring. Still divided for ownership and administrative purposes into Upper and Lower sections, each with their own management trust, the river is a delightful waterway, peaceful and unspoilt, with the added bonus of Stratford-upon-Avon at its eastern end.

Contact: *Lower*: 01386 552517 *Upper*: 01386 870526.

BASINGSTOKE CANAL

Length: 31 miles from River Wey to Greywell
Locks: 29
Maximum dimensions of vessel:
Length: 70ft *Beam*: 13ft 6in *Draught*: 2ft 6in *Height*: 6–9ft

Running from the River Wey into the Surrey and Hampshire countryside, this canal was derelict for many years, but re-opened after a voluntary restoration project, in 1991. Water shortages restrict the number of boat movements, and there is conflict with nature conservationists who want to see it revert to a 'natural' state. The present limit of navigation is the collapsed Greywell Tunnel.

Contact: 01252 370073.

BIRMINGHAM CANAL NAVIGATIONS (BCN)

Length: over 120 miles
Locks: 190
Maximum dimensions of vessel:
Length: 70ft *Beam*: 7ft *Draught*: 2ft 6in *Height*: 6ft 6in

Running round and through Birmingham and the Midlands, this network provides a fascinating opportunity to look at our industrial heritage. Much of it runs through derelict or run-down areas, but a section in the centre of Birmingham has been the subject of an ambitious waterfront restoration project. The network forms part of the through route from the South to the North-West.

Contact: 0121 506 1300.

BRIDGEWATER CANAL

Length: 28 miles from Wigan to Preston Brook
Locks: None
Maximum dimensions of vessel:
Length: 70ft *Beam*: 14ft 9in *Draught*: 4ft *Height*: 11ft

The first canal of the new era, this famous waterway was built by the third Duke of Bridgewater to carry coal from his mines at Worsley, where there were another 40 miles of canal underground. It is also renowned for the Barton Swing Aqueduct. Bridgewater links the western end of the Leeds & Liverpool Canal with the system, and forms part of the Cheshire Ring.

Contact: 0161 872 2411.

BRIDGWATER & TAUNTON CANAL

Length: 14^1/$_2$ miles from Bridgwater to Taunton
Locks: 6
Maximum dimensions of vessel:
Length: 50ft *Beam*: 10ft *Draught*: 3ft *Height*: 6ft 6in

Subject of a restoration project, only one low bridge now requires to be raised. This will then open up a delightful stretch of water, which may eventually link with 200 miles of the Somerset Levels which are currently being investigated for possible navigation. Trailer boats can launch at Taunton.

Contact: 01873 830328.

CALDER & HEBBLE CANAL

Length: 21½ miles from Sowerby Bridge to the Aire & Calder Canal
Locks: 39
Maximum dimensions of vessel:
Length: 57ft 6in *Beam*: 14ft 2in *Draught*: 3ft 9in *Height*: 9ft

Running up into the Pennines, the lower reaches of this canal are industrial, and still have some commercial traffic, but you quickly emerge into superb countryside, with the canal buildings and locks built from the local stone.

Contact: 01977 554351.

RIVER CAM

Length: 14 miles from the River Ouse to Cambridge
Locks: 3
Maximum dimensions of vessel:
Length: 100ft *Beam*: 14ft *Draught*: 4ft *Height*: 9ft

Part of the Fenland Navigations, the Cam is a delightful river. Cambridge is internationally famous, and well worth the visit. Abandon your cruiser and take to a punt to explore the backwaters, or Backs, behind the colleges. The Fenland Navigations are connected to the main system by the short Northampton Arm, but this is only narrow beam. Otherwise, you have to come in by sea. You will then have almost 250 miles of varied and uncrowded waterways to cruise, or you can leave your boat permanently here. As we describe under the River Great Ouse, there is a proposal for a broad-beam connection between the Fenland Waterways and the Grand Union Canal, between Bedford and Milton Keynes.

Contact: 01223 58977.

CHELMER & BLACKWATER NAVIGATION

**Length: 14 miles from Chelmsford to the sea
Locks: 13
Maximum dimensions of vessel:
Length: 60ft *Beam*: 16ft *Draught*: 2ft *Height*: 6ft**

An isolated stretch of canalised river, this connects to the sea at Heybridge Basin, and is still navigable. It is a pretty river, mostly known only to local boat-owners. The draught, at 2ft, is the lowest statutory depth of any navigation, and led to the development of a unique design of wide, flat barge.

Contact: 01245 222025.

CHESTERFIELD CANAL

**Length: 45 miles from Chesterfield to the River Trent,
31 miles navigable
Locks: 65 (46 restored)
Maximum dimensions of vessel:
Length: 72ft *Beam*: 7ft *Draught*: 2ft 6in *Height*: 7ft**

This joins the River Trent at West Stockwith, and can only be reached from here by well-found craft able to handle strong river currents. At the time of writing, it is restored to the eastern end of the collapsed Norwood Tunnel, and some stretches to Chesterfield can also be navigated.

Contact: 01636 704481.

COVENTRY CANAL

**Length: 38 miles
Locks: 13
Maximum dimensions of vessel:
Length: 70ft *Beam*: 7ft *Draught*: 2ft 6in *Height*: 6ft 6in**

This links the Trent & Mersey with the North Oxford Canal, and forms part of the Midlands Ring. Apart from one main flight, it is a substantially lock-free canal in some pleasant countryside.

Contact: 01283 790236.

RIVER DEE

Length: 12 miles from Chester to Farndon
Locks: None
Maximum dimensions of vessel:
Length: no limit *Beam*: no limit *Draught*: 3ft *Height*: 10ft

Another isolated waterway, the Dee winds its way through pleasant country-side and is worth a visit by trailer boaters. Its estuary was a very old naviga-tion, but the river is now cut off from this by the weir at Chester. Craft up to 2ft in draught can, in fact, sail over the weir at the top of spring tides, in theory gaining access to the Shropshire Union Canal via the Chester Lock, but, in practice, this is difficult.

Contact: 01925 653999.

RIVER DERWENT

Length: 21 miles from the Yorkshire Ouse to Stamford Bridge
Locks: 2
Maximum dimensions of vessel:
Length: 55ft *Beam*: 14ft *Height*: 6–10ft *Draught*: 4ft

The Derwent is navigable for its first 15 miles from the barrage at Barmby to Sutton-on-Derwent; the original navigation continued for another 23 miles, but at present the rights to continued navigation have been the subject of protracted legal wrangling between the Inland Waterways Association and the landowners on either side, in a test case that could have repercussions throughout the rest of the system where old navigation rights exist.

Contact: 01904 659570.

EXETER SHIP CANAL

Length: 5 miles from the estuary of the Exe to Exeter
Locks: 2
Maximum dimensions of vessel:
Length: 122ft *Beam*: 25ft *Draught*: 10ft 6in *Height*: no limit

Begun in 1563, this was the first canal to be dug in England since Roman times. It was once a busy commercial waterway, and for pleasure-boat use, the tolls are still high.

Contact: 01392 74306.

FOSSDYKE & WITHAM NAVIGATION

Length: 45 miles from the River Trent to the Wash
Locks: 4
Maximum dimensions of vessel:
Length: 74ft 6in *Beam*: 15ft 2in *Draught*: 5ft *Height*: 8ft l0in

Strictly speaking, this is two navigations. The Fossdyke is one of Britain's oldest waterways, being cut by the Romans in about AD 120 to link the Trent with the River Witham. They pass through Lincoln and Boston on the way to the sea.

Contact: 01636 704481.

GLOUCESTER & SHARPNESS CANAL

Length: 17 miles from Sharpness to Gloucester
Locks: 2
Maximum dimensions of vessel:
Length: 144ft *Beam*: 22ft *Draught*: 10ft *Height*: no limit

This is a ship canal, cut to avoid the often treacherous lower reaches of the tidal Severn, including its fearsome bore, or tidal wave. It enables ships to reach Gloucester docks and is still used commercially. There are 16 swing bridges, all of which are manned. Private vessels can use the canal with care. It is connected to the now disused Stroudwater Canal and thence the disused Thames & Severn Canal both subject to major restoration projects.

Contact: 01452 319000.

GRAND UNION CANAL

**Length: 137 miles from London to Birmingham, plus 42 miles
to Leicester, and the 35 mile Northampton Arm
Locks: over 250 on all sections
Maximum dimensions of vessel:**
Length: 70ft *Beam*: 12ft 6in (London–Birmingham) 7ft (Leicester)
Draught: 3ft 6in *Height*: 7ft

The Grand Union was the major artery of the canal system. It linked London and Birmingham, with further arms going to Leicester, Aylesbury and Northampton. Much of it was originally 14ft beam, and more was widened in 1932 in an attempt to improve movement of cargo. This was meant to allow the use of wider barges, and to allow two narrow barges to pass through a lock at once. However, key sections, including part of the Leicester Arm, and the Northampton Arm remained narrow, strangling the trade. In theory, craft up to 14ft can navigate, but in fact 12ft 6in is the practical maximum, and then only on certain sections. The canal also includes the Regent's Canal, which runs through north London, and links with the River Lee. At its lower end, it joins the Thames at Brentford, allowing boats from the Thames to enter the canal system. Along its length, the Grand Union offers a variety of countryside and features – including the Blisworth Tunnel and Hatton Flight – making it both varied and rewarding.

Contact: *North*: **0121 506 1300.**
Central: **01908 302500.**
South: **0207 985 7780.**

GRAND WESTERN CANAL

**Length: 10 miles from Loudwell to Tiverton
Locks: None
Maximum dimensions of vessel:**
Length: no limit *Beam*: 7ft *Draught*: 2ft 6in *Height*: 7ft

Originally connected to Taunton and thence Bridgwater, only 10 miles now remain. These are the subject of an enthusiastic restoration programme, fully supported by Devon County Council, who see the canal as an important amenity.

Contact: 01392 77977.

HUDDERSFIELD CANAL

Length: Huddersfield Narrow: 40 miles from Dukinfield Junction to Huddersfield. Huddersfield Broad: 4 miles from Huddersfield to the Calder & Hebble Navigation.
Locks: 74 narrow, 9 broad
Maximum dimensions of vessel:
Narrow Section: *Length*: **70ft** *Beam*: **7ft**
Broad Section: *Length*: **58ft 6in (60ft for narrowboats)** *Beam*: **14ft**

Strictly two separate canals, the Huddersfield Broad is also known as Sir John Ramsden's Canal, and links the town to the Calder & Hebble. It has always been navigable for its short 4 mile length. The Huddersfield Narrow, however, was derelict for many years, but was re-opened in one of the celebrated Millennium Restorations. Completed in 2001, its 74 locks straddle the Pennines, cutting through the summit in the Standedge Tunnel, at 5698 yards, the longest on the British waterways system. The length of the Broad Locks will restrict the size of narrowboats that can carry on round the Pennine Ring and the Rochdale Canal to 60ft.

Contact: 0161 819 5847.

RIVER IDLE

Length: 10 miles from Bawtry to the River Trent
Locks: None
Maximum dimensions of vessel:
Length: **no limit** *Beam*: **18ft** *Draught*: **2ft 6in** *Height*: **9ft**

This runs from the River Trent at West Stockwith to Bawtry. Entry is by a sluice, which only opens at high water. The shallows at Misson can be as low as 18 inches. Tolls for opening the sluice are expensive, but the local boat club organises regular cruises to maintain the navigation.

Contact: 01543 444161.

KENNET & AVON NAVIGATION

Length: 86½ miles from Reading to Bristol
Locks: 86
Maximum dimensions of vessel:
Length: 72ft *Beam*: 13ft 10in *Draught*: 3ft *Height*: 7ft

One of the three great trans-England navigations, the Kennet & Avon Navigation links London with Bristol via the Thames, the Kennet, the Avon and the Kennet & Avon Canal. Its prosperity was quickly challenged by the Great Western Railway that ran alongside, and navigation finally ceased in 1951. Since then, one of the best-organised and successful restoration campaigns raised over £2,000,000 and culminated in an opening by Her Majesty The Queen in 1990.

The canal runs through superb countryside, and has two notable engineering features: the Caen Hill flight at Devizes, with 29 locks, 16 of them in a dead-straight line, and the Dundas Aqueduct. The entry into Bath is one of the most spectacular on the system. Because of its broad beam and good headroom, the canal is accessible to many river cruisers from the Thames and Avon. Previously, water-shortages on the top pound caused severe restrictions to navigation, but these have now been solved by a back-pumping scheme.

Contact: 01380 722859.

LANCASTER CANAL

Length: 42 miles from Preston to Tewitfield
Locks: None
Maximum dimensions of vessel:
Length: 72ft *Beam*: 14ft 6in *Draught*: 3ft *Height*: 8ft

Once an isolated canal, this originally ran from Kendal in Cumbria to Preston. It was then intended to join the Leeds & Liverpool Canal, but this was never carried out. There are presently 42 miles navigable, plus a link with the sea at Glasson Basin. However, in 2002, the short Ribble Link joined it to the rest of the system, and there are also plans to re-open the Northern Section to Kendal.

Contact: 01524 751888.

RIVERS LEE & STORT

Length: 40 miles from the Thames to Bishop's Stortford
Locks: 36
Maximum dimensions of vessel:
Length: 86ft *Beam*: 13ft 4in *Draught*: 3ft *Height*: 6ft

The River Lee joins the Thames at Limehouse Basin and Bow Creek and, for the first few miles, it runs through depressing East London scenery. But it quickly reaches pleasant, open countryside, on its way to Hertford and Bishop's Stortford, the latter via the particularly attractive River Stort. It also links to the rest of the national system via the Regent's Canal.

Contact: 01932 788375.

LEEDS & LIVERPOOL CANAL

Length: 127 miles from Leeds to Liverpool
Locks: 91
Maximum dimensions of vessel:
Length: 62ft *Beam*: 14ft *Draught*: 3ft 6in *Height*: 7ft 6in

Three trans-Pennine canals were built, and the Leeds & Liverpool was until recently the last remaining navigable one, but the others, the Rochdale & Huddersfield, were restored in 2001 and 2002. It is a majestic canal, rising high into the hills, and travelling across some of the magnificent moorland made famous by Charlotte Brontë. The locks may be broad but, by a quirk, they were made to a length of 62ft rather than the universal 70ft. Narrowboats up to 62ft can just negotiate these by going in diagonally. Features include the Bingley Five-Rise: five locks interlinked in a staircase rather than a flight; and the awesome Wigan Flight. The Burnley Straight is an embankment that runs for 1256 yards above the rooftops of Burnley, and had to be drained on occasions during the war for fear it would be bombed and flood the town.

Contact: East: 01274 611303 West: 01942 242239.

LLANGOLLEN CANAL

Length: 46 miles
Locks: 21
Maximum dimensions of vessel:
Length: 70ft *Beam*: 7ft *Draught*: 2ft–2ft 3in

The Llangollen is probably our most popular cruising canal, and justly so. More correctly, it should be described as the Welsh Branch of the Shropshire Union Canal, because that is what it joins. It contains some of the most spectacular scenery on the system, as it winds up from the fertile Cheshire Plain into the mountains of Wales. It is the engineering feats, however, that rank it alongside the wonders of the waterway world. These include tunnels blasted out of rocks, and staircase flights of locks, but the Pontcysyllte Aqueduct wins the prize: 126ft high, and 1007ft long, this strides out across the valley of the Dee, carrying the canal in a cast-iron trough that is little wider than your boat. As you stand at the tiller, just inches from a sheer drop, the feeling is awesome. And, incredibly, the canal then turns through 90° so you can look back and get the full effect! The Llangollen is shallow, and vessels with draughts over 2ft will not get up the last stretch after the aqueduct.

Contact: 01244 390372.

MACCLESFIELD CANAL

Length: 26½ miles
Locks: 13
Maximum dimensions of vessel:
Length: 70ft *Beam*: 7ft *Draught*: 2ft 9in *Height*: 6ft 6in

The Macclesfield links the Trent & Mersey with the Peak Forest Canal, and is part of the Cheshire Ring. It runs under the shadow of the Peak District through green and unspoilt countryside. A special feature are the stone roving bridges that allowed the horse to change sides of the canal without untying the rope.

Contact: 01782 785703.

The Llangollen Canal is justifiably one of our most popular cruising waterways, and the Pontcysyllte Aqueduct is one of the wonders of the canal system. 1007ft long, and 126ft high, it strides across the Valley of the Dee. All crew should remain in the cockpit while crossing.

MANCHESTER SHIP CANAL

Length: 26 miles
Locks: 4
Maximum dimensions of vessel:
Length: 600ft *Beam*: 65ft *Draught*: 30ft *Height*: 70ft

The Manchester Ship Canal was not designed for use by pleasure craft, but the decline during recent years in commercial shipping has led the company to look at the possibility of encouraging greater use by private boats. Seaworthy craft wishing to navigate the canal should telephone first.

Contact: 0151 327 1461.

RIVER MEDWAY

Length: 43 miles from Tonbridge to Sheerness
Locks: 10
Maximum dimensions of vessel:
Length: 80ft *Beam*: 18ft 6in *Draught*: 4ft *Height*: 8ft 6in

The Medway runs through Kent to the Thames Estuary. Its lower reaches are tidal and not particularly attractive, but the 17 miles above Allington Lock, through Maidstone to Tonbridge, are very pleasant; there is a good population of private cruisers.

Contact: 01903 832000.

MIDDLE LEVEL NAVIGATIONS

Length: 90 miles
Locks: 7
Maximum dimensions of vessel:
Length: 80ft *Beam*: 11ft 6in *Draught*: 2ft 3in *Height*: 6–7ft

The principal purpose of these channels is drainage and flood prevention for the low-lying surrounding Fens, but they also provide a link between the River Nene, and the Great Ouse and Cam. The scenery is flat, often hidden behind high banks but, even so, these areas have an attraction of their own, similar to Holland; some places even having Dutch names. Few boats travel these waters, so you need to ring the lock-keepers in advance, particularly when entering and leaving the system; the tide in the River Ouse governs the time when you can pass through. Presently no licence is needed, and there are no tolls.

Contact: 01354 653232.

MONMOUTH & BRECON CANAL

Length: 35 miles from Brecon to Cwmbran
Locks: 6
Maximum dimensions of vessel:
Length: **43ft** *Beam*: **8ft 6in** *Draught*: **2ft 6in** *Height*: **5ft 10in**

This isolated, but idyllic, canal runs through the beautiful Brecon Beacons National Park of South Wales. Originally, it joined the sea at Newport, but now it is accessible to trailable boats only. It does, however, have a series of charging points for electric boats, and a fleet of hire cruisers. Restoration schemes are afoot to connect it to the adjacent Crumlin Branch.

Contact: 01873 830328.

RIVER NENE

Length: 91 miles from Northampton to the Wash
Locks: 38
Maximum dimensions of vessel:
Length: **78ft** *Beam*: **13ft** *Draught*: **4ft** *Height*: **7ft**

Considering its length and pleasant surroundings, the Nene is a little-used river. This is partly due to the narrow beam length of the Northampton Arm that links it to the central system, and partly to its locks. These have a unique system of guillotine lower gates, that require nearly 100 turns of a handle to open; this puts off all but the most active of crews. Gradually these locks are being electrified, thereby easing the problem, and it is hoped that this will encourage people to use it. This will be good, because it is an attractive waterway, wide enough for cruisers as well as narrowboats.

Contact: 01733 371811.

NORFOLK & SUFFOLK BROADS

Length: 125 miles in total
Locks: None
Maximum dimensions of vessel:
Length: **no limit** *Beam*: **16ft** *Draught*: **3–5ft** *Height*: **6ft 6in***

The Broads is the name generally used to describe the whole of the system of navigable rivers and lakes of Suffolk and Norfolk. Technically, a broad is a wide, shallow lake, but the name applies now to the whole network, which includes the rivers Ant, Bure, Thurne, Waveney and Yare, plus the dozen or so broads. The area is hugely popular for hire boats, and justly so. The slow-moving rivers and soft banks are forgiving for beginners, and the absence of locks make them ideal for all age-groups. The waters can get busy in the peak of the summer, but you can usually find somewhere quiet to escape the crowds.

* Minimum bridge heights are those at Potter Heigham: 6ft 6in, and Wroxham: 7ft 3in. Otherwise they are 7ft 6in for the rest of the northern rivers and unlimited heights for the Yare to Norwich.

Contact: 01603 610734.

GREAT OUSE

Length: 85 miles from Bedford to King's Lynn
Locks: 16
Maximum dimensions of vessel:
Length: **70ft** *Beam*: **10ft 6in** *Draught*: **3ft 3in** *Height*: **7ft 6in**

The Great Ouse, and its associated tributaries the Cam, the Lark, the Little Ouse and the Wissey, form a most attractive cruising ground. Lazy flowing rivers, varied scenery, plentiful villages and towns alongside, and no over-crowding. Connected to the rest of the system by a narrow-beam stretch of canal, it is still probably the second most popular cruising river after the Thames. The locks are large enough for cruisers, but not as wide as the Thames and care must be taken to ensure that your craft will fit. There are ambitious plans for a new wide-beam link from Bedford to the Grand Union Canal at Milton Keynes.

Contact: 01733 371811.

YORKSHIRE OUSE

Length: 70 miles from Ripon to Trent Falls
Locks: 5
Maximum dimensions of vessel:
Length: 60ft *Beam*: 14ft 6in *Draught*: 3–4ft *Height*: 8ft 6in

The Yorkshire Ouse, together with the Ure and the Ripon Canal, total 70 miles in all. The lower 30 miles are tidal, and more difficult for navigation and less interesting than the upper reaches, from York onwards. York itself is well worth a visit, especially from the water.

Contact: 01904 728229.

OXFORD CANAL

Length: 77 miles
Locks: 46
Maximum dimensions of vessel:
Length: 70ft *Beam*: 7ft *Draught*: 3ft *Height*: 7ft

The Oxford Canal, particularly its southern section, is one of our most popular cruising canals. Meandering through typical English countryside, scattered with villages and pubs, it provides the ideal relaxed holiday. Linking with the Thames at Oxford it provides a through route from north to south for narrow-beam craft. The summit levels can suffer from water shortages in the height of the summer months, but this situation is gradually being improved with back-pumping projects.

Contact: 01788 890666.

PEAK FOREST CANAL

Length: 15 miles
Locks: 16
Maximum dimensions of vessel:
Length: 70ft *Beam*: 7ft *Draught*: 2ft 9in *Height*: 6ft

Another restored canal, Peak Forest includes in its length the magnificent Marple Flight. Climbing up to Whaley Bridge, it clings to the hillside, affording wonderful views below.

Contact: 01782 785703.

REGENT'S CANAL see GRAND UNION CANAL

ROCHDALE CANAL

Length: 33 miles from Manchester to Sowerby Bridge
Locks: 91
Maximum dimensions of vessel:
Length: **74ft** *Beam*: **14ft 2in** *Draught*: **4ft** *Height*: **9ft**

Until recently, the only part of this canal remaining navigable were two crucial miles through and under the streets of Manchester, providing a vital link in the Cheshire Ring. For this you paid a princely sum in tolls. However, in 2002 the whole canal was re-opened.

Contact: 01422 844990.

RIVER SEVERN

Length: 42 miles navigable from Gloucester to Stourport on Severn
Locks: 5
Maximum dimensions of vessel:
Length: **88ft** *Beam*: **18ft** *Draught*: **6ft** *Height* **21ft**

The mighty Severn is the longest river in England and Wales and used to be navigable for over 100 miles up to Welshpool. It is now restricted to the lower 42 miles. Below this the lower reaches are tidal to the Bristol Channel with fierce currents. The five locks are all manned, and capable of taking commercial vessels, though few use it now. The river is beautiful and secluded in the summer, but with winter rains it can rise 15ft or more. It forms part of the Avon Ring, and also links to the Worcester & Birmingham, and Staffordshire & Worcestershire canals.

Contact: 01452 318000.

SHEFFIELD & SOUTH YORKSHIRE NAVIGATION

Length: 42 miles from Sheffield to the River Trent
Locks: 26
Maximum dimensions of vessel:
Length: 61ft *Beam*: 15ft 3in *Draught*: 4ft 6in *Height*: 10ft

Until recently still a commercial waterway, this is gradually losing its traffic, particularly on the upper sections. The lower section forms part of the link between the Leeds & Liverpool and the Trent.

Contact: 01636 704481.

SHROPSHIRE UNION CANAL

Length: Main line 66½ miles from Ellesmere Port to Wolverhampton
Locks: 46
Maximum dimensions of vessel:
Length: 70ft *Beam*: 7ft *Draught*: 3ft 3in *Height*: 8ft

One of the prettiest canals, the Shropshire Union runs from Ellesmere Port, on the Manchester Ship Canal, down nearly to Birmingham. The upper section through Chester to Nantwich has broad locks, but from there they become narrow. The Welsh section or Llangollen Canal leaves at Hurleston Junction. It forms part of the Shropshire Ring, which able crews can do in a one-week hire.

Contact: 01786 284253.

STAFFORDSHIRE & WORCESTERSHIRE CANAL

Length: 46 miles
Locks: 31
Maximum dimensions of vessel:
Length: 70ft *Beam*: 7ft *Draught*: 2ft 6in *Height*: 6ft 3in

Joining the River Severn at the bustling Stourport Basin, this canal climbs up to Wolverhampton, passing through rolling countryside on its completely rural route. Kidderminster is the terminus of the Severn Valley Steam Railway, which makes a good day trip away from the boat.

Contact: 01785 284253.

RIVER STOUR (SUFFOLK)

Length: 23½ miles from Sudbury to Manningtree (restricted navigation)
Locks: 15 (3 restored) 10ft beam
Maximum dimensions of vessel:
Length: **50ft**

The Suffolk Stour was made famous by John Constable's paintings, and is typical of many partially restored waterways today. Its 15 locks fell into disuse in the 1930s, and through navigation was restricted to unpowered craft in 1967, but a thriving River Stour Trust campaigns for its full restoration and navigation. Three locks have been rebuilt, and powered craft can use certain sections.

Contact: 01473 727712.

STOURBRIDGE CANAL

Length: 5¾ miles
Locks: 20
Maximum dimensions of vessel:
Length: **70ft** *Beam*: **7ft** *Draught*: **2ft 6in** *Height*: **6ft**

A short canal linking the Staffordshire & Worcestershire Canal to the Birmingham Canal Navigations, the Stourbridge still packs in a string of locks alongside some of the few remaining glassworks in this area. A trip to the local museum and shop is recommended.

Contact: 0121 506 1300.

STRATFORD-UPON-AVON CANAL

Length: 25½ miles from Kings Norton to Stratford
Locks: 55
Maximum dimensions of vessel:
Length: **70ft** *Beam*: **7ft** *Draught*: **2ft 6in** *Height*: **6ft**

The Stratford is a fascinating little canal. The subject of another renowned restoration, its southern section was opened by the Queen Mother in 1964. The canal is completely rural with barrel-shaped lock cottages and split bridges to allow the tow-rope through. Stratford-upon-Avon is at its bottom end, which makes it a popular (though busy) cruising canal, the canal basin allowing you to moor right opposite the Shakespeare Theatre. Here it also connects to the River Avon, forming part of the Avon Ring.

Contact: 01564 784634.

Narrowboats can travel on the tidal lower stretches of our rivers, provided the boat and crew are fully prepared, and preferably travel in convoy for security. Here a fleet passes through London under Tower Bridge. Photo: Anne Kelly.

RIVER THAMES

Length: 143 miles from Lechlade to London Bridge
Locks: 44
Maximum dimensions of vessel:
To Oxford *Length*: **120ft** *Beam*: **17ft** *Draught*: **4ft** *Height*: **11ft**
Above Oxford *Length*: **109ft** *Beam*: **14ft** *Draught*: **3ft** *Height*: **7ft 6in**

England's Royal River, the Thames fully justifies its name. It offers 140 miles of the most varied cruising, from the placid headwaters to the centre of our capital; today few commercial vessels use the river except in the tidal lower reaches. The Thames began to attract pleasure boating from the turn of the last century when the London masses flocked to such spots as Boulters Lock at Maidenhead to take to the water in canoes, punts and skiffs. Today there are still 18,000 vessels registered, of which 12,000 are motorboats – most for private use but also with many hire craft. While it is well locked, they are all manned, making this one of the easiest waterways to cruise and explaining its popularity. It is possible to connect with the rest of the system, via the narrow-beam Oxford Canal, or the broad Grand Union in London. Well-found craft can negotiate the London section, providing the crew is prepared to make a 250-mile cruising ring.

Contact: 0118 953 5000.

RIVER TRENT

Length: 81 miles from Trent Falls to Nottingham; 36 miles from Nottingham to Leicester (River Soar)
Locks: 7 to Nottingham; 22 to Leicester
Maximum dimensions of vessel:
To Nottingham *Length*: 145ft *Beam*: 18ft 6in *Draught*: 6ft
***Height*: 12ft 3in**
To Leicester *Length*: 70ft *Beam*: 10ft 6in *Draught*: 3ft Headroom: 7ft 6in

The Trent has historically been one of our major navigations, forming a natural north-south highway, and a geographical boundary. Until recently, it was a busy commercial waterway, as the size of the locks indicates but, latterly, much of this trade has fallen away. Nevertheless, large barges and coasters can still suddenly appear round a bend, and must be given a wide berth. The first 50 miles are tidal, with strong currents. However, it forms a vital link down the east side of the system, and pleasure craft still use its waters. Unless your craft has sea-going power, you should plan all trips with the tide, ensuring that your vessel complies with the regulations. The upper reaches to Nottingham are broad and picturesque; beyond that the Trent & Mersey Canal and the River Soar take you into the rest of the system.

Contact: 01636 704481.

TRENT & MERSEY CANAL

Length: 93 miles from Preston Brook to the River Trent
Locks: 76
Maximum dimensions of vessel:
***Length*: 70ft *Beam*: 7ft *Draught*: 2ft 6in *Height*: 5ft 9in**

One of the great cross-country canals, and also one of the most successful, the Trent & Mersey linked many centres of industry and commerce. These included the Potteries, steel-works, and the cities of Liverpool and Nottingham. The canal scenery is varied, ranging from rural to industrial landscapes, and includes such notable features as Harecastle Tunnel, and the Anderton Lift – this lowered boats vertically to the River Weaver, and has for many years been disused, but was restored and working again in 2002.

Contact: 01283 790236.

RIVER WEY

Length: 19½ miles from the Thames to Godalming
Locks: 16
Maximum dimensions of vessel:
Length: **73ft 6in** *Beam*: **13ft 9in** *Draught*: **2ft 6in** *Height*: **7ft to**
Guildford; 6ft to Godalming

One of our earliest navigations (opened in 1653), the Wey is a charming and peaceful waterway that winds through the Surrey countryside. Despite being connected to the Thames at Weybridge, it is not over-populated with boats, possibly because of its low headroom and the occasional dilapidated lock. It was bequeathed by Harry Stevens to the National Trust, who now administer it. The river used to be connected to the River Arun, by the Wey and Arun Canal, forming a through-route from London to the south coast. It still gives access to the Basingstoke Canal. Guildford is well worth the visit by water.

Contact: 01483 561389.

WORCESTER & BIRMINGHAM CANAL

Length: 30 miles from Birmingham to the River Severn
Locks: 58
Maximum dimensions of vessel:
Length: **70ft** *Beam*: **7ft** *Draught*: **2ft 6in** *Height*: **6ft**

One of Birmingham's routes to the sea, the Worcester and Birmingham is a mainly rural canal, except for its section out of the city. Its main claim to fame is the Tardebigge Flight – 30 locks in a single flight. The cathedral city of Worcester at its western end is an attractive historic town; here the canal joins the River Severn, forming part of the Warwickshire Ring.

Contact: 01564 784634.

SCOTLAND'S WATERWAYS

Scotland has many locks and lakes, but just four canals, all of which are now navigable. The Caledonian Canal is a masterpiece of engineering, originally built to allow sea-going vessels to avoid the stormy passage round the north of Scotland. As such it can accommodate craft 150ft x 35ft, but is now mainly used by pleasure boats. Its 60 miles and 29 locks link Inverness and Fort William, via 21 miles of canal, and Loch Oich, Loch Lochy and Loch Ness, whose waters can occasionally be stormy and grey. The Crinan Canal is a short sea-canal. The Forth & Clyde Canal linked Edinburgh to Glasgow, and its 35 miles are now restored to navigation. Similarly, the Union Canal, 31 miles long between Edinburgh and Falkirk, is now restored, with the two linked by the magnificent new Falkirk Wheel.

Contact: 0141 332 6936.

IRELAND'S WATERWAYS

Ireland is studded with rivers and lakes, many of which were made navigable over the centuries and linked with canals. The whole system has been the subject of major restoration projects over the past 15 years, and an extensive network is now open to navigation, covering Northern Ireland and the Republic of Ireland, with many hire-cruiser bases throughout. The Shannon is the largest navigation, at 140 miles, and includes wide sections of river, plus Lough Ree and Lough Derg, which are broad enough to get rough in high winds. The Shannon–Erne navigation joins this to the River Erne system, which links two large lakes, Lough Erne and Lough Allen. Lough Neagh is the largest lake in the British Isles, and joins the sea via the River Bann. The Grand Canal runs from Dublin to the Shannon, and is fully navigable. Similarly the Barrow Navigation and the River Barrow link the Grand Canal to Waterford. The Royal Canal from Dublin to the Shannon is nearly fully restored.

Contact: Waterways Ireland: +353 (0) 1868 0148
www.waterwaysireland.org

Millennium Restorations

A wave of new canal restorations has been funded by the Heritage Lottery Fund, and the Millennium Commission, with further proposals from the Waterways Trust. These are briefly described below.

The Huddersfield Narrow Canal

20 miles, from the Ashton Canal, Manchester, to Huddersfield. 74 locks, and one tunnel, Standedge, at 5698 yards, the longest in Britain. The locks are 72ft x 7ft. The project was completed in 2001.

The Rochdale Canal

33 miles, from Manchester to Sowerby Bridge, including the already restored section. 91 locks, 74ft x 14ft. With the Huddersfield, and the Leeds & Liverpool, this completes the three trans-Pennine waterways.

The Forth & Clyde and Union Canals

70 miles, and with 40 locks, 66ft x 19ft 8in, and 66ft x 11ft 3in, these join Edinburgh to Glasgow. The most spectacular structure is the Falkirk Wheel, that lifts boats from one level to another, eliminating a flight of locks.

The Falkirk Wheel in Scotland is one of the modern wonders of the waterways. Built in 2000, it links the newly restored Forth & Clyde and Union Canals, with two rotating caissons that carry boats from one level to the other.

The Ribble Link

Just 4 miles long, with 9 locks, in 2000 this finally connected the Lancaster Canal to the rest of the system, via the River Ribble, and thence to the Leeds & Liverpool Canal.

The Anderton Lift

This magnificent steel structure originally lifted boats from the River Weaver up to the Trent & Mersey Canal in Cheshire. It was closed for 18 years, but was restored to full operation in 2002.

The Cotswold Canals

More correctly this is the joint name for the Thames & Severn Canal, and the Stroudwater Navigation. Together they linked the River Thames to the River Severn, via the Gloucester & Sharpness Canal. 37 miles long, with 56 locks, 74ft x 12ft 9in, and 70ft x 16ft, they include the stunning Sapperton Tunnel, at 3808 yards the third longest in Britain, hewn from the native rock. Restoration to date has been restricted to short sections, but plans are in train for its complete opening within 10 years.

Foxton Inclined Plane

Another engineering masterpiece, this lifted boats past the flight of staircase locks at Foxton on the Leicester Line of the Grand Union. It was built in 1900, but fell into disuse in 1910. It is another proposal for restoration by the Waterways Trust, and should be completed within the next few years.

The Bedford Link

This is an ambitious proposal for a completely new canal to link the Grand Union Canal at Milton Keynes to the River Ouse at Bedford. It will allow broad-beam boats to reach the Anglian waterways from the main system. At present it is a proposal only, with no date set.

Appendix I Useful addresses

APCO, Association of Pleasure Craft Operators
Audley Avenue, Newport, Shropshire, TF10 7BX
Tel: 01952 813572   Fax: 01952 820363   apco@britishmarine.co.uk

AWCC, Association of Waterways Cruising Clubs
69 Downs Drive, West Timperley, Altrincham, Cheshire, WA14 5QT
Tel: 0161 9693776   www.awcc.org.uk

British Marine Federation and Boatline Information Service
Meadlake Place, Thorpe Lea Road, Egham, Surrey, TW20 8BF
Tel: 01784 223600   Fax: 01784 439678   Boatline Tel: 01784 472222
www.britishmarine.co.uk

British Waterways
Willow Grange, Church Road, Watford, Hertfordshire, WD17 4QA
Tel: 01923 201101   Fax: 01923 201300   www.britishwaterways. co.uk
& www.waterscape.com

Inland Waterways Association
P.O. Box 114, Rickmansworth, WD3 1ZY
Tel: 01923 711114   Fax: 01923 897000   www.waterways.org.uk

Environment Agency
Rivers House, Waterside Drive, Aztec West, Almonsbury, Bristol, BS12 4UD
Tel: 01454 624400   www.environment-agency/gov.uk

Royal Yachting Association
Ensign Way, Hamble, Southampton, Hampshire, SO31 4YA
Tel: 023 8060 4100   Fax: 023 8060 4299   www.rya.org.uk

NABO, National Association of Boat Owners
111 Maas Road, Northfield, Birmingham, B31 2PP
Tel: 0121 475 6273   www.nabo.org.uk

Yacht Designers & Surveyors Association
The Glass Works, Penns Road, Petersfield, GU32 2EW
Tel: 01730 710425   Fax: 01730 710423   info@ybdsa.co.uk

Appendix II Major boat shows and events

The dates for these are only approximate, as they alter from year to year. For more up-to-date information, contact the BMF Boatline Service on 01784 472222.

In addition, the IWA organises many smaller rallies and events, and can supply an up-to-date list.

January ◆ London International Boat Show, Excel

February ◆ Birmingham Boat Show

April ◆ Beaulieu Boat Jumble

May ◆ Crick Boat Show, Crick, Northants.
◆ Inland Waterways Association Trailboat Rally
(Different location each year)

June ◆ Beale Park Thames Boat Show, Pangbourne, Berkshire

August ◆ Inland Waterways Association National Rally and Boat Show
(Different location each year)

September ◆ Southampton International Boat Show

Appendix III Books, maps & guides, magazines, DVDs & video tapes

Books

There are a great many descriptive books on the inland waterways and their history and also cruising guides. Some are available from chandleries while a larger selection is available from the IWA (Inland Waterways Association) who have stands at the major boat shows plus a mail order service.

For general boating books, particularly out-of-print titles, try the Warsash Nautical Book Shop, 6 Dibles Road, Warsash, Southampton SO3 9HZ. Tel: 01489 572384.

Adlard Coles Nautical have their own general boating catalogue and website: www.adlardcoles.com plus a series covering all practical aspects of boating on inland waterways and the sea. Titles include: *The RYA Book of Buying Your First Motor Cruiser*, *Practical Motor Cruising*, *Marine Inboard Engines*, *The Adlard Coles Book of Outboard Motors*, *The Adlard Coles Book of Diesel Engines*, *Skipper's On-board Diesel Guide*, *The Power Boater's Guide*, *Motorboat Electrical and Electronics Manual*, *The Adlard Coles Book of EuroRegs for Inland Waterways*, *The Ups and Downs of a Lockkeeper*, and *25 Years of Motor Cruisers*, the latter being particularly useful for tracking down information on out-of-production boats. These can be bought from book-stores or chandleries.

Maps and guides

Detailed maps and guides are available for most individual waterways, but three series will cover most general needs. Nicholsons Guides have been the bible for boaters for many years, and they cover almost all of the system in seven volumes. Waterways they do not cover include the Anglian rivers and the Norfolk Broads.

Geoprojects have a growing list of waterway maps, currently 23, but with more being added every month. They include comprehensive navigation notes and local information on each map.

Pearsons produce 11 waterway guides, whose idiosyncratic style is popular with many readers.

Additionally, the Lockmaster series has maps of 26 waterways.

Magazines

Canal Boat & Inland Waterways, edited for nine years by Emrhys Barrell, is aimed at both newcomers to the waterways, and experienced boaters. Coverage is divided between the rivers and canals of Great Britain, with additional articles on the popular overseas waterways.

Waterways World is the longest established of the inland magazines.

Coverage is mainly narrowboats and canals, but with some river and overseas articles.

Canal & Riverboat is evenly divided in its coverage, and includes contributions from the now defunct *Practical Motor Cruiser.*

Motorboats Monthly covers mainly sea-going boats, plus occasional articles on rivers and broad canals.

Motor Boat & Yachting covers mainly sea-going boats, plus some inland cruise features.

Practical Boat Owner covers mainly sea-going sailing boats, but its detailed coverage of basic seamanship and equipment is often of interest to all owners.

Boat Mart covers sportsboats, small cruisers and trailer boats. It has a large classified Boats for Sale section.

Buy a Boat is a classified magazine for all boats under £20,000.

DVDs and video tapes

Another development are DVDs and video tapes covering individual waterways. These are basically of the travelogue style, but give you some navigation information, plus local points of interest, and generally give you an overall feel for the canal or river. They are ideal for winter arm-chair viewing, or planning a holiday trip. The main supplier is Videoactive, but other companies are now also joining the market.

Index